THE PSYCHOLOGY OF HUNGER AND STARVATION

Hunger and starvation have significantly shaped the human condition. The imprints of past famines continue to cast lasting shadows on our evolutionary relationship with food, highlighting starvation as a powerful cognitive force. This book explores the nature of human hunger primarily from a psychological perspective, covering its basis in the brain, its critical dependence on learning and memory, and the dramatic effect of starvation on morality and behaviour. It connects the biology and psychology of hunger with historical and social examples, including hunger strikers, hunger artists, disordered eating, and hunger as a weapon. Human experimental studies of deep starvation are also analysed, alongside case studies of the 'super hungers' in Prader–Willi syndrome, binge eating, and dementia. Delivering a comprehensive and interdisciplinary picture of human hunger and starvation, this book is an ideal resource for students and researchers interested in ingestive behaviour from a multidisciplinary perspective.

RICHARD J. STEVENSON is a professor in the School of Psychological Science at Macquarie University. He has worked in both applied and academic settings, with a current research focus on hunger and interoceptive processing.

THE PSYCHOLOGY OF HUNGER AND STARVATION

RICHARD J. STEVENSON

Macquarie University, Sydney

Shaftesbury Road, Cambridge CB2 8EA, United Kingdom

One Liberty Plaza, 20th Floor, New York, NY 10006, USA

477 Williamstown Road, Port Melbourne, VIC 3207, Australia

314–321, 3rd Floor, Plot 3, Splendor Forum, Jasola District Centre, New Delhi – 110025, India

Cambridge University Press is part of Cambridge University Press & Assessment, a department of the University of Cambridge.

We share the University's mission to contribute to society through the pursuit of education, learning and research at the highest international levels of excellence.

www.cambridge.org
Information on this title: www.cambridge.org/9781009445146

DOI: 10.1017/9781009445139

When citing this work, please include a reference to the DOI 10.1017/9781009445139

First published 2026

Cover image: *The Man with Two Loaves of Bread* by Jean Francois Raffaelli (1879). Christie's Images/ Bridgeman Images

A catalogue record for this publication is available from the British Library

A Cataloging-in-Publication data record for this book is available from the Library of Congress

ISBN 978-1-009-44514-6 Hardback
ISBN 978-1-009-44516-0 Paperback

Contents

Figures

Tables

Boxes

Preface

A few years ago, I was chatting to a student who had recently completed my third-year course on eating and drinking. He remarked how glad he was that I had not set an exam question on hunger, because he did not really understand what it was. Some comments really invite reflection, and the more I thought about it, the more I came to the view that I did not really understand it either. This was the start of both my interest in hunger and, ultimately, this book.

Many people have helped make this book happen. I would particularly like to thank Nori Geary for his detailed critique of Chapter 2 and for the feedback provided by two anonymous expert readers for Cambridge University Press. The original idea for basing hunger around the declarative memory system arose from work with my long-time collaborators Heather Francis and Martin Yeomans, in addition to the valuable insights and criticisms from Kerry Boutelle, Bob Boakes, Terry Davidson, Jon Mond, Tuki Attuquayefio, and Supreet Saluja. I would also like to thank Viv Wuthrich for inviting me to join the Lifespan Health and Wellbeing Research Centre and for sparking my interest in dementia and feeding. The assistance of Daiana Martin-Rivera with the references list is also gratefully acknowledged. Support from the Australian Research Council contributed significantly to the genesis of this book. I would also like to thank my family for their support – Caroline, Gemma, Lucy, Harry, Chris, and Mike – and especially Rosie and Bailey – because dogs still have so much to teach us about hunger. Finally, I would like to thank the team at Cambridge University Press, especially Stephen Acerra for his unwavering support and Anna Hubbard for her patience.

CHAPTER 1

Introduction

1.0 Introduction and Approach

This book has two aims. The first is to present a psychological theory of human hunger based on learning and memory. In essence this theory proposes: (1) that a range of events, some in the environment (e.g., seeing your favourite food; knowing that it is lunchtime) and some arising in the body (e.g., an empty rumbling stomach), serve as cues for hunger; (2) that the meaning of these cues are learned, especially during childhood; and (3) that these cues come to predict either that a particular food will be good to eat now or that food in general will be good to eat now (definitions of hunger are considered further below).

To establish why a psychological theory of hunger is needed, Chapter 2 examines biologically orientated explanations of hunger, their limitations, and why they necessitate a particular type of psychological model based on learning and memory. Biological explanations of hunger have completely dominated the theoretical landscape, and there are no psychological models that *focus* solely on explaining hunger. While many psychological models include hunger as a component (e.g., Wardle's behavioural susceptibility to obesity model) – and particularly so when dealing with hunger for high-palatability foods (often termed appetite) – for hunger in general, explanations just defer back to biological processes. In contrast, this book presents a psychological account of hunger that shares features in common with psychological models of motivation. There is an emphasis on the distinction between anticipatory (wanting/desire) states such as hunger, and consummatory states, such as the sensory pleasure of eating. There is also an emphasis on the affective nature of wanting, and most importantly of all a basic dependence on learning and memory processes. Chapter 3 describes this model, along with the supporting evidence.

The learning and memory model then forms the theoretical basis for the remainder of the book – Chapters 4–9 – which collectively address the second aim, namely, to explore all the various facets of human hunger and starvation. Chapter 4 reviews the effects of hunger and starvation on the mind, covering preoccupation with food and especially immorality and crime. Chapter 5 explores the definition, epidemiology, and causes of famine and starvation, using the Irish potato famine of 1845–1849 and the Great Chinese Famine of 1959–1961 as examples. Chapter 6 examines the effect of voluntary restriction of food intake, in hunger strikes, dieting for weight loss, semi-starvation and longevity, and religious fasting. Chapter 7 investigates the imposition of hunger, in animal studies of food deprivation, in the experimental semi-starvation studies of Benedict and Keys, and the use of hunger as a weapon of war. Chapter 8 focusses on reductions or loss of hunger in anorexia nervosa, in constitutional thinness, cachexia, stress, and avoidant and restrictive food intake disorder. Chapter 9 surveys 'strong' hungers, in obesity, and in genetic, medical, psychiatric, and neurological populations, and the use of drugs and other techniques to augment hunger. Finally, Chapter 10 discusses predictions of the learning and memory model of hunger, as well as identifying other areas of hunger research that require attention.

1.1 What Is Hunger and What Is Not

Formally, human hunger has a three-fold scientific definition: (1) the meaning of certain bodily sensations such as a rumbling stomach; (2) a mental state of positive anticipation that food will be good to eat now; and (3) an organising principle that serves to prioritise feeding (Cofer & Appley, 1964; Reber, 1985). This definition can be simplified to just 'a mental state of positive anticipation that food will be good to eat now'. There are two reasons for this. First, definition (1) concerns '*the meaning*' of certain bodily (i.e., interoceptive) sensations. That *meaning* is definition (2) – a theme developed further in Chapter 3. Second, the effect of having 'a mental state of positive anticipation that food will be good to eat now' is often to go and seek food. Thus definition (3) is the sometime consequence of definition (2). So, for the purposes of this book definition (2) is the focus. Note that this definition implies that hunger is affective (i.e., '*positive* anticipation', '*good* to eat'), explicitly meaningful (i.e., '*knowing* that food will be good to eat now'), and anticipatory.

Four aspects of this scientific definition warrant comment. The first concerns the distinction between specific and general hunger. Specific hunger (often known as appetite and, when very intense, craving) is used here to refer to 'a mental state of positive anticipation *that a particular food (or category of food* (e.g., chocolate)) will be good to eat now'. In contrast, general hunger is 'a mental state of positive anticipation that *any* reasonable (i.e., basically edible/palatable) food will be good to eat now'. This distinction reflects a more specific focus on *a food* or a restricted food category, in contrast to food in general (see Watts et al., 2022, for a similar distinction). A second issue involves situations that include both specific and general hunger or where they are not easily distinguished, and here the overarching term hunger is used.

A third aspect of this definition concerns *when* hunger occurs. Hunger is constrained to the time *between* eating bouts (i.e., it is anticipatory). This reflects the long-standing distinction (i.e., W. Craig, 1917) between appetitive (i.e., hunger/desire/wanting/foraging) and consummatory (i.e., eating/sensory pleasure/liking) processes in ingestive behaviour. Relatedly, this also acknowledges that during eating there is gustatory, oral-tactile, and retronasal olfactory stimulation, which at least in the case of gustation, and possibly for the other two senses in the context of eating, may innately invoke pleasure (e.g., J. E. Steiner et al., 2001). Outside of eating – and thus in the appetitive phase – identifying whether a food, or food in general, will be good to eat, must involve memory (i.e., prior learning that the food had a pleasant taste and positive post-ingestive consequences (or not)).

A fourth issue concerns some of the chapters dealing with malnutrition and famine. One common usage of hunger is to mean lack of food, such as in phrases like 'world hunger', 'hunger indexes', and the like. It is usually very apparent from the context if this 'lack of food' meaning applies to the use of hunger in this book.

Finally, it is important to delineate what is not included as hunger in this book. Hunger has yet another usage, as applied to nutrient-specific desires to consume salts, perhaps other macro or micronutrients, or non-foods such as ice or clay (i.e., picas). There is certainly robust evidence that people can have a specific hunger for salt (Grove & Knight, 2024), but this falls outside of the domain of the book, because the focus here is not on specific nutrients per se, but rather on food in general. This also rules out the inclusion of picas, which are strong, often compulsive hungers, to eat a substance generally considered inedible (Leung & Hon, 2019). Claims have also been made that deficits in certain micronutrients (e.g., thiamine) can result in specific hungers for foods that may contain them (e.g., peas are a good source of thiamine). Not only are there grounds to be sceptical about such claims (Galef, 1991), but it seems that in many instances, notably for iron, vitamin B12, zinc, calcium, and copper, deficits are more likely to induce a pica (e.g., Borga-Pignati & Zanella, 2016; Miao et al.,

2015). With these concerns, and with the focus being on food in general, hungers for specific nutrients are not considered here.

1.2 A Short Social History of Hunger

The closest one can get to the experience of hunger in our ancestral past is from cave paintings, the oldest of which date from around 40,000 years ago. These paintings are dominated by animals, especially large herbivores such as bison, horse, and auroch, which were hunted for food, although depictions of the hunters themselves are rare. Strangely, there do not seem to be any pictures of gathering fruit or tubers, and so on, nor of the preparation of food, and while deer seemed to have been the most hunted animal, based on palaeolithic bones dumps, they do not predominate in the paintings. So, while these depictions could be primarily functional – in a magical sense – to make a hunt successful and so bestowing that most nutritious of foods, meat, on our ancestors, these strange inconsistencies have suggested to some an alternative explanation. Rather than helping to satisfy hunger, the paintings may have a shamanistic origin, aimed at satisfying a deeper need (Clottes, 2016).

While some have suggested, based on studies of hunter-gatherers, that their lifestyle was leisurely with little want, the shift from a nomadic lifestyle to farming seems to have brought with it periodic hunger, and even famine (Prentice, 2001). Indeed, the spectre of hunger and famine hangs heavily over our past. Revelations, in the Bible, describes the four horsemen of the apocalypse, the third being famine and hunger, represented as a merchant with weighing scales riding a black horse. Later, in contrast, Revelations 7:16 reassuringly notes that there is no hunger in heaven.

In the Middle Ages, a popular meme in Europe was the land of Cockaigne, a place where food was delicious, easily available, cheap – or even free. This land was celebrated in popular poems and songs, and is depicted in Bruegel's phantasmagorical work of 1550 (see Figure 1.1). Here the three central characters lie sated on the ground, rotund from consuming the food all about them. This depiction of gluttony and abundance was, of course, in stark contrast to most people's lives.

Concerns about the plight of the hungry have continued into modern times and still find expression in literature and art. In literary work, hunger emerges in three forms. First, as a protest against the injustices of poverty. In the nineteenth century, this spanned Victor Hugo's hero Jean Valjean imprisoned for stealing a loaf of bread to feed his starving sister, to Oliver

Figure 1.1 *The Land of Cockaigne* by Pieter Brueghel the Elder (1550).
Source: Bavarian State Painting Collections – Alte Pinakothek Munich. https://www.sammlung.pinakothek.de/de/artwork/01G1P9YLkE

Twist, in Dickens' eponymous novel. Oliver has the temerity to ask the workhouse master for more food, having been selected by drawing straws with the other boys in the workhouse. As Dickens vividly describes, all these children are experiencing slow starvation. An equally bleak depiction of poverty, food deprivation, and starvation in England is provided by Jack London's *The People of the Abyss*. Jack London visited England in 1902 to cover the coronation of Edward VII but instead spent long periods living rough in the East End of London. By the 1930s, with the Great Depression, mass unemployment, and widespread poverty, hunger manifested as a key theme in many works. Two notables are Steinbeck's *The Grapes of Wrath* and Bukowski's *Ham on Rye*. Bukowski grew up in Los Angeles during the Great Depression, with a diet often consisting of 'luncheon meat'. In the UK, George Orwell powerfully described the gnawing boredom of slow starvation, with the bread, margarine, and tea diet of homeless men and women in *Down and Out in Paris and London*.

Two other strands of hunger literature also emerged in the nineteenth century. One, still popular today, is the survival story, either biographical, embellished, or fictional. Many examples exist, but notables in this genre are Daniel Defoe's *Robinson Crusoe* (1719) and Herman Melville's *Typee*

(1846), both of which feature a protagonist wrestling (successfully) with food deprivation and hunger. Modern forms, with chronic hunger as a backdrop to the whole story, include Solzhenitsyn's *One Day in the Life of Ivan Denisovich* (1962) and Cormac McCarthy's *The Road* (2006). A final strand uses hunger as an allegory for the plight of the artist, with Knut Hamsun's *Hunger* (1890) and Franz Kafka's very depressing *A Hunger Artist* (1924) as the most famous examples.

Painting is a powerful medium to express social concern, including hunger, and echoes many of the sentiments seen in nineteenth- and twentieth-century literature. Millet's *The Gleaners* (1857) depicts three women picking over a field after a rich harvest – seen in the distance – and trying to find any remaining sheafs of wheat to use as food. Van Gogh's *The Potato Eaters* (1885) also depicts the harsh reality of rural life, and indeed van Gogh much admired Millet's work. The Irish potato famine was a powerful artistic stimulus, and one of the works it generated was De Scott Evans' *The Irish Question* (c. 1880), which is pictured in

Figure 1.2 *The Irish Question* by De Scott Evans (c. 1880). Purchased with funds provided by Carol W. Wardlaw and Jill Burnside Zeno; Roger and J. Peter McCormick Endowment Fund.

Figure 1.2. Kathe Kollwitz's *Misery (In Need)* (1897) shows a mother bent over her dead child, a consequence of starvation from striking in the Weavers' Rebellion of 1844.

This artistic concern for poverty and starvation, which was directed at European and American countries, has changed in more recent times. As hunger in Westernised nations got replaced by abundance, attention has shifted to other parts of the world (e.g., Bob Geldof and Band Aid, in 1984). And while the dream of the Middle Ages – the land of Cockaigne – has come true, popular culture remains preoccupied with overindulgence. Modern audiences pay to watch people binge eat junk food (the *mukbang* phenomenon – of Korean origin, meaning a broadcast while someone eats (a lot)). Professional and semi-professional food athletes engage in competitive eating, and this is attracting a growing public. And when people have a moment, they may watch one of the many cooking shows that first emerged as a genre in the nineteenth century or they may be viewing 'food porn' (i.e., glamourised pictures of highly palatable food) on their device.

1.3 A Short History of the Scientific Understanding of Hunger

Several contemporary ideas about hunger echo themes that have been present since the earliest recorded thinking on this topic. Both Aristotle (384–322 BC) in *On the Soul* and Epicurus (341–270 BC) in his surviving writings suggest a distinction between 'appetite' and 'hunger'. Epicurus described appetite as a desire that was 'ornamental and superfluous', with Aristotle linking it strongly to pleasure. Both thought 'hunger' also involved pleasure but importantly this was of a more wholesome, natural, and healthier kind. Aristotle, and Plato (428–328 BC) in *Timaeus*, both agreed that hunger was experienced in the stomach, so making the connection between a key organ of digestion and the desire to eat.

The Greek and Roman doctor, and natural philosopher, Galen (126–216 AD) also distinguished between 'appetite' and 'hunger', and suggested that each had discrete anatomical locations (and hence presumably discrete causes), with 'hunger' in the stomach and 'appetite' in the liver (from *Doctrines of Hippocrates and Plato*). The first explicit biological theory of hunger comes from the Muslim doctor and polymath Ibn Sina (Avicenna; 980–1037), in *The Cannon of Medicine*. Here, excitation in the liver triggers activity in the spleen, manifesting as 'hunger' felt in the stomach and mouth. This chain of activation is inhibited by the detection of food in the gut. Ibn Sina similarly distinguished 'hunger' from 'appetite' and noted the importance of a cold temperature in exciting 'hunger'.

Figure 1.3 Drawing of Anthelme Brillat-Savarin (1755–1826).
Source: GetArchive

Of these natural philosophers, one stands out above all others in his reflections on hunger, and this is the French pioneer of gastronomy Brillat-Savarin (1755–1826; see Figure 1.3). Brillat-Savarin in his book *The Physiology of Taste* (1825) started by identifying a very contemporary homeostatic theory of hunger, based on energy depletion: 'Motion and life occasion in the animal portion of all that lives, a constant loss of substance, and the human body, that most complicated of machines, would soon be unfit for use, did not providence provide it with a mark to inform it of the very moment when its powers are no longer in equilibrium with its wants' (Meditation IV). In contrast to earlier theorists, Brillat-Savarin regarded 'appetite' and 'hunger' as dimensional, with 'appetite' being a 'small hunger' and, with greater deprivation, 'hunger' then emerged. Most notably from the perspective of this book, he identified the importance of learning and memory, describing their use in recalling 'food that has flattered its tastes' and the related process of imagination, and its capacity to recreate the eating experience – anticipating contemporary models of specific hunger (or appetite). He also seems to have recognised the importance of the cephalic phase response – anticipatory salivation and gastric activity when food is imminent – and the importance of time of day in dictating hunger. And while these ideas foreshadow many of the themes discussed later in this book, it is not until people started doing experiments that things moved from natural philosophy to science. A clear point of demarcation in this regard comes with the work of Ivan Petrovich Pavlov and Walter Bradford Cannon, which is where the scientific record, and this book, really start.

CHAPTER 2

Biological Approaches to General Hunger

2.0 Introduction

This chapter examines biological models that attempt, directly or more often indirectly, to explain the cause of hunger for food in general. The reason for this focus is that in most discussions of hunger since Cannon, general hunger has been regarded as having a biological cause, while specific hunger has been thought to have a psychological one. This chapter argues that this view is incorrect, and that a psychological explanation is also required for general hunger. Importantly, this does not negate the key role of brain systems in supporting hunger, rather it shows that any causal explanation of hunger needs psychology and, in particular, associative learning and memory processes.

2.1 Energy Control (or Homeostatic) Models of General Hunger

Cells require energy, and so fuel supplies at the cellular level are under tight homeostatic control (Berthoud et al., 2017; Geary, 2023; Watts et al., 2022). In animals, at the level of the organism, the primary source of fuel is food. Thus, one means (there are several others) of regulating fuel supply at the organism level is to control the amount eaten by increasing or decreasing general hunger. Thus, a control (or homeostatic) model of general hunger is one where a departure from the usual level of some index of bodily fuel status *causes* a compensatory response, manifesting as either an increase or decrease in general hunger. Such models of general hunger are popular in the psychological literature and also reflect the public's understanding of its cause (Assanand et al., 1998). This is because the idea has intuitive appeal, for it seemingly parallels, at the organism level, the homeostatic process known to occur at the cellular level.

Historically, one form of control model has been that using a 'set point' (Mrosovsky & Powley, 1977). The set point provides a reference signal, such as, for example, a measure of bodily energy reserves (e.g., fat).

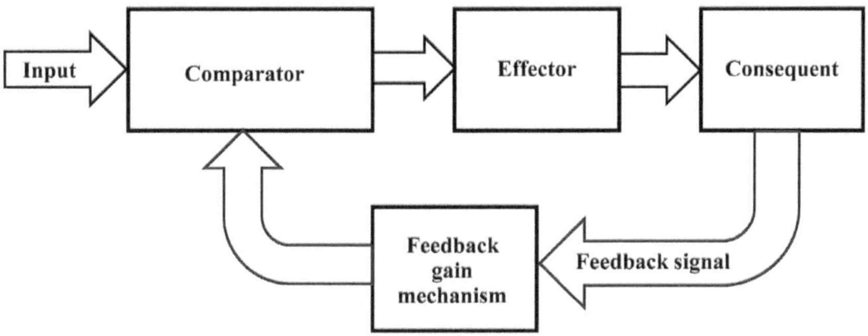

Figure 2.1 A control model of energy regulation.

A comparator examines whether the feedback signal – in this example the quantity of fat tissue – is greater, the same, or less than the set point. If the feedback signal is greater or less than the set point, then the comparator instructs the effector to remedy this. The remedy in this case would include either an increase or decrease in general hunger, which would then affect food intake, and thus the quantity of fat tissue in the body – the consequent.

While set-point models have been widely used, homeostatic regulation of a parameter can be achieved without a set point (Geary, 2023). One type of 'set-point-free' control model is illustrated in Figure 2.1. Here the critical difference is the presence of a feedback gain mechanism, which can modify the feedback signal in several ways (e.g., accumulate information about changes in the feedback signal over time, amplify its effect, etc.), to drive general hunger, and so achieve energy regulation.

Control models using a set point had their heyday in the 1950s. The basic approach was to select an appropriate type of set point to regulate, one which is a proxy for either energy storage or usage. Four basic models emerged. Three focussed on energy (fuel) sources – either carbohydrates, proteins, or fats. The fourth utilised body temperature as the set point, with this serving as an indicator for energy usage (i.e., heat, a by-product of metabolism). Each model is discussed next, followed by a broader examination of the ability of energy control models to provide a cause for general hunger.

2.1.1 *Carbohydrates*

Of the three energy reservoirs in the body, there are several reasons why variation in the carbohydrate one might be good to monitor and regulate.

Carbohydrate stores fluctuate more over a day than do stores of fats or proteins, and so this variation could drive general hunger, which also varies across the day (e.g., Mattes, 2010). Of the various bodily carbohydrates, glucose (or blood sugar) is the primary fuel for the brain and so its availability is carefully monitored by the body. From these observations came the idea that when blood glucose declines general hunger starts, and when blood glucose recovers general hunger ends. An immediate problem with this version of events is that diabetics can have persistently elevated blood sugar but still feel hungry.

To remedy this, Mayer (1953) proposed the glucostatic model. Here, glucose utilisation is the key, with this being indexed by the disparity in blood glucose between the arteries and veins. When utilisation is high (i.e., arterial blood glucose > venous blood glucose) the person will not be hungry. However, when utilisation is low (i.e., arterial blood glucose = venous blood glucose) this will cause general hunger. Initial data supported this model, with pharmaceutical agents that block glucose utilisation able to produce feeding even in sated animals. In contrast, later work often failed to support key model predictions (Levitsky et al., 2022). For example, meta-analysis reveals no relationship in normal weight participants between changes in hunger and changes in blood glucose (Flint et al., 2007). Moreover, in animals and humans, glucose utilisation often *increases* just prior to eating a meal, which is not a good time to stop being hungry. Daily fluctuations in blood glucose are not the cause of general hunger.

Notwithstanding this conclusion, there is no doubt that glucose regulation is critical to normal metabolic function, with sensors located throughout the brain (Levin et al., 2011). Indeed, Flint et al. (2007) found that higher post-meal insulin levels were correlated with reduced general hunger. Such a finding might suggest that changes in insulin are themselves a cause of general hunger. Setting aside that the studies in Flint et al.'s (2007) meta-analysis are correlational, even if insulin injections resulted in increased general hunger this would still not necessarily indicate causality. This is because people have to learn that a particular bodily feeling (i.e., the one associated here with an increase in insulin) *means hunger*. This important issue is considered at several further points in this chapter, and in Chapter 3.

2.1.2 *Protein*

By mass, protein forms the largest energy reservoir of the human body (around 17 per cent or 10.5 kg for a 70 kg person). Tissues rich in protein, such as muscle, which comprises over a quarter of all cells in the body, are also the most metabolically active. Protein then offers another potential route to match food intake, and hence general hunger, to energy needs and reserves. The first protein-based set-point model was proposed by Mellinkoff et al. (1956), who reported that levels of serum amino acids (the building blocks of protein) were correlated with reports of hunger. Interest in protein-based models has rekindled with the discovery of a correlation between a person's lean body mass (essentially a protein store measure), general hunger, and food intake (Blundell et al., 2015; Hopkins et al., 2017; Hopkins et al., 2019; Weise et al., 2014). Around 7 per cent of the variability in reported hunger is accounted for by an index of lean body mass (Caudwell et al., 2013).

Lean body mass accounts for a large portion of the energy expended each day on maintaining routine cellular function – basal metabolic rate – which in turn comprises 60–75 per cent of daily energy requirements. So, if basal metabolic demands are high, as in people with a lean muscular body, general hunger will typically be higher than in a person with a greater proportion of their tissue as fat, which is less metabolically active. Blundell and colleagues (e.g., Blundell et al., 2015; Casanova et al., 2019; Hopkins et al., 2017) suggest that lean body mass exerts a moderating effect on general hunger. There are several ways this could be enacted, such as by adding a constant to each daily episode of hunger or, indirectly, by reducing inhibition on general hunger (see Chapter 3).

In sum, while these findings suggest that greater lean body mass is correlated with general hunger, it does not follow that general hunger is caused by lean body mass. Indeed, there is no evidence that variation in protein stores causes general hunger. As argued earlier for insulin, even if a chemo-signature for lean body mass was identified, and its administration resulted in greater hunger, this still may not indicate causation. This is because the meaning of biological signals is learned during development – a person has to know that the associated feeling generated by the signal means if I eat now food will be rewarding.

2.1.3 Body Temperature

There is a clear relationship between thermogenic and protein energy control models. This arises from the correlation between body temperature, basal metabolic rate, and lean body mass. While the initial conceptualisation (Brobeck, 1948) regarded food intake as a means of *regulating* body temperature, it is not much of a stretch to see that body temperature could form a hypothetical set point for food intake. Changes in body temperature, reflecting the thermic effects of food or from reductions in basal metabolic rate (e.g., as an adaptation to starvation) *could* index fuel usage, and so cause changes to general hunger, and hence food intake (e.g., decreases in body temperature engendering increases in food intake and vice versa). However, body temperature is tightly regulated and so only has a small range, making it a poor candidate to serve as an index of fuel usage. It is more likely that body temperature either moderates hunger (as suggested for lean body mass earlier) and/or that people learn that eating when feeling cold is rewarding, while eating when feeling hot is not.

2.1.4 *Fat*

Fat is the body's long-term energy store, so if this store starts being used for fuel, and becomes depleted, this should be associated with an increase in general hunger and hence food intake. This type of model was first proposed by Kennedy (1953), who suggested that some 'circulating metabolite' (i.e., a chemo-signal) indexed the body's fat reserves, with general hunger increasing or decreasing, dependent on increasing or decreasing adiposity – a lipostatic model. In the mid 1990s Friedman discovered leptin, a peptide hormone secreted by adipose tissue, whose circulating levels increase with greater adiposity and decrease with reduced adiposity.

The discovery of leptin reinvigorated interest in lipostatic models. Circulating leptin levels broadly reflect the degree of adiposity (Wynne et al., 2005), and changes in leptin levels also correlate with changes in general hunger (e.g., Mars et al., 2006) – at least when fat mass is lost. Further interest was generated by the discovery that mice lacking the capacity to produce leptin were hyperphagic and rapidly became obese (see Figure 2.2). However, several more recent findings are problematic for leptin serving as a feedback signal for a lipostatic model. First, people with obesity have high circulating levels of leptin but this does not seem to affect their general hunger or food intake, contrary to what the lipostatic model would suggest. Second, much larger falls in leptin are observed in short-term fasting than would be expected if its levels were solely yoked to degradation of fat stores (e.g., Mars et al., 2005). Paralleling this is the finding that leptin concentrations tend to return to 'normal' long before fat stores have recovered. Third, even providing doses of leptin some 400 times the typical circulating level does not impact body mass in people who are overweight (Levitsky et al., 2022). These findings suggest that leptin is not functioning as the type of feedback signal that the lipostatic model envisaged.

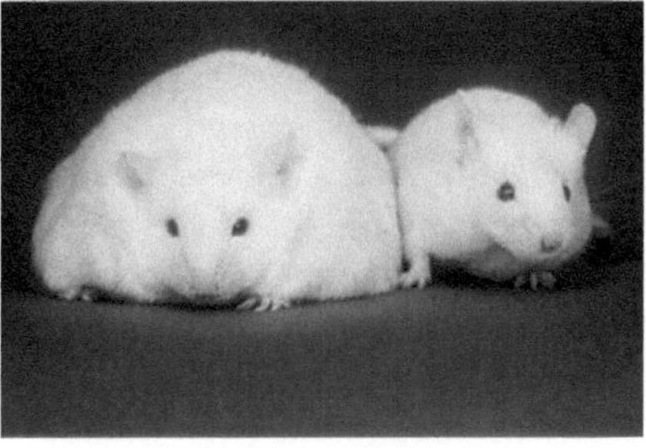

Figure 2.2 The ob/ob mouse (left) and its lean litter mate.
Source: Figure 3 in Sanches, S. C., Ramalho, L. N., Augusto, M. J., da Silva, D. M., & Ramalho, F. S. (2015). Nonalcoholic steatohepatitis: A search for factual animal models. *BioMed Research International*, 574832. https://doi.org/10.1155/2015/574832

2.1.5 Problems with Control Models of General Hunger

All control models of general hunger (i.e., homeostatic accounts) have several problems, both from theoretical and empirical perspectives (de Castro & Plunkett, 2002). These problems suggest they are not the cause of general hunger.

2.1.5.1 Problem 1: Fuel Depletion

Control models cause general hunger when there is *some* depletion of fuel reserves. In either a set-point conception or using a control model without a set point, the comparator reacts to a disparity and instructs the effector to remedy it. This is problematic for all three fuel types, but for different reasons. For carbohydrates, it is misleading because the body can maintain an adequate supply of fuel to the cells for days or even weeks without food (i.e., it accesses long-term energy stores from fat and protein) – including provision of glucose for the brain and other glucose-requiring tissues. Strictly speaking there is no running out of fuel and especially so on a day-to-day basis – the time span where general hunger is felt. In addition, on the rare occasions that carbohydrates become unavailable, such as with diabetic hypoglycaemia or with complete depletion of glycogen stores during endurance sport, the resulting state is not generally reported to *feel* like hunger (Rogers & Brunstrom, 2016). Finally, for proteins and fats, there is a different problem. In most healthy people these stores never become depleted, and so if one were reliant on them to generate hunger one would have to start losing weight (i.e., burning these stores). Overall, it makes more sense to anticipate energy needs rather than react to them (Geary, 2023; Watts et al., 2022).

2.1.5.2 *Problem 2: Regulatory Time Course*

In the natural environment there is a lot of variation in the amount that a person (or animal) eats from day to day (Speakman et al., 2011). They may be unwell and eat less for a few days, they may eat more because it's Christmas or their birthday, and there are many other variables that can drive up or down short-term food intake (e.g., number of people at a meal, portion size, mood, stress, etc.; Berthoud, 2004). Controlled studies have explored the effects of these short-term influences of food intake on body weight. The general finding from both under- and overfeeding experiments is of weak compensation – if people are overfed then they tend to eat less in the following days, but not less enough to compensate for the overfeeding period (e.g., Edholm et al., 1970; Speakman et al., 2011). The same holds for underfeeding, which is also followed by imperfect compensation. People are then generally poor compensators for all the myriad variations in food intake that occur over the short term.

Poor short-term compensation has led to the suggestion that homeostatic regulation of energy (i.e., as indexed by body weight, adiposity, etc.) – should it exist – probably works over longer periods of time (weeks/months). This is also a problematic notion. First, most of the purported feedback signals (e.g., glucose, leptin) vary over the short term. This raises the troubling issue of how they can vary in the short term but only regulate in the long term (Speakman et al., 2011). Second, body weight regulation in the longer term is also imperfect. The strongest piece of evidence for this is the obesity epidemic. That is, over the longer term, adult body weight in developed countries tends to drift upwards at around 0.5 kg/year (Levitsky et al., 2022). This relatively modest year-by-year change is sometimes taken as an indication of successful homeostatic regulation, as a 0.5 kg increase per year represents only an additional 1 per cent of total energy intake. However, as outlined later this *apparent* 'regulation' may be achieved – although this is contentious in some quarters – with no regulatory mechanism at all.

2.1.5.3 *Problem 3: Regulatory Asymmetry*

When food is readily available people do not typically become thinner, they become fatter. This has led to the observation that perhaps there is strict regulation of energy, but only at the 'depleted end'. That is, when fat and protein stores start to become depleted, body weight is falling, and the risk of starvation looms large – biological regulatory mechanisms kick in (Berthoud, 2004). It has been argued that the reason for this asymmetry is because in our ancestral past incidents of famine were common, and so people who were able to accumulate fat rapidly in the good times and were metabolically thrifty in the bad times had a selective advantage. There was then little selection pressure *against* excess weight gain, as the environment rarely provided the conditions for it to occur (i.e., we did not evolve in a Garden of Eden, but rather where the four horsemen of the apocalypse roamed; Mrosovsky & Powley, 1977). In contrast, in modern times, food is highly palatable, cheap, and easily available, so the environment is optimal for excess weight gain to occur, with many people having few physiological mechanisms to guard against this happening.

This theory has been termed the thrifty gene hypothesis (Neel, 1962). The thrifty gene hypothesis has mixed support (e.g., G. Wang & Speakman, 2016; L. Wang et al., 2020; and see Section 5.2.1 for an extended discussion of this issue) and so there *may* not be selection for genes favouring rapid fat storage during times of plenty. However, the idea that body weight is vigorously defended at low weights still stands. As a control model of general hunger dictates that increases or decreases in energy stores will elicit appropriate compensatory responses, clearly this is not the case.

2.1.5.4 Problem 4: Small Animals and Large Humans

In humans, the shorter the time a biological need can be deferred seems to be linked to greater non-volitional (i.e., deterministic) control. For example, if you hold your breath you may pass out, but the biological systems that control breathing will then kick in to ensure you breathe whether you like it or not. In contrast, a healthy adult can go several weeks without food, and as hunger strikers attest (see Chapter 6), if a person chooses not to eat, they will ultimately die. The point here is that humans have substantial reserves of energy, in contrast to oxygen, so volition is allowable for the former in a way that it is not for the latter.

The reason why this issue is important is because at least some of what we know about the biology of human hunger and food intake is based on studies of rats and mice. Rats and mice have different energy economies to humans. First, these animals need to devote far more of their daily energy expenditure to maintaining body temperature, due to their higher surface-area-to-body-weight ratio (Watts et al., 2022). Second, rats and mice have much smaller fat reserves than humans (a couple of days for the mouse, several days for the rat), probably because if they gain weight too readily when food is available this would confer a serious risk of death from predation or impaired heat dissipation. In other words, these energy-hungry small animals are (in nature) under strong selection pressure from two directions – the Scylla of starvation and the Charybdis of predation. This set of circumstances would favour far stricter control of body weight than in humans (Kelley et al., 2005). Consequently, data from rat or mouse models of feeding may lend itself to deterministic control models, reflecting the biology of small mammals but not necessarily our biology.

2.1.5.5 Problem 5: Models with No Regulation

Some authors have questioned whether the notion of a set point is even falsifiable (Mrosovsky & Powley, 1977). This is because if one accepts that there is such a thing as a set point, it is clearly not that set as it can change with pregnancy, lactation, illness, and excess weight gain – and the defence of a new higher body weight too (Hao et al., 2016). Of course, this is not a problem for set-point-free control models (see Figure 2.1), as various changes can be instantiated by alterations to the feedback gain mechanism. Nonetheless, this set-point-free model still suffers from problems 1–4 identified earlier, at least when it serves as an explanation for general hunger.

Some authors have suggested abandoning the notion of regulation (with this rebutted by others – see Watts et al., 2022). One such model was outlined by Levitsky et al. (2022), where increases in energy intake result in rises in lean and fat mass, which then increase energy usage (via more metabolically active tissue), and so dampen any further weight gain even if the higher energy intake is maintained. Similarly, if energy intake decreases, there is a gradual loss of fat and lean mass, and hence a reduction in energy needs and so the system will adjust to a lower point of energy balance. Computational modelling indicates that such a system behaves, in terms of body weight, rather like free-living human beings.

This type of model has been described more generally by Speakman et al. (2011) and is illustrated in Figure 2.3. These so-called dynamic equilibrium models have certain features (Speakman & Hall, 2023). They have an unregulated parameter, which in this case is food intake. Food intake then fills a hypothetical energy reservoir. This energy reservoir then affects one parameter, which in this example is energy expenditure (i.e., basal metabolic rate). When this model is put into simulated operation it maintains a broadly stable point in the energy reservoir, because when more food 'pours in', more energy 'flows out' in the form of increased metabolic costs. When less food 'pours in' and the reservoir is depleted,

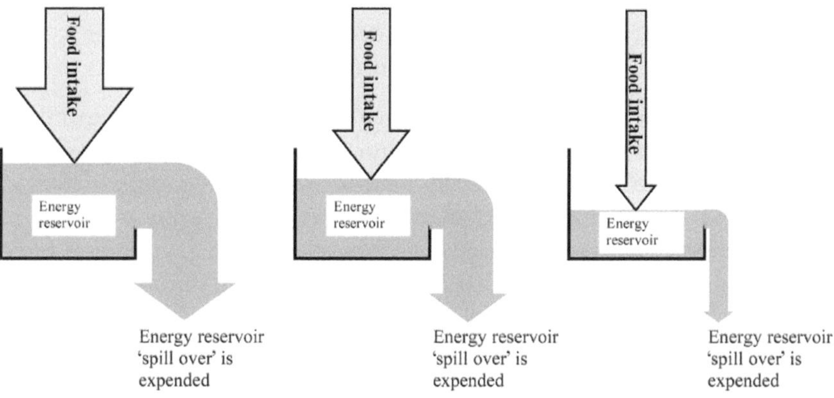

Figure 2.3 A dynamic equilibrium model.

less energy 'flows out' due to decreased metabolic costs. Whatever its benefits, this model does not constrain food intake, and so offers no cause for general hunger.

2.1.6 Why Energy-Based Control Models Do Not Offer a Cause for General Hunger

Energy control models do not offer a convincing cause of general hunger because daily energy fluctuations in healthy humans, relative to total energy reserves, are small. In addition, energy consumption in humans is typically anticipatory (e.g., Geary, 2023; Watts et al., 2022), occurring before any deficit arises, which again points strongly away from a reactive energy control perspective. The literature clearly identifies several biological variables that are correlated with general hunger (e.g., insulin, leptin, lean body mass, body temperature). However, even if it were to be shown that the manipulation of these (or other) biological agents produces general hunger, this still would not be enough to claim that agent as a cause. This is because of evidence examined in Section 2.2 and in Chapter 3, which suggests a critical role for development, namely learning the predictive value of biological and environmental events (i.e., what they mean). Rather than being a cause, these biological correlates may instead be either direct moderators of hunger, or indirect ones via inhibitory processes – something that is also discussed further in Chapter 3. In sum, energy control (i.e., homeostatic) models do not explain general hunger.

2.2 Hormones and Neurotransmitters as a Cause for General Hunger

The model under examination here is that a hormone or neurotransmitter is released, which then causes general hunger. While readers may feel this crudely represents what is generally held to be a more complex process, that has not been my reading of many papers that invoke this type of model. Several such agents have been discovered that when administered boost food intake, suggesting that they stimulate general hunger. There are some significant empirical and theoretical problems with this type of model (some already alluded to in Section 2.1.6). Here, each of the main orexigenic (i.e., hunger-inducing) hormone/neurotransmitters are examined, followed by a discussion of this approach.

2.2.1 Ghrelin

Ghrelin is a peptide hormone released from several different sites in the body, with the principal one being the stomach (Kojima & Kangawa, 2005). It exerts its orexigenic effects in the brain possibly via ghrelin receptors on vagal afferents, and by crossing the blood–brain barrier and binding to receptor sites located in several regions linked to feeding (Hsu et al., 2016). An early discovery was that injection of ghrelin into the brains of animals or into their peripheral circulation led to a powerful short-term increase in feeding (e.g., Wren et al., 2001). Paralleling this was the observation that circulating ghrelin levels correlate with general hunger, and increase just prior to feeding, and fall off during and after a meal (e.g., Cummings et al., 2001). While ghrelin release is not always perfectly correlated with feeding (e.g., Nymo et al., 2018) one conclusion has been that ghrelin is a key biological signal for hunger. This has often been extended to concluding that ghrelin causes hunger.

Whatever functions ghrelin serves in explaining feeding behaviour and hunger – and it clearly has a role – it is unlikely to be *the* cause of general hunger. There are two reasons for this (and see Watts et al., 2022 for several more). First, it is possible to genetically engineer germ-line knockout mice that do not produce ghrelin or that lack the growth hormone receptor that it uses (e.g., Sun et al., 2003). Sun et al. (2003) vividly describe the impact of such manipulations: 'In contrast to the predictions made from the pharmacology of ghrelin, ghrelin-null mice are not anorexic dwarfs; their size, growth rate, food intake, body composition, reproduction, gross behavior and tissue pathology are indistinguishable from wild type littermates'

(p. 7973). While later gene-manipulation studies reveal some broader impacts on growth and physiology, after eliminating ghrelin or its receptors these ghrelin-less animals still grow and gain weight much like their intact littermates (e.g., Peris-Sampedro et al., 2021; see Figure 2.4).

A second reason to doubt that ghrelin causes general hunger comes from studying people who have had their stomach removed, either following, or to prevent, cancer. Gastrectomy causes major reductions in general hunger and eating post-surgery, but it is unclear if (or how much) this is driven by changes in ghrelin secretion. Some findings suggest ghrelin plays a role and others that it does not (Wagner et al., 2022). Moreover, some gastrectomy

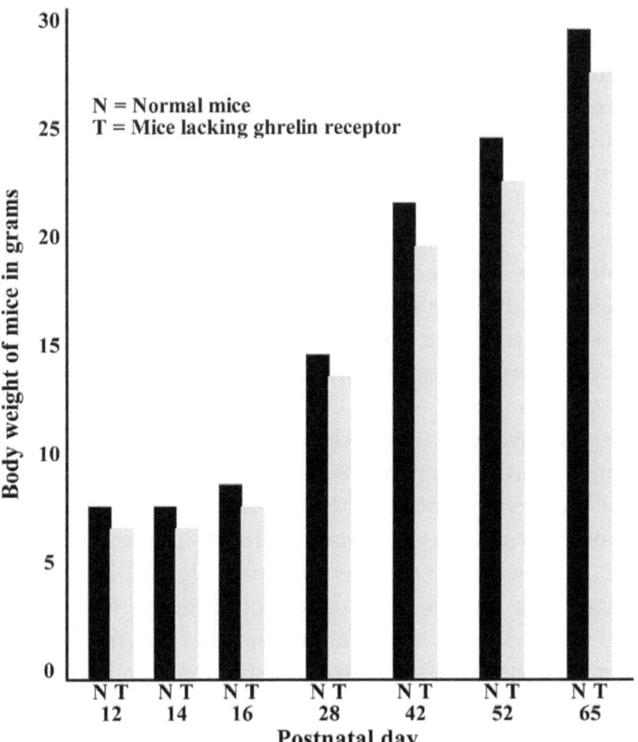

Figure 2.4 Growth of mice either with (control mice) or without the receptor for ghrelin (target mice).

Source: Data from Figure 5.c in Peris-Sampedro, F., Stoltenborg, I., Le May, M. V., Zigman, J. M., Adan, R. A. H., & Dickson, S. L. (2021). Genetic deletion of the ghrelin receptor (GHSR) impairs growth and blunts endocrine response to fasting in Ghsr-IRES-Cre mice. *Molecular Metabolism*, *51*, 101223. https://doi.org/10.1016/j.molmet.2021.101223

patients report never experiencing general hunger again following surgery, while others report that general hunger returns to normal (Hallowell et al., 2021; Wangensteen & Carlson, 1931). The failure of general hunger to reappear (or not) needs to be interpreted in the context that ghrelin levels eventually return to pre-surgical values (presumably from up-regulation of non-gastric sources). Thus, if ghrelin is present so should general hunger be, but this assumes that the non-gastric release of ghrelin (e.g., timing and time course) affects general hunger in the same way as gastric release does – and the chemical form of ghrelin too. Animal data also bear on these issues. Ghrelin knockout mice who undergo 'bariatric surgery', eliminating part of their stomach, still demonstrate the same degree of weight loss as their intact littermates, suggesting ghrelin does not play a major role in bariatric surgery outcomes (Woods et al., 2018). As one review indicated in its title 'From "Hunger Hormone" to "It's Complicated"...' (Deschaine & Leggio, 2022) – there is no simple linkage between ghrelin and general hunger.

Some functions of ghrelin are now understood. It maintains a euglycemic state in starvation, which ghrelin knockout mice are impaired at surviving. It also enhances gastric motility, and stimulates growth hormone release (Deschaine & Leggio, 2022). In regard to hunger, two more nuanced roles have emerged. The first is that ghrelin release serves as a teaching signal so that the brain can learn whether the expected energy value of a food matches the observed (i.e., signalled) value. Favourable to this view is the unusual biochemistry of ghrelin, namely that its activated form is acyl-ghrelin (T. D. Müller et al., 2015). To become acylated there must be nutrients available (fatty acids), so the active form of this hormone is consequently nutrient dependent. Consistent with this perspective is a study by Callahan et al. (2004). They found that for a drink of set volume but of varying caloric value, acyl-ghrelin release was proportional to energy content (i.e., it appeared to serve as a nutrient signal). However, there are animal studies that seem to contradict this finding, with sham feeding triggering ghrelin release in the same manner as a real meal – clearly not a nutrient signal – and others that suggest different orally presented nutrients can affect ghrelin release during sham feeding (Hsu et al., 2016).

The second view is that ghrelin is released in anticipation of feeding (see Watts et al., 2022). There is certainly evidence favourable to this idea (but also contradictory data – see, for example, Dailey et al., 2016), with animals fed at certain times entraining ghrelin release at those times (e.g., Sugino et al., 2002). As many feeding-related hormones are released prior to food intake – the cephalic phase response – this observation is not perhaps surprising. However, what is more interesting is that ghrelin knockout mice have abnormal time-entrained feeding behaviour, which may suggest that ghrelin is involved in learning this type of relationship (Müller et al., 2015). Indeed, there is evidence that ghrelin actively promotes long-term potentiation in the brain, and synaptogenesis, which is consistent with a learning function. So perhaps in addition to being part of the cephalic phase response, ghrelin release augments learning about the circumstances surrounding feeding (e.g., place and time). This may not be its only learning-related feeding role, as it is also involved in the higher-order modulation of responsiveness to learned food cues (Hsu et al., 2016) – namely, when a food cue is present, indicating whether the associated food will be rewarding to eat.

In sum, rather than being the 'hunger hormone', ghrelin's role seems to be better characterised by learning: learning about when and where eating might occur, modulation of learned cues, and the likely reward value of a food. It may be for these reasons that ghrelin receptors are in the hippocampus, in brain reward areas, and in the hypothalamus (Abizaid, 2009; Hsu et al., 2016).

2.2.2 *Orexin*

Orexin is a neuropeptide transmitter secreted by around 50–80,000 specialised neurons located in the hypothalamic area of the brain (Scammell & Winrow, 2011). Interest in its capacity to affect general hunger arose from injecting orexin directly into the brain, which served to increase food intake in rats, but only when they normally do *not* feed (i.e., during the day). Orexin antagonists also decrease food intake (Peleg-Raibstein et al., 2023). In terms of its functional role, orexin is involved in glucose metabolism, wakefulness, and locomotion. This may facilitate the search for food when protein and fat stores are being metabolised for energy – that is, under conditions of starvation (Sakurai, 2014). Under normal conditions, eliminating orexin in germ-line knockout mice has a small negative impact on food intake, with them eating about 5 per cent less than their healthy littermates. Orexin is then orexigenic, but clearly animals lacking this neuropeptide can still eat, suggesting that it does not serve as *the* cause of general hunger. Rather, its role in feeding seems more strongly linked to survival under conditions of starvation.

2.2.3 *Agouti-Related Peptide (AgRP) and Neuropeptide Y (NPY)*

The principal orexigenic effects of agouti-related peptide (AgRP) and neuropeptide Y (NPY) occur in one of the nuclei of the hypothalamus – the focus of a later part of this chapter (see Section 2.3). NPY is abundant throughout the brain, while AgRP is more restricted, being localised to neurons in the arcuate nucleus of the hypothalamus – but noting that these project to several other brain areas. Around 10,000 neurons deploy AgRP as a neuropeptide transmitter, alongside NPY (and gamma aminobutyric acid (GABA); Zhang et al., 2019). If NPY release is stimulated in this region (or if NPY is injected), there is a short-term increase in feeding. The same manipulations for AgRP produce a different temporal pattern, with feeding elevated for a week (Zhang et al., 2019). Thus, both these neuropeptides exert an orexigenic effect.

The impact of eliminating AgRP and NPY from the mouse brain has been examined using germ-line knockout mice. Individual (i.e., NPY or AgRP) or joint knockout mice are completely normal as long as they have continuous access to food (Qian et al., 2002). However, they are unable to adapt to time-restricted feeding schedules (Zhang et al., 2019). If the knockout of both neuropeptides occurs in adulthood (i.e., as the mouse develops, the NPY/AgRP neurons are functionally normal) the impact is catastrophic, with the animals starving to death – pointing to the critical role for developmental processes. As with the other hormones and neurotransmitters examined in this section, it is problematic to just regard them as causes of hunger or 'hunger' peptides. Their function is more nuanced.

Three interrelated functions have emerged for AgRP/NPY (Deem et al., 2022). First, under conditions of starvation the AgRP/NPY system is involved in facilitating adaptations to energy shortage by slowing metabolic processes, altering glucose homeostasis, reducing anxiety (i.e., to promote riskier foraging), enhancing wakefulness, and promoting aggression and territoriality (i.e., to defend resources). Second, there is emerging evidence that AgRP/NPY is involved in circadian entrainment of eating behaviour, which may be why animals lacking this system are unable to adapt to time-restricted feeding. Third, AgRP/NPY are stimulated by both low body temperature and food deprivation/fasting/starvation, which then triggers foraging (and the suite of behaviours identified under the first point here). AgRP/NPY release is then shut down either by encountering a learned food cue or by eating food. Deem et al. (2022) suggest that while the AgRP/NPY system has an important reactive component (i.e., response to starvation), the more critical and less studied function is likely to be its role in coordinating foraging behaviour in the anticipation of energy needs (see Ramsay & Woods, 2014 – and the related notion of allostasis). Note that anticipating something is dependent on prior experience, pointing again to the importance of learning.

2.2.4 *Asprosin*

Asprosin is an orexigenic peptide hormone secreted by white adipose tissue that can cross the blood–brain barrier and activate AgRP/NPY neurons (Duerrschmid et al., 2017). It is rapidly released during food deprivation and decreases upon refeeding. Administration of asprosin stimulates hunger, and the release of glucose from the liver. It has been suggested that asprosin functions as part of the broader system to manage food deprivation/starvation, by maintaining euglycemia and stimulating behaviour necessary to procure food.

2.2.5 *Discussion: Hormones and Neurotransmitters as a Cause of General Hunger*

The tacit model explored in this section is that a particular hormone or neurotransmitter is the cause of hunger (and see Woods et al., 2018, for a discussion on this same issue in relation to satiation/satiety). The data described earlier do not support this type of deterministic model, as knocking out individual genes coding for different peptides does not have the catastrophic effect that it should have if an agent was *the cause* of general hunger. Moreover, the data, and especially that for AgRP/NPY, suggest the importance of development in making an agent an orexigenic agent. If AgRP/NPY is eliminated in adult animals, the result is death from starvation. If an animal grows without AgRP/NPY, its development is effectively normal. This suggests that events in development (e.g., learning) are critical for establishing an agent's orexigenic role.

As each orexigenic peptide is studied in greater depth, two things seem to emerge. The first concerns learning. For ghrelin and AgRP/NPY, the most studied agents, this is already clear. Ghrelin facilitates learning about when and where food is, possibly its nutrient value, it modulates response to food, and is involved in circadian entrainment (i.e., adjusting to feeding in a time window). AgRP/NPY also seems to be involved in circadian entrainment, food selection learning, and in the anticipatory coordination of foraging. As Deem et al. (2022) noted, it is more important to anticipate energy deficits than to react to them, and while a function of all the agents here was reactive, in assisting survival during severe energy depletion – famine – the major function was ensuring this never occurred. Such anticipatory behaviour requires a period of development, that is, time for the organism to interact with the environment and to learn. Once an anticipatory signal is established, it then becomes part of the feeding architecture.

A final point concerns the chain of causality, which places an interesting constraint on any orexigenic agent endogenous to the brain (i.e., such as AgRP/NPY). Whatever the orexigenic agent, something must occur before it, to cause its release. In most cases this initial cause is likely to be a signal originating from outside the brain. This signal must have predictive validity – it might predict food will be available at this time, in this place, after this event, or perhaps that soon a lot of energy will be used, and so on. This would suggest that no orexigenic agent, endogenous to the brain, can serve as a primary cause of hunger.

In sum, orexigenic agents do not cause general hunger. Indeed, those endogenous to the brain require another cause to initiate their release. The evidence suggests that orexigenic agents' role in hunger is connected to the anticipation and avoidance of an energy deficit, an ability that seems to critically depend on learning and development – as exemplified by the impact of knocking out AgRP/NPY in adults versus in the germ line.

2.3 The Brain and General Hunger

Brain-based models of general hunger and feeding are dominated by a two-process model (for an example, see Fig 1b in Volkow et al., 2011) where excitatory processes promote hunger, foraging, and feeding, while inhibitory processes retard them. Initially, the excitatory process, and the inhibitory process, were thought to have discrete neuroanatomical locations. However, as knowledge has increased, the excitatory and inhibitory processes fractionated into multiple anatomical locations, with these now being viewed as distributed interacting networks. While this has produced a more complex picture, it is still one fundamentally characterised by opposing forces of excitation (hunger, foraging, and feeding) and inhibition (satiation and satiety).

The brain area that has consistently attracted the most attention regarding feeding is the hypothalamus (see Figure 2.5). Early conceptions of the neural basis of hunger and feeding centred on this structure, but with time this has expanded to include several other brain areas/systems, which are examined in Section 2.3.2 (before the hypothalamus) and Section 2.3.3 (after the hypothalamus). A section on neurotransmitter systems is also included here, as serotonin, dopamine, and norepinephrine have at different times been thought to exert opposing excitatory and inhibitory influences on feeding. Finally, in considering the neural substrates of excitation and inhibition, this section also includes the circadian entrainment of hunger. This is an important biological account and is placed in this section due to its links to the hypothalamus.

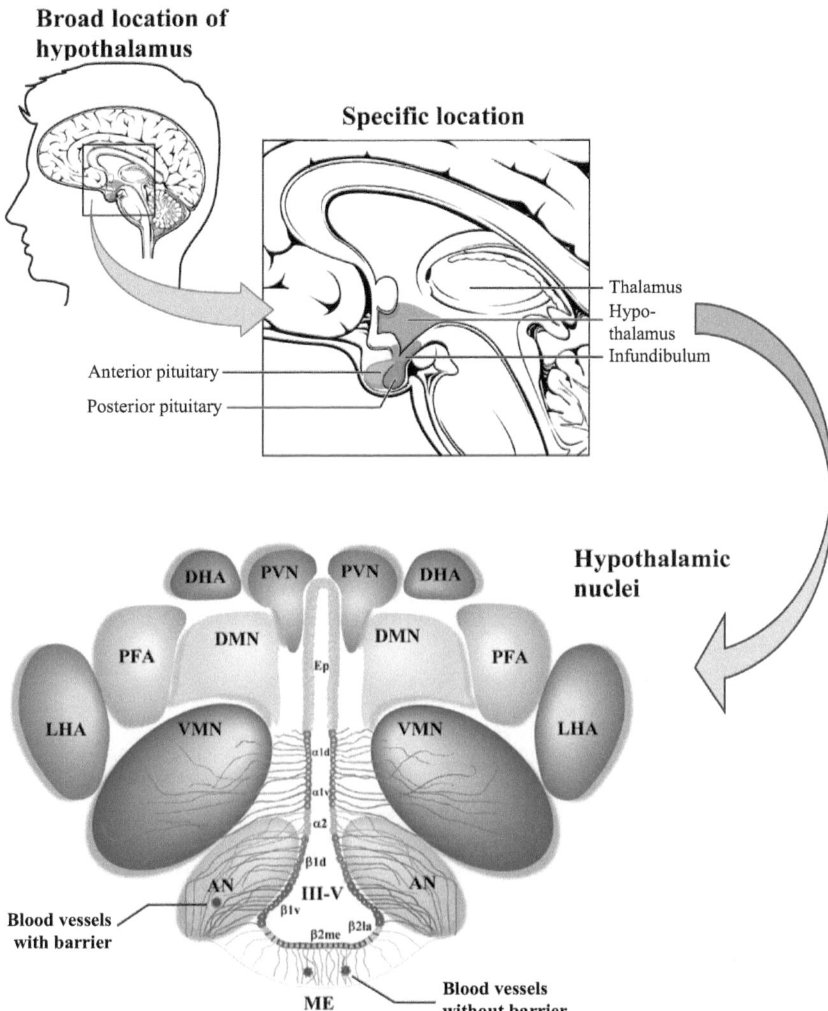

Figure 2.5 The location of the hypothalamus in the brain and its principal nuclei.
Notes: AN: arcuate nucleus; VMN: ventromedial nucleus; DMN: dorsomedial nucleus; PVN: periventricular nucleus; DHA: dorsal hypothalamic area; PFA: perifornical area; LHA: lateral hypothalamic area; SCN: suprachiasmatic nucleus; SON: supraoptic nucleus; POA: preoptic area; MB: mammillary bodies; ME: median eminence; III-V: third ventricle.
Source: Anatomy & Physiology, Connexions website by OpenStax College; and Elizondo-Vega, R., Cortes-Campos, C., Barahona, M. J., Oyarce, K. A., Carril, C. A., & García-Robles, M. A. (2015). The role of tanycytes in hypothalamic glucosensing. *Journal of Cellular and Molecular Medicine*, *19*(7), 1471–1482. https://doi.org/10.1111/jcmm.12590. www.ncbi.nlm.nih.gov/pmc/articles/PMC4511346

2.3.1 *The Hypothalamus*

An influential dual-process model of general hunger was proposed by Stellar (1954) and is illustrated in Figure 2.6. The model envisaged two centres located within the hypothalamus; these having been identified by electrical stimulation and lesion studies. One centre was excitatory (LHA in Figure 2.5), initiating general hunger and feeding, the other was inhibitory (VMN in Figure 2.5), shutting the former down. Inputs to the centres came from both internal and external sources. The internal sources differentially affected the centres (e.g., some cues excite one and inhibit the other, and vice versa). The external sources reflected sensory inputs, including the capacity of learned cues to serve as excitatory inputs. The model also acknowledged other controlling influences on feeding (i.e., cortical), and these were considered to have access to the same inputs as the hypothalamic centres. In sum, feeding (and general hunger) in this model are the outcome of these two opposing centres. While more refined lesion techniques indicated that the anatomical detail of the model was incorrect, its conceptualisation of general hunger/feeding as being the product of two opposing forces remains highly influential, as does its recognition of the hypothalamus as an important feeding control region of the brain.

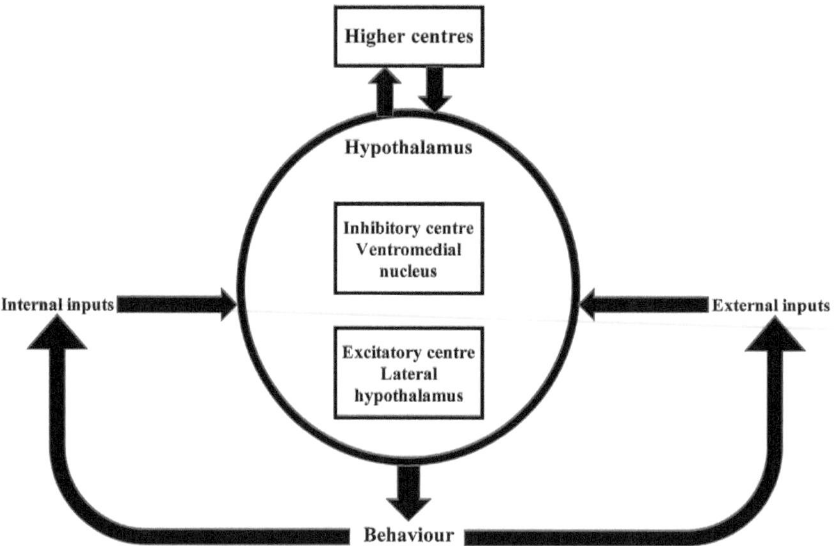

Figure 2.6 Stellar's (1954) hypothalamic model.

Hypothalamic models of general hunger and feeding now focus on the arcuate nucleus (e.g., Sternson, 2013; Subramaniapillai & McIntyre, 2017; see Figure 2.5 for its location and that of the other nuclei). There are good reasons for this, as the orexigenic neurons that jointly express the neuropeptides AgRP and NPY are located here, as are anorexigenic neurons that jointly express the neuropeptides pro-opiomelanocortin (POMC) and cocaine- and amphetamine-regulated transcript (CART) – see Figure 2.7. While the orexigenic AgRP/NPY neurons serve to excite general hunger and feeding, POMC/CART neurons serve to inhibit it. Each set of neurons is in turn excited or inhibited by many of the agents described earlier in this chapter, such as ghrelin, leptin, glucose, and insulin. The arcuate nucleus also has a special connection with the median eminence, where there is no blood–brain barrier, allowing it to 'sample' metabolic events in the body. Stellar's model proposed discrete excitatory and inhibitory centres within the hypothalamus, with links to other brain areas. The arcuate nucleus contains both excitatory and inhibitory neurons within it, with all these neurons also receiving both excitatory and inhibitory inputs, and with multiple links to other brain areas.

2.3.2 *Before the Hypothalamus*

In Sternson and Eiselt's (2017) 'three pillars of appetite control', two of the three pillars are in the hypothalamus, but the third is in the brain stem. The brain stem is involved in the initiation and control of feeding most notably in the consummatory phase, where it coordinates chewing, swallowing, and the digestive process. It has several relevant nuclei (notably the parabrachial with its role in inhibiting food intake; Sternson & Eiselt, 2017), and it serves as the initial entry point for vagal afferents from the digestive system as well as possessing most of the same feeding-related receptors as the hypothalamus (Grill & Hayes, 2012). It connects extensively to the hypothalamus, and to structures beyond it.

2.3.3 *Beyond the Hypothalamus*

Beyond the hypothalamus, the most studied networks concern reward processing and brain areas linked to conscious-regulatory control over feeding (i.e., self-control, restraint, dieting, long-term consequences of eating *this*). These can respectively be construed as excitatory (reward) and inhibitory (self-control/satiation) processes (e.g., Cassidy & Tong, 2017). A key advance in understanding the neural basis of reward

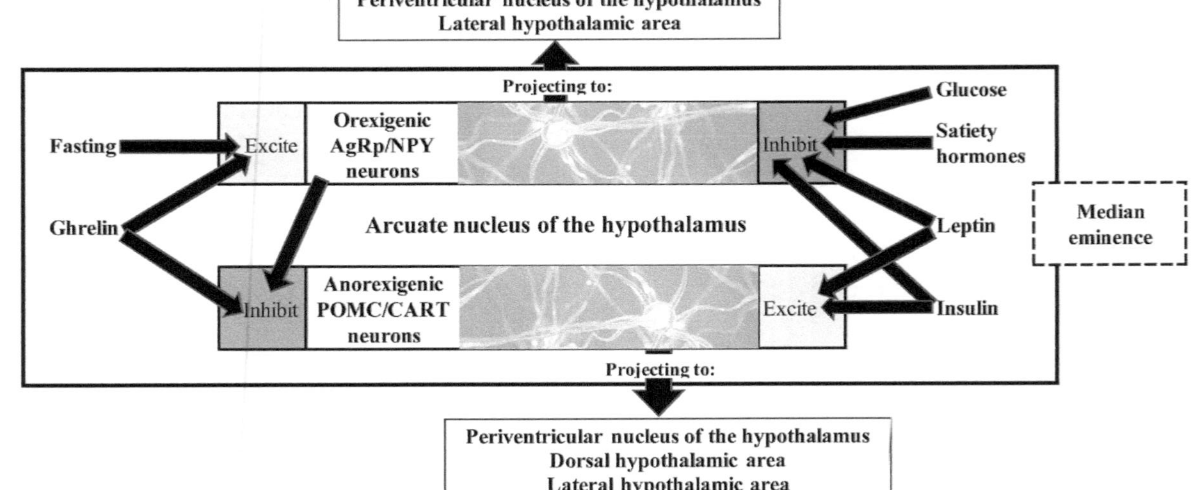

Figure 2.7 A current conception of the hypothalamic model.

(Berridge, 1996) has been to differentiate between its anticipation (termed wanting) and the consummatory pleasure that ensues when the reward is consumed (termed liking, affect, hedonics). Wanting is thought to be mediated by a network involving the ventral tegmental area and liking by the one including the shell of the nucleus accumbens. Conscious control of food intake has often been attributed to frontal cortical areas (Ferrario et al., 2016). A further consideration is decision-making between competing anticipated rewards. This seems to be subserved by a variety of other frontal structure, including the orbitofrontal cortex (E. T. Rolls, 2016). All these areas, for wanting, liking, self-control, and reward decision-making, are interconnected, and share many of the same inputs with the brain stem and hypothalamus (Azevedo et al., 2022).

Two less studied networks subserve feeding-related interoception and learning. Learning is a critical enabler of excitatory and inhibitory processing (more later), and the focus of Chapter 3. Interoception concerns the perception, modelling, and anticipation of internal bodily states. Interoception also encapsulates certain experiential aspects of general hunger (e.g., an empty rumbling stomach) and satiety (e.g., bloated full stomach). There is agreement that one important neural substrate for interoceptive processing is the insular cortex (e.g., Haruki & Ogawa, 2021). For learning and memory, a network involving the anterior and media temporal lobes, and limbic system structures – the hippocampus, septum and amygdala – are all relevant (e.g., Kanoski & Grill, 2017).

The number of brain areas implicated in feeding has increased considerably since the 1950s. However, the picture that emerges is still reminiscent of Stellar's (1954) model but with a distributed network of excitatory and inhibitory processes. There is a competition between these excitatory and inhibitory networks, with the outcome being general hunger/feeding (or not). While there is nothing controversial or new about characterising brain function in this way, tipping the system towards excitation (or inhibition) still requires a cause. In just the same way as something must cause the release of an endogenous orexigenic agent, with that 'something' typically being external to the brain, tipping the brain towards excitation and hunger also requires that initial external 'something' as well.

2.3.4 Neurotransmitter Systems

In an early model Leibowitz and Shor-Posner (1986) proposed that norepinephrine, binding to the α2 receptor in the paraventricular nucleus of the hypothalamus, served as the excitatory cause for food intake, with serotonin providing an inhibitory countereffect. That serotonin exhibits some form of anorexigenic effect in the brain continues to be well supported. There are seven serotonin receptors, with multiple subtypes, and while the 2c receptor has been repeatedly linked to an inhibitory effect on feeding, manipulating *most* of the other receptor types exerts a similar effect (Shin et al., 2023). It is then not surprising that serotonin has been the focus of much research in the hunt for an effective weight-loss drug (Simansky, 1996). The serotonergic pathways that promote this inhibitory effect arise in the raphe nuclei of the brain stem, and project into the arcuate nucleus of the hypothalamus, the ventral tegmental area, and the nucleus accumbens (van Galen et al., 2021). In the arcuate nucleus they inhibit AgRP/NPY neurons and excite POMC/CART neurons – consistent with an inhibitory role in hunger and feeding. Similarly, they exert an inhibitory effect on brain areas linked to wanting and liking. The raphe nuclei are themselves subject to inhibition by ghrelin, and also excitation from both gut-released satiety hormones, and prefrontal cortical activity.

The brain has four main dopaminergic pathways, of which the mesolimbic (ventral tegmental area projecting to the nucleus accumbens) and nigrostriatal (substantia nigra projecting to the dorsal striatum) ones are the most important here. While the mesolimbic pathway was discussed earlier in relation to reward processing (i.e., wanting and liking), the nigrostriatal pathway is critical for goal-directed movement, including towards food. An excitatory role for the mesolimbic pathway was originally envisaged. Direct injection of dopamine into the nucleus accumbens promoted feeding, gene inactivation of dopamine reduced feeding, and extracellular dopamine levels increased in the nucleus accumbens in anticipation of food – all suggesting an excitatory function (Joshi et al., 2022). There has also been related interest in the D2 receptor, and its role in promoting consumption of palatable food. However, there are many contradictory findings, and dopamine's role in feeding is more complex than once envisaged (Joshi et al., 2022). In sum, serotonin and dopamine slot into the broader neural model, pitting excitatory appetitive influences against inhibitory ones. The same concerns identified earlier arise here as well, namely the problem of initial cause – *something* needs to tip the balance towards excitation.

2.3.5 Circadian Rhythms

Mammals have a master internal clock located in the suprachiasmatic nucleus of the anterior hypothalamus, which is entrained by exposure to the light/dark cycle. This clock exerts multiple influences: (1) it coordinates other cellular clocks, which in turn produce the circadian release patterns observed for leptin, insulin, and ghrelin; and (2) it regulates metabolic processes and the activity of the gut microbiome (Laermans & Depoortere, 2016). The most obvious impact of the master clock is that in humans, hunger and feeding typically occur during the day, while in laboratory rats and mice, which are nocturnal, hunger and feeding occur at night (Strubbe & Woods, 2004). The importance of this biological coordination of activity, relative to the external environment, is illustrated by what happens when it is disrupted. Mice who have a key gene of the master clock knocked out exhibit hyperphagia, develop metabolic disorder, and become obese. A parallel can be seen in human shift workers, who are at increased risk of obesity and metabolic disorder (Pickel & Sung, 2020). The overarching coordination of physiological activity based on the light/dark cycle reflects a clear biological constraint on hunger and feeding. More importantly, it could also be thought of as a rather distal 'initial cause' pushing the brain towards excitation, and hence hunger, and food intake, during the light cycle.

When the environment dictates that food is available at a particular time, and perhaps for a set period, animals and people learn to anticipate its arrival (Mistlberger, 1994). In animals, this anticipation manifests as increased activity, such as wheel running, lever pressing, approaching a feeder, pacing, and drinking. In humans, increased activity may also occur, but the more reportable aspect may be the experience of general hunger and the overt anticipation of food (i.e., it's nearly lunchtime!). The mechanisms responsible for food anticipatory activity have been studied extensively in animals, and there are at least three contributory mechanisms. Each involves different learning processes. In just the same way that there is a master clock entrained with the day/light cycle, there are also internal clocks that are specifically entrained by the time that food becomes available (although nobody knows where they are, the hypothalamus would seem a likely guess). Animals are also able to 'read off' time from the master clock when a food event – and this can include linking it to a location in space as well – and this information can then accumulate in memory and be used to predict the occurrence of food when that clock time (and place) approaches. There are also several Pavlovian models of time-based learning, which can explain an animal's capacity to anticipate the arrival of food. None of these mechanisms can account for all anticipatory phenomena, but all contribute in some degree (Mistlberger, 1994).

Two important conclusions emerge from this section. First, the master internal clock dictates the broad period in which feeding will occur, and so arguably serves as an endogenous but distal initial cause for hunger, in that hunger becomes more likely in the light cycle. Second, for anticipatory feeding behaviour, the environment provides the initial cause (i.e., food consistently available at this time), and if this changes, then the brain adjusts by learning the new relationship. What is so surprising is how understudied this all is in humans, even though we exhibit (at least in industrial societies) several time-dependent hunger and feeding patterns, which in Western culture have the familiar names of breakfast, lunch, and dinner.

2.3.6 Discussion: The Brain and General Hunger

The focus of this chapter has been the biological causes of general hunger. Cause is rather difficult to discern for the excitation/inhibition model, which dominates thinking about feeding (and by implication hunger) and the brain. This is because except for hunger being more likely during the waking part of the day – a consequence of an endogenous rhythm (i.e., a distal internal cause) – the cause of hunger must lie outside of the brain, namely in whatever input *causes* the system to tip towards excitation. Critical inputs could come from the body or from the environment (e.g., food being available at a certain time).

A further issue is whether excitatory brain areas in adults are similarly excitatory at birth. The germ-line knockout mice data described earlier indicate that at least for orexigenic peptides, developmental processes are seemingly critical for these agents to function in an excitatory manner. This would explain why eliminating an orexigenic peptide in adulthood can be catastrophic, in a way that it is not for the knockout animals that never possessed it as an excitatory cue. If development really is the critical step where neural processing is first linked with environmental and bodily inputs, this points to a central dependence on learning.

2.4 Conclusion: Biological Causes of General Hunger

Four models of general hunger emerge from this examination of its biological basis. The first is the energy control model (or homeostatic account), where a departure from the usual level (historically a set point) of some index of bodily fuel status causes a compensatory response, namely an increase or decrease in general hunger. The second is the biological agent account, where release of an agent causes general hunger. The third is the excitation–inhibition account, where general hunger arises from tipping the balance towards excitation, with these processes instantiated in the neuroanatomy and neurochemistry of the brain. The fourth model, which could be encompassed within the third, is the circadian account, namely that one cause of general hunger arises from the brain's timekeeping mechanisms.

The first model, the energy control account, no longer offers a plausible model of general hunger. It has many empirical and theoretical problems, which were detailed in Sections 2.1.5 and 2.1.6. Here, only the most critical are summarised. First, in healthy people, daily energy fluctuations are small relative to total energy reserves, making a control model based on identifying a deficit, and remedying it with hunger, unlikely. Second, eating is typically anticipatory, occurring well before any energy deficit arises. Third, even if in the future a signal is discovered that both reliably indicates bodily energy status and precedes general hunger, this would not be enough to claim causation. This is because it runs into the same problem identified for the biological agent model considered next, namely developmental processes – presumably involving learning – seem critical to establishing a functional hunger signal (i.e., you must learn what it means).

The second model, the biological agent account, is also unviable. Germline knockout mice indicate that an animal can feed effectively (albeit with certain impairments) without these orexigenic agents, suggesting that each one is not the cause of general hunger. Importantly, what this body of work reveals is that eliminating some of these agents in adulthood can have catastrophic effects on feeding, and hence on general hunger. This would suggest that during development, some association is made between feeding-related events in the environment and/or the body, and the presence/action of the agent in the brain. Moreover, there is evidence from the most well-studied orexigenic agents that they also facilitate food-related learning processes, including anticipatory and time-based forms.

The third model, the excitation–inhibition account, is also unviable as a causal explanation of general hunger *on its own*. There is of course overwhelming amount of evidence that the brain has multiple excitatory processes that serve to increase general hunger and food intake, and multiple inhibitory processes that serve to shut these down. The principal problem with this type of model is that it does not provide an initial cause for general hunger, because this initial cause is nearly always located *outside* of the model (i.e., of the brain), namely in what are often euphemistically labelled as 'inputs' to the excitatory process(es). No input means no tipping towards excitation, and hence no general hunger. A further problem is that the most well-understood excitatory and inhibitory circuits, located in the arcuate nucleus, can be lost in knockout mice, yet the system still functions effectively (i.e., the animals will feed and thrive, etc.). Not only does this suggest that learning during development is critical for these brain systems to function appropriately, but it also points to another finding that characterises current knowledge. This is the multiplicity of brain areas and networks involved in exciting and inhibiting feeding, and it is presumably these that satisfactorily substitute for those lost to the gene knockout process.

The fourth model, the circadian account, is really an extension of the excitation–inhibition account. Circadian rhythms impose a general biological constraint on when feeding and hence general hunger can occur, and this could be construed as an endogenous initial cause – solving a key problem of the excitation–inhibition account. However, this needs to be tempered by the distinctly distal nature of this initial cause, because hunger is typically episodic during the day (e.g., Mattes, 2010; Reichenberger et al., 2018), and presumably the master circadian clock plays no role in causing each episode of hunger. Humans and animals also use time cues to anticipate the arrival of food, and this certainly can explain certain episodes

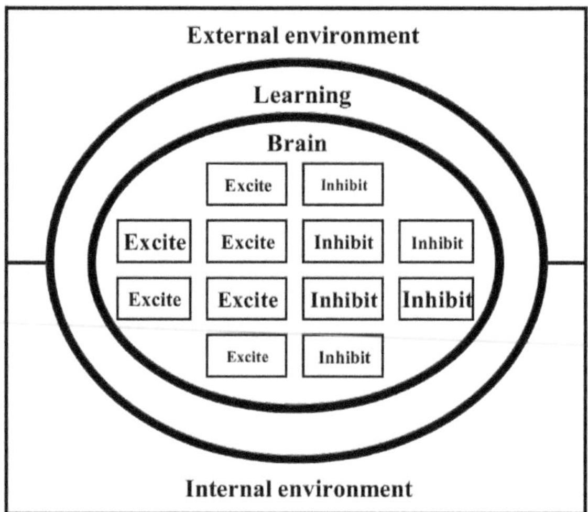

Figure 2.8 A conceptual model of hunger (and feeding) in which learning mediates the relationship between the environment (internal (i.e., body) and external (i.e., world)) and neural processes (multiple excitatory and inhibitory elements).

of hunger within the active part of a day. There are several learning-based mechanisms that can account for time-anticipatory feeding. Each mechanism captures features of the environment that predict food, and then use these to tip the neural balance towards excitation, hunger, and feeding. In this case, the primary cause of general hunger lies in the environment.

Aside from time, many other environmental variables are predictive of food (e.g., place, objects, smells, sounds, etc.), and similarly many internal events are predictive that food will probably be good (or not) to eat now (e.g., many of the biological signals examined in this chapter can function this way). Learning about all these events can provide a highly flexible and adaptive causal account of general hunger, one that links the brain's excitatory processes to predictive events outside of the brain (and for some of the inhibitory processes too). A generalised version of this model is illustrated in Figure 2.8. Here, multiple excitatory and inhibitory processes are available to control feeding (and general hunger) located in the brain (i.e., plenty of redundancy), and which become linked during development (and in some cases continuing into adulthood) to events in both the internal bodily milieu and the external environment, via learning. A learning-based model of hunger forms the focus of Chapter 3.

CHAPTER 3

Psychological Approaches to Hunger

3.0 Introduction

Chapter 2 presented several biological accounts that could potentially explain general hunger. It was concluded that except for the circadian account, none of the models, on their own, offered an adequate causal explanation of hunger. This chapter presents an account of hunger based on learning and memory. It starts by outlining why learning and memory are important for understanding hunger. It then presents a psychological model of hunger and identifies its linkages back to the biological accounts in Chapter 2.

3.1 Challenges from Neuropsychology

Even if Chapter 2 did not provide enough grounds for questioning a wholly biological approach to general hunger, evidence from neuropsychology is even more problematic. This is because the observed neuropsychological deficits are utterly unanticipated by all biological approaches, albeit with some interesting caveats.

In 1953 Henry Molaison (HM) underwent a bilateral temporal lobectomy for intractable epilepsy (Corkin, 2013). This procedure, while reducing his seizure frequency, left him profoundly amnesic. He was no longer able to form new memories about events in his life, such as what he ate for dinner (i.e., episodic memories), nor store new information about the world, such as what McDonald's is (i.e., semantic memories). From the late 1950s until HM's death in 2008 he was the subject of extensive scientific investigation, which included long sessions of sometimes tedious psychological testing. It was noticed that even if testing went over a mealtime, he never complained of hunger (Corkin, 2013). This led to two studies exploring HM's capacity to experience hunger. The first asked HM, at several times in the day, including before and after meals, to rate how hungry/full he currently felt on a bipolar line scale with anchors of hungry and full (and neither hungry nor full in the middle). Irrespective of when these ratings were obtained, HM consistently reported feeling neither hungry nor full (Hebben et al., 1985). A second study tested whether these self-reports of hunger reflected HM's appetite for food. HM was offered his dinner at the usual time, which he ate with relish and in full. Just a few minutes later he was offered the *same dinner again.* He ate all of it except for the salad. Ratings of hunger/fullness were obtained across this testing session, and while there was no change in his self-report across the first meal, the second one led to a small shift towards the 'full' end of the scale – the *only* hunger rating change observed in this report (Hebben et al., 1985).

These observations are interesting for several reasons. First, HM's surgical lesion did not affect the hypothalamus nor other areas of the brain that are generally considered to control ingestive behaviour (Annese et al., 2014). This is why the loss of hunger in HM is largely unanticipated by the biological accounts presented in Chapter 2. Second, HM's reports of hunger did not seem sensitive to either the passage of time or to interoceptive cues that might signal that food would be good to eat now (e.g., an empty rumbling stomach, fatigue, etc.). Additional testing revealed that HM was also impaired in judging elapsed time, with an hour appearing to HM as just the passage of a few minutes (Richards, 1973). HM was also less able to feel pain and fatigue than controls, suggesting a broader impairment in interoceptive processing (Hebben et al., 1985).

Together, this suggests: (1) that even if several hours had passed since his last meal, this is probably not how it felt; and (2) that interoceptive cues such as a full or empty stomach might either have lost their meaning and/or were perhaps less perceptible. Third, his willingness to eat a second main meal almost immediately after a first is perhaps the most abnormal feature identified by Hebben et al. (1985). This finding has since been replicated in other patients with lesions to the medial temporal lobe (and hence with amnesia like HM's). The bizarreness of this finding is nicely illustrated in one of these follow-up studies. Rozin et al. (1998) reported the incredulity of brain-injured controls, when they were offered an identical second main meal just moments after consuming their first. Needless to say, they did not want more. This capacity of HM and similar cases to immediately eat a second main meal likely reflects a combination of factors: (1) no episodic memory of having just eaten; (2) no appreciation of how much time has passed since last eating; (3) no experience of hunger; and (4) difficulty in comprehending the meaning of and/or perceiving interoceptive feedback from the stomach and gut, limiting the experience of fullness.

While there has not been much research into neuropsychological patients with similar damage to HM, what has been done has confirmed his general impairment with hunger. In one study, Berriman informally talked to patients and carers about their experiences of hunger after the formal experimental phase was complete (Berriman et al., 2016). One patient, the one with the most marked abnormalities on testing, was described by her carer as not showing any signs of hunger nor of reporting hunger. This same patient had recently lost weight and had to be reminded to eat and drink. While this patient was not as seriously impaired as HM and lived semi-independently, it is noteworthy that HM resided in a care facility where all his meals were provided (Corkin, 2013). Indeed, if HM had not been living in such a structured environment, he may have died of inanition. Such is the importance of learning and memory to hunger and eating.

3.2 The Importance of Memory

Hunger can arise from: (1) seeing a particular food; (2) thinking about food; (3) seeing a food-related logo; (4) feeling/hearing a rumbling stomach (or other bodily cues); and (5) knowing it is a mealtime. There may be others too, such as place-based and event-based hungers. The commonality across these diverse situations is that hunger is a state of *knowing* that food will be good to eat *now*. The information being used to arrive at this state of knowing is unlikely to be something one is born with; rather it is acquired. Consider in more detail the examples (1) to (5): (1) to know that a food you are *just* looking at will be good to eat requires access to information about prior encounters with it, especially its flavour, and post-ingestive consequences – all of these are products of memory; (2) in thinking about food, one needs to draw upon knowledge of what food is and what it is like to eat – again products of memory; (3) in seeing a food logo, its meaning requires both knowing the food(s) associated with that brand and what they are like to eat – again products of memory; (4) a rumbling stomach means nothing unless you know what it signals – again a product of memory; and (5) a mealtime is only a mealtime because one has learned that at this time of day people eat, and that they eat particular sorts of food – again these are products of memory. Without wishing to labour the point, all these examples involve memory, and hence learning, as the basis for this knowledge.

While memory may serve up a representation of a food, this is not much use unless one can also evaluate whether that food will be good to eat *now*. Certain types of cue are very helpful in this regard, such as knowing that: it is lunchtime; several hours have elapsed since last eating; the food is palatable (who can refuse a morsel of chocolate?); or that the stomach feels empty. In all these examples, the cue *signals* that food will be good to eat now. This too is learned (i.e., is one *really* born knowing that noon is lunchtime, and that 3–4 hours have likely passed since breakfast and so the stomach will probably be empty?). Although there is more to be said later about how these learning and memory processes operate, two things should be apparent now: (1) damage to brain areas that support learning and memory produce significant impairments in hunger; and (2) on logical grounds alone, memory, and hence learning, are involved in routine manifestations of hunger. There is then an important reliance on learning and memory processes when a person becomes hungry. Historically, this has not always been remembered or appreciated.

3.3 The Two Hungers

Since the initial experimental investigations of hunger by Cannon and Washburn (1912) – and earlier (see Chapter 1) – there has been a recognition that there are two main forms of hunger (e.g., see Castonguay et al., 1983; Lowe & Butryn, 2007; May et al., 2012; Mayer, 1953; Weingarten, 1985). The first is termed here specific hunger (also known as 'appetite', 'hedonic hunger', 'head hunger' and in its strongest form 'craving'). It refers to a desire to eat one specific type (or category; e.g., chocolate) of palatable food. Cannon and Washburn (1912) attributed the discovery of specific hunger to the Russian physiologist Ivan Pavlov, thereby firmly setting it within a framework of associative (i.e., Pavlovian) learning. In essence, specific hunger occurs because a person (or dog in Pavlov's case) has learned an association between a cue (e.g., a bell, logo, sight of food, etc. (i.e., the conditioned stimulus, CS)) and the rewarding orosensory and post-ingestive consequences of consuming a particular food (i.e., what that food tastes like and its caloric density (the unconditioned stimulus, US); e.g., Sclafani, 2004). Cannon and Washburn (1912) suggested, as have later proponents of specific hunger, that it is generally for palatable foods, namely those that taste good because they pack a caloric punch (i.e., sweet, sweet-fatty, salty-fatty). Seeing or smelling the food, or its other associated cues (e.g., a logo) then leads to the retrieval of pleasant memories of eating it. This indicates it would be good to eat now – hunger, in other words.

The second form of hunger has generally been regarded as a direct product of biological processes and was the focus of Chapter 2. There is considerable confusion around most aspects of this type of hunger – particularly its phenomenology (i.e., what is/are its psychological manifestation), what causes it to arise, and its developmental origins. However, there is widespread agreement that this form of hunger reflects a need to eat *any type* of wholesome food (e.g., see Cannon & Washburn, 1912; Castonguay et al., 1983; May et al., 2012; Mayer, 1953). For this reason, it is termed general hunger. When people talk about the biological processes causing hunger, it is general hunger they are usually referring to. One such biological conception of general hunger is that it manifests as sensations *in the body* (e.g., fatigue, muscle weakness, etc.), reflecting its basis in *bodily physiology* resulting from an energy deficit (e.g., Siemian et al., 2021). The typically unstated presumption here is that as the energy deficit occurs in the body, so then do the feelings that indicate this state. There is an assumption built into this presumption, namely that people just innately *know* that a particularly bodily feeling connotes hunger (see Harshaw, 2008; Woods et al., 2018, for further discussion of this issue). Although the energy control model (i.e., homeostatic) of hunger is incorrect, it is undisputedly true that there are multiple bodily sensations *associated* with both changes in alimentary physiology and energy metabolism. Whether these bodily sensations are innately meaningful is, however, an assumption, and one that is very possibly wrong.

Notice that the conception of general hunger presented earlier completely excludes the circadian account – that is, time-related hunger. This is probably because the time-related hunger literature has generally had little penetration into the literature dealing with hunger, body weight regulation, and ingestive behaviour – albeit with some important exceptions (see Strubbe & Woods, 2004; Weingarten, 1985). In terms of more recent biological models, such as the biological agent or excitation–inhibition accounts (see Chapter 2), their conceptualisation of general hunger seems different again. As both these biological accounts are 'more' brain-based, hunger seemingly manifests as a mental state without a bodily location – in contrast to a mental state 'located' in the body (e.g., felt in the stomach). However, these are all *my presumptions*, because while it is easy to say that: (1) something causes hunger (e.g., ghrelin, or ARC-AgRP neurons) and (2) it leads to greater food intake, this is unrevealing as to what psychological processes may be occurring – hence one has to *presume* how physiologists, and so on, think hunger occurs (e.g., see Lowell, 2019). And of course, as concluded at the end of Chapter 2, only the circadian account in and of itself seems to offer a viable biological model of hunger. In contrast, there are good grounds to set aside energy control models and, without significant modification, the biological agent account, and the excitation–inhibition accounts of hunger as well. In sum, apart from agreeing that general hunger reflects a need to eat some form of wholesome food, what it is (phenomenally), what causes it, and how it develops – remain largely unanswered questions.

3.4 A Declarative Memory Perspective on Hunger

The following two sections provide an account of specific and general hunger from a declarative learning and memory perspective (e.g., Stevenson, 2024; Stevenson, Yeomans, & Francis, 2024). While this is uncontentious for specific hunger (with at least four similar existing psychological models), for general hunger it reflects a very different approach to thinking about what it is and how it operates. Indeed, the literature to date has only offered biologically based motivational models of food intake (e.g., Le Magnen, 1981; Toates, 1986) – of the kind described in Chapter 2 – and even then, it is often necessary to assume how these models instantiate general hunger. There are of course general psychological models of motivation, notably based on the idea of incentive salience (e.g., Bindra, 1974), and the model of general and specific hunger proposed here is related to this conception in integrating physiology, learning, and internal and external cues. However, there do not appear to be any competing *psychological* models of general hunger, nor models that attempt to place general and specific hunger in a common conceptual framework. This comment may induce surprise, but of the many theories that utilise hunger (e.g., Booth, 2008; Herman & Polivy, 1983; Wardle & Carnell, 2009), either appetite (i.e., specific hunger) is their focus or, if it is general hunger, then it is simply conceived as being of biological origin.

3.4.1 Specific Hunger

3.4.1.1 Previous Models

The brief description of specific hunger provided by Cannon and Washburn (1912) is worth repeating. This is because of its fundamental similarity to all the contemporary models that have followed:

> Appetite [i.e., specific hunger] is related to previous sensations of the taste and smell of food; it has therefore, as Pawlow [i.e., Pavlov] has shown, important psychic elements. It may exist separate from hunger [i.e., general hunger], as, for example when we eat delectable dainties merely to please the palate. Sensory associations, delightful or disgusting, determine the appetite for any edible substance, and either memory or present stimulation can thus arouse desire or dislike for food. (p. 441)

The essence then of specific hunger is twofold – its basis in experience (i.e., learning and memory) and its sensory-affective phenomenology.

There are at least four contemporary models that share the same essential features identified by Cannon and Washburn (1912). The first was the Hoch and Loewenstein (1991) model. They envisaged two forces. One was driven by imagination with the person 'vividly simulating the experience…' and this being synonymous with desire. The other force regulated this – willpower. This account was followed by the elaborated intrusion model, which was initially developed to account for drug craving (Kavanagh et al., 2005). It has been readily adapted for palatable foods (e.g., May et al., 2012), with cues (e.g., logos, names, pictures, etc.) for such foods automatically triggering thoughts/images about them. This hypothetical process can stop at this point, or it can be continued by a process of voluntary elaboration in which the person forms an 'image of desire' – that is, they imagine what it would be like to eat the food (i.e., mental imagery of its appearance, taste, and smell). This elaborative process induces desire via recalling the food's affective properties and, if this recall process is potent enough, this constitutes a craving. The model's focus on mental imagery has been particularly generative, revealing that people do form 'images of desire', that better mental imagery is linked to greater body weight (Patel et al., 2015), and that disrupting 'images of desire' reduces craving (e.g., Kemps & Tiggemann, 2007).

A further model emerged termed hedonic hunger (Lowe & Butryn, 2007). According to this model, encountering a cue to a palatable food brings to mind what it would be like to eat. These associations are strengthened by further pairings of the cue and palatable food, and weakened when the cue is no longer followed by that food (i.e., extinction). More recent iterations of this model have tied it to the neural concept of wanting, mentioned in Chapter 2. Thus, a learned association between a cue and a palatable food induces wanting (desire) for that food (Espel-Huynh et al., 2018). The most recent model is the simulation account (Papies et al., 2020). Here, a palatable food cue automatically activates a process of mental simulation of eating that food, which draws upon memory of prior eating experiences, including motor, sensory, and affective imagery. This can (but does not have to) produce explicit mental content, namely what it would be like to eat this food (i.e., mental imagery and affect). The model has three noteworthy features. First, it draws a similar distinction to Hoch and Loewenstein (1991), between process simulation (what has been discussed so far – that is, the *process* of eating the food) versus outcome simulation. Outcome simulations are reflections on the *consequence* of eating the food, which, for calorically dense palatable food, might be weight gain. Outcome simulation can be likened to the opposing force of willpower. A second feature is that, like the elaborated intrusion model, perceiving a food cue will not automatically lead to a conscious desire for food. And third, this model has also been generative, especially in demonstrating a causal pathway from the experience of a food cue to simulation/imagery and to desire (e.g., Devos et al., 2022).

3.4.1.2 A Declarative Memory Model of Specific Hunger

The model of specific hunger favoured here (see Figure 3.1, upper part) is a distillation of the ideas outlined earlier but placed in the context of human memory research (Stevenson, 2024; Stevenson, Yeomans, & Francis, 2024). Three major sub-divisions of memory are relevant here (Squire et al., 2004). The first is between short-term (seconds and minutes) and long-term (hours, days, months, years) memory. Interest here is mainly on prior experiences of eating, so long-term memory is most relevant. Long-term memory can be divided into declarative (i.e., consciously examinable) and non-declarative (i.e., not consciously examinable) forms (Tulving, 1983). As all the models involve declarative memory processes in the final stage/s of generating a specific hunger (i.e., it is consciously examinable), then declarative memory systems are the relevant form here. Finally, declarative memory can be subdivided into two forms, episodic (i.e., the re-experiencing of an event) and semantic (i.e., knowledge about the world). Episodic memory is most relevant to specific hunger, as it involves the re-experiencing of an event (i.e., eating a particular food). Semantic memory (i.e., acquired meaning) is very important too, but for general hunger, and this is discussed later in the chapter.

Encountering an environmental cue for a particular high palatability food can lead to the retrieval of episodic memories of prior consumption of that food. Episodic memories can be retrieved voluntarily (e.g., thinking about something) or involuntarily (e.g., encountering an environmental food cue; e.g., Hall et al., 2014). This leaves open the possibility that people can make themselves specifically hungry without the need for an

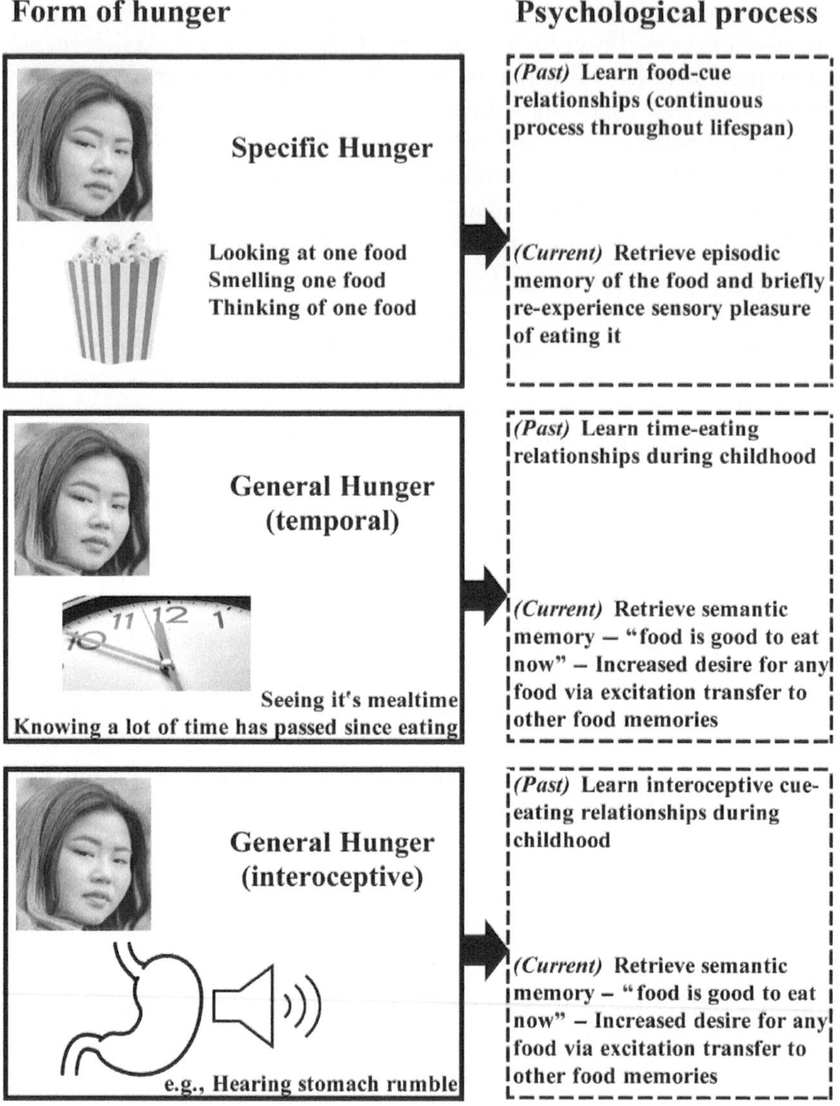

Figure 3.1 A declarative memory model of hunger.

external stimulus, but via voluntary retrieval alone – perhaps when bored, daydreaming, and so on. Voluntary retrieval could also support a process of elaboration (as in the eponymous model). Irrespective of how the episodic memory is retrieved, such recollections are characterised by: (1) the feeling that the remembered event is happening to the person now (i.e., first-person perspective); (2) the involvement of sensory imagery and affect (i.e., as if it were being experienced); and (3) a brief time course (i.e., akin to having just a quick 'taste' of a food), relative to that of the actual event (Conway, 2009). When such an episodic memory of consuming a palatable food occurs, this constitutes specific hunger.

Episodic recollections of eating specific foods have not been a major focus of memory research, so relatively little is known about their properties. Episodic memories of life experiences are typically specific to a personal event, which in turn is often constrained to one discrete time (e.g., a birth, a marriage, a death, etc.). In contrast, the format for episodic memories of food seems to be for eating a *particular food*, and this constitutes the personal event. While this is not constrained by time (i.e., it probably reflects an integration of one or more experiences with that food across multiple occasions), it may be constrained by other factors. These include: (1) place (e.g., see Papies, Claassen, et al., 2022; Papies, van Stekelenburg, et al., 2022), as what a person likes in one context may not be the same in another (e.g., a hospital beef casserole versus a beef casserole from a Michelin-starred restaurant); and (2) who prepared the food (i.e., for the same reasons as with place). A further consideration, and one alluded to by Papies et al. (2020) is the nature of the 'food memory landscape' that each person establishes. Each person builds a set of cue–food relationships, unique to them. If a person's diet comes mainly from pre-prepared food from grocery stores or fast-food chains, then almost everything eaten will have an associated logo, advertising jingle/tag line, brand, and imagery. As such foods are often heavily advertised (Berthoud et al., 2017) – a city dweller may see 5,000 such adverts in a day (Larson et al., 2014) – the upshot of this would be frequent specific hunger, occurring whenever a logo/advert for a consumed food is seen/heard. This is an awful lot of specific hunger. In contrast, someone who prepares their own food from raw ingredients is less likely to come across cues to trigger specific hunger. So, they may have less temptation to eat.

Although much remains to be learned about episodic memories for food, and specific hunger more broadly, some aspects are understood primarily because of the findings generated by the models listed earlier. One robust observation is the centrality of mental imagery and affect in specific hunger. In addition, plenty of experimental work shows that people readily form memories of their food experiences, especially the sensory and affective components (e.g., Rode et al., 2006).

3.4.1.3 Specific Hunger and the Medial Temporal Lobes

Framing specific hunger in terms of an established human memory model (i.e., episodic memory) is parsimonious both because it does not require a separate system, and as it offers a point of convergence for all the models described in Section 3.4.1.1 (i.e., two forces, elaborated intrusions, hedonic hunger, simulation). A similar point of convergence is reached if the neural basis of each of these models is considered. Episodic memory relies upon the medial temporal lobes (see Figure 3.2), and especially the hippocampal formation (Squire & Zola-Morgan, 1991) – some of the same brain areas that were lost when HM had his temporal lobectomy. As Suzanne Corkin (2013) recalled, HM loved eating, and he generally only ate 'healthily' because his intake was controlled by a dietician. When he was due to attend a testing session at MIT in Boston, he would be picked up from his care home to make the two-hour drive. On one such journey, Howard Eichenbaum had stopped to get coffee at McDonald's before collecting HM, and so the branded cup was sitting in the car when HM got in. When HM saw the cup, he remarked: 'Hey, I knew a fellow named John McDonald when I was a boy!' (Corkin, 2013, p. 84). Why is this interesting? McDonald's did not open its first franchise east of the Mississippi River until 1955, two years after HM's surgery, so he would probably not have encountered and hence *learned about* this now ubiquitous fast-food chain. For many people the distinctive rounded letter M logo is a cue for McDonald's food be it fries, nuggets, or burgers. Rather than the cup serving as a hunger cue, as it would for many people – and probably to an intact HM too – instead, all it brought to mind was a childhood memory. This is one way in which damage to the medial temporal lobes can impair learning and memory, and hence specific hunger.

While none of the models described in Section 3.4.1.1 (i.e., two forces, elaborated intrusions, hedonic hunger, simulation) directly focus on episodic memory, they nonetheless draw upon memory processes that would utilise episodic memory and hence the medial temporal lobes. The construction of a mental image seemingly utilises episodes from personal memory. Mental imagery features directly in the elaborated intrusion model (May et al., 2012), and indirectly in all of the other models – namely, in anticipating the consumption of palatable food for hedonic hunger (Espel-Huynh et al., 2018), simulating eating in the simulation model (which explicitly includes its sensory and affective components; Papies et al., 2020), and 'vividly simulating the experience' in Hoch and Loewenstein's (1991) model. Not surprisingly then, asking participants to form mental images while in an MRI scanner indicates that it draws upon

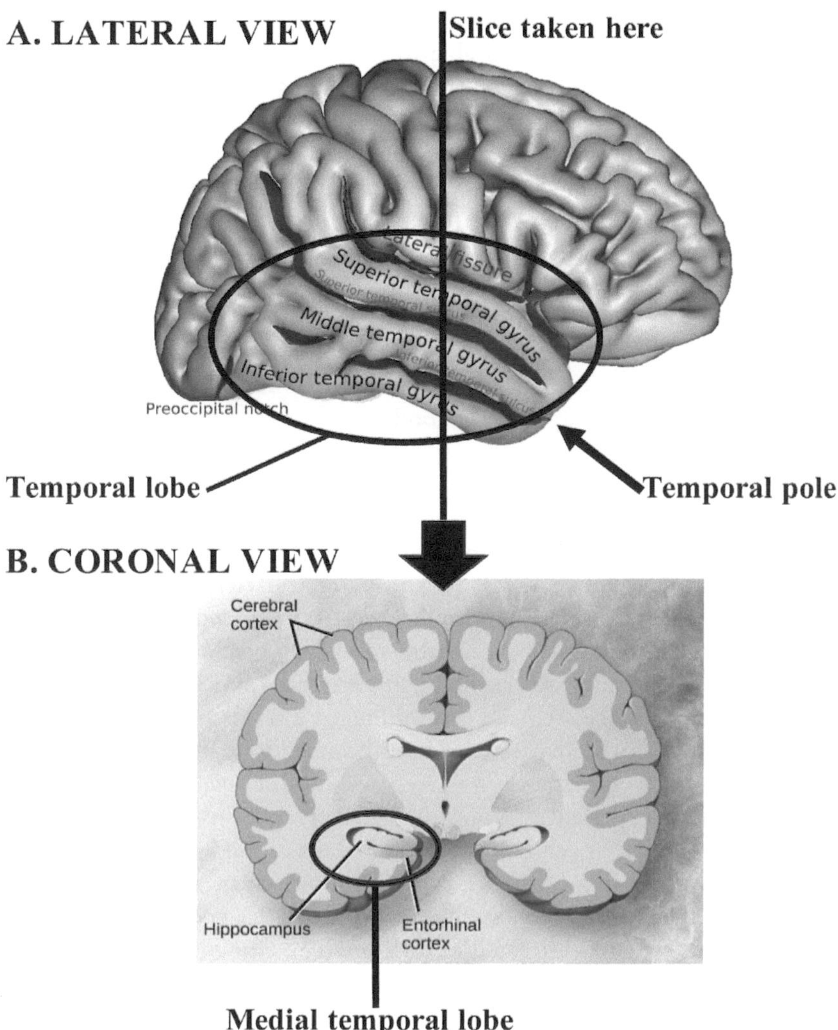

Figure 3.2 (a) Lateral view of the human brain showing the temporal lobe (circled) and indicating the temporal pole. The brain is then sliced where indicated to present a coronal view in (b), revealing in this coronal slice the medial temporal lobe (circled), with two of its key constituents – the hippocampus and entorhinal cortex.
Source: OpenStax Biology

the medial temporal lobe (e.g., Buckner, 2010; Maguire et al., 2010). Relatedly, the capacity for mental imagery is also impaired by damage to the medial temporal lobe (e.g., Gilboa et al., 2006; McCormick et al., 2018). This would suggest that even if HM had eaten at McDonald's prior to his surgery and so knew that it meant burger and fries (or whatever), he would probably not have been able to fully imagine what this would be like to eat. A further impairment of specific hunger.

3.4.1.4 Specific Hunger: Conclusion

A specific hunger occurs when an episodic food memory is retrieved, either automatically when a cue is encountered in the environment for a particular food (or category; e.g., chocolate) or from thinking about one. Retrieval generates a brief sensory-affective experience of what it would be like to eat the food now. This experience can be voluntarily elaborated or ignored. The medial temporal lobes support learning and retrieval of these episodic memories and of the related process of mental imagery that accompanies re-experiencing eating a particular food.

3.4.2 General Hunger

3.4.2.1 A Learning and Memory Perspective

The process under study in this section is the capacity to feel hunger for food in general. The solution adopted here is one based on learning and memory, and it follows on from the model of specific hunger already described. Certain cues can come to predict that food in general will be good to eat now. If the stomach is rumbling or it is lunchtime, both events will in the past (for many people) have been followed by eating, and so would have involved many *different* types of food. However, each of these different eating experiences would likely have one key similarity – they would generally have been enjoyable. This leads to the following proposal. What is learned is that a cue – a rumbling stomach or a time of day – is *predictive* that food in general will be enjoyable (i.e., good, rewarding) to eat now. This type of abstracted knowledge (i.e., enjoyment across lots of different eating bouts with lots of sensorily different foods) is an example of semantic memory (i.e., facts about the world – eating *now* will be good). This type of process can also be framed in another way, as a particular form of associative learning called feature-positive occasion setting (Fraser & Holland, 2019). Here, a cue (e.g., a rumbling stomach or a time of day) sets the occasion that an activity (eating) will be rewarding now.

Knowing that food will be good to eat now when experiencing a rumbling stomach or noticing it is lunchtime could mean just that – 'I know these things mean it is time to eat' in the same way I know that Paris is the capital of France. While people clearly do have this knowledge, the type of knowing that is envisaged for a rumbling stomach or that it is lunchtime is different. The knowing referred to here is an affective experience (Osgood et al., 1957), with this feeling connoting 'food will be good to eat now'. This affective feeling, which is a semantic memory, is composed of hundreds or even thousands of prior positive affective experiences of eating with or after the cue (e.g., a rumbling stomach or lunchtime). Not only may this generate a brief burst of positive affect that connotes food will be good to eat now, it has a further putative consequence – excitation transfer.

Imagine that your stomach rumbles or it is lunchtime. You will experience a brief burst of affect indicating that food will be good to eat now, at the same time as you are thinking about food. If this thinking about food leads to the retrieval of an episodic memory of a particular food, then this general excitation can be transferred to the re-experiencing of the episodic food memory. So, if the person sees it's lunchtime and then thinks of a banana, the affect (i.e., excitation) generated by the cue 'lunchtime' (i.e., the semantic memory) is transferred to the episodic memory of the banana. When the person then imagines eating the banana the affect they experience is augmented because of this transfer of excitation (i.e., positive affect) from the semantic memory. The consequence of this is that the banana is experienced as far more desirable than it would normally be. General hunger is then both a cue-retrieved semantic memory – a positive affective feeling of knowing that food will be good to eat now – and a capacity to transfer this excitatory state to other food-related memories.

The two example cues – a rumbling stomach and lunchtime – were selected deliberately, because for general hunger there are two major classes of cue. One concerns interoceptive signals (such as a rumbling stomach) and the other temporal cues (such as it's lunchtime). Each is examined in turn (and see Figure 3.1, lower parts).

3.4.2.2 Interoceptive Cues for General Hunger

Interest in hunger started with interoceptive cues, in particular the sensation linked to the muscular contractions of the stomach (i.e., phase III of the migrating motor complex; Deloose et al., 2012) and how these might cause hunger (Cannon & Washburn, 1912). The next major investigation of interoceptive hunger was initiated by Jean Mayer (Monello & Mayer, 1967), who was perhaps searching for the interoceptive correlates of glucostatic theory. Instead, what his study revealed was surprising, because it demonstrated that there was *a lot* of variation in the way that general hunger makes itself manifest in the body. This interoceptive variability has been confirmed in several later studies. Harris and Wardle (1987), who undertook two well-powered studies, concluded: 'It proved impossible to identify a specific subset or constellation of hunger symptoms which were characteristically experienced by hungry people and no evidence was found for a dimensional structure for hunger' (p. 154).

A more recent study confirmed the general character of these older observations, namely that the interoceptive experience of hunger is surprisingly varied. Stevenson, Hill, et al. (2023) asked participants to describe their interoceptive hunger sensations using the questionnaire developed by Monello and Mayer (1967). These data were then factor analysed, revealing eleven dimensions – that is, (crudely) eleven manifestations of interoceptive hunger (see Figure 3.3). These included moods, emotions, oropharyngeal, oral, and abdominal sensations, headache, fatigue, irritability, dizziness, and nausea, among other things, as interoceptive hunger cues. Perhaps surprisingly given the strong association that is believed to exist between the stomach and hunger, around 20 per cent of this sample did not use stomach contractions as an interoceptive hunger cue. The average person in this sample had four main interoceptive hunger cues (some people only had one and others had ten), which typically included a focal (i.e., location-specific) bodily cue (e.g., stomach-related), a diffuse (i.e., whole-body) bodily cue (e.g., tiredness), and an affective state (e.g., low mood). For everyone, these interoceptive hunger cues remained stable over a four-week period indicating good reliability. In other words, variability in interoceptive hunger cues between one person and another was not a consequence of noisy responding – individuals were consistent – and hence reliably different from one another.

This variability in interoceptive hunger cues is important. This is because it points to how these cues may develop, and the linkage between this developmental pathway and their function in adults as feature-positive occasion setters (i.e., an interoceptive cue evokes an affective semantic memory (food is good to eat now), and this excitation can transfer to food-cue induced episodic memories). It has been hypothesised that parents may train their children to attend to particular interoceptive cues and teach them that these signals mean you are hungry (Stevenson, 2024; Stevenson, Yeomans, & Francis, 2024). What these signals of course actually mean is that food will be good to eat now, and many of the interoceptive cues are hence correlates of an empty stomach and upper gastrointestinal tract. Alternatively, the interoceptive states can be low mood, tiredness, and irritability, where eating may have served to temporarily improve these experiences. So, if the child eats shortly after encountering an interoceptive cue that their parent tells them means hunger, and eating food is then a

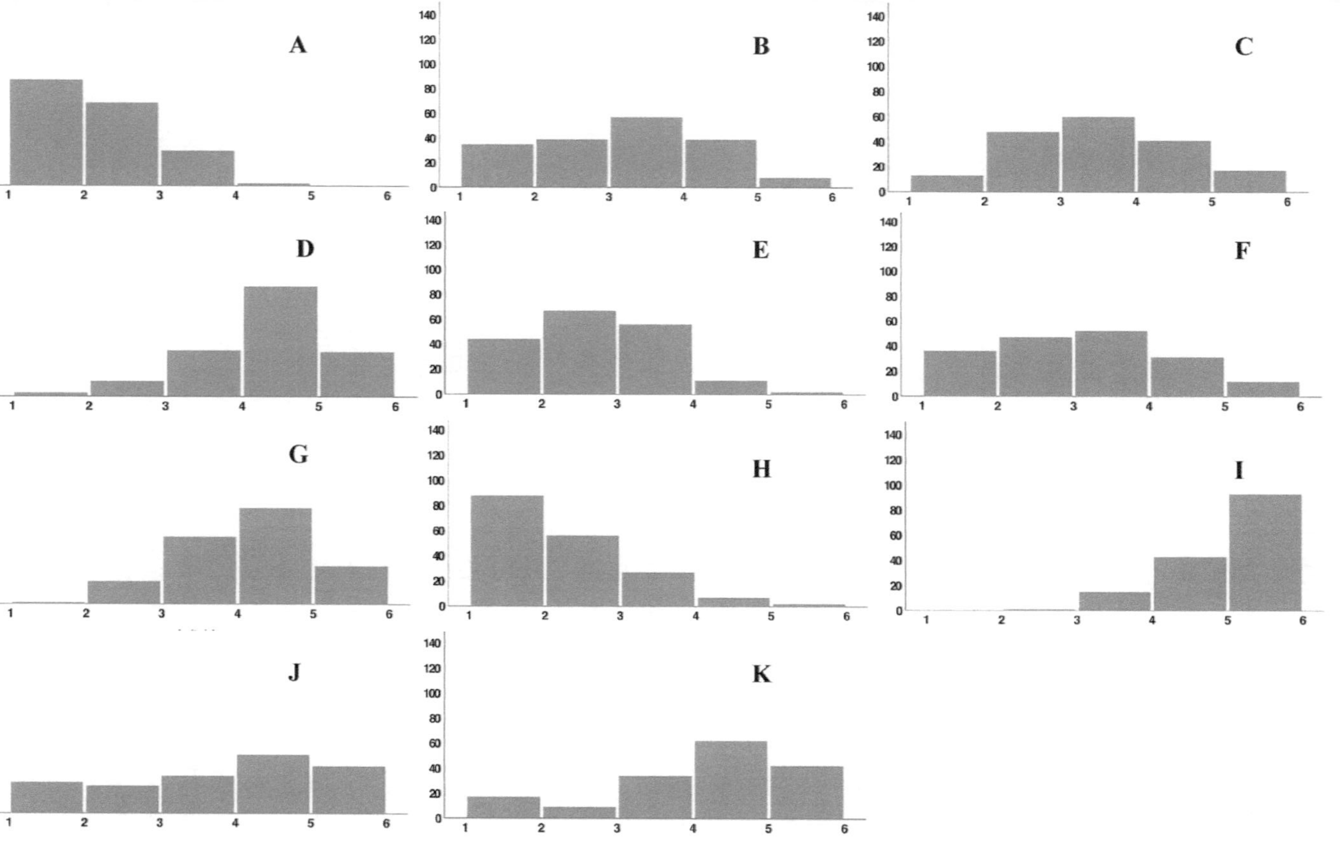

Figure 3.3 Different forms of interoceptive hunger, derived from factor analysis. Each individual histogram shows the distribution of how intensely that factor is experienced by the participants in this survey (absent (1) to very strong (6)). The interoceptive hunger factors are: a) positive feelings; b) oropharynx sensations; c) nausea; d) fatigue; e) positive mood; f) cold/tension; g) irritable; h) stomach full; i) cold/empty stomach; j) boredom; k) salivation.

Note: The y axes signify number of participants and the x axes signify the intensity of the hunger signal.

pleasant experience, they start to learn an association between that interoceptive cue, and 'that food will be good to eat now'.

There is remarkably little study of the type of process outlined in the preceding paragraph for the simple reason that many people have assumed (probably wrongly; Harshaw, 2008) that children (and animals) are born knowing the bodily cues that indicate hunger. From the perspective of an energy control (homeostatic) model of general hunger, where the focus is on replenishing energy after fuel supplies run low, it makes sense that one should automatically know the signal for 'energy running low' – after all, this is something of an emergency. However, as pointed out in Chapter 2, this is not how things operate for humans, at least. It makes more evolutionary sense to anticipate and hence avoid energy deficits by eating when food is available, assuming of course that this will not overload and damage the gut/body. From this perspective there is no imperative to tie certain bodily sensations to certain feelings such as hunger or actions such as food seeking (see Harshaw, 2008).

What animal literature there is, is consistent with this idea. In an early study, supervised by Donald Hebb, his student Ghent (1951) reported how deprivation-naïve rats took a few days to adjust to eating within a set period, suggesting they had to learn what feeling 'food deprived' meant (i.e., eating now will be rewarding). In a later series of studies, Changizi et al. (2002) demonstrated that food-deprived rat pups did not respond appropriately (i.e., search for food) to the internal state associated with being food deprived, until they had sampled food *in that state*. It seemed again they had to learn what that internal state meant – food is good to eat now. A few other studies have drawn the same inference for thirst (Changizi et al., 2002; W. Craig, 1912; Myers & Hall, 2001). The meaning of deprivation states does not appear to be innate; it is learned.

In humans, if parents do teach their children about interoceptive hunger cues, it might be expected that parental hunger cues should be more like those of *their* child, than of a stranger's child. This was tested by asking students, and their parent who was the primary caregiver when they were a young child, to complete the Monello and Mayer (1967) hunger survey. As predicted, there was significantly greater similarity between parent–child pairs than between random pairings of parents and children (Stevenson, Bartlett, et al., 2023). Looking at the correlations between the different individual interoceptive hunger dimensions mentioned earlier, these were all positive, varying between 0.07 and 0.44, with a median r of 0.27. An obvious counter to the suggestion that this reflects the influence of learning (i.e., parents teaching their children what these cues mean) is that these associations could instead reflect shared genetic similarity. Clearly, genes influence hunger in many ways (e.g., Llewellyn & Wardle, 2015; Wardle & Carnell, 2009; see Chapter 9), almost certainly including interoceptive capacities, but there was additional evidence in these data that argued strongly for a learning-based account. Participants (both parents and their offspring) were asked to complete a questionnaire about the causes of hunger, including if they believed in an energy control model (homeostatic) of general hunger. Parental beliefs about the causes of hunger strongly influenced the type and strength of interoceptive hunger cues present in their offspring. While this does not exclude genetic influences, it strongly suggests that parents influence the interoceptive hunger cues of their children. Moreover, it is consistent with them doing so along the lines described earlier (i.e., parent detects cue (e.g., hears their stomach rumble), tells the child 'you must be hungry', the child eats, enjoys the experience, and associates the cue with food tasting good now). Indeed, parents report noticing interoceptive hunger cues in their children (e.g., hearing their stomach rumble, noticing fatigue and irritability) and they respond appropriately to the child's perceived need (e.g., asking if they are hungry, offering food, etc.; Stevenson, Serebro, et al., 2024).

While there has been some progress in examining the development of interoceptive hunger cues, far less is known about their basis in semantic memory or their capacity for excitation transfer. For this last-mentioned question, some data pertinent to it have now been collected. Participants were asked to listen to various sounds while simultaneously viewing pictures of food. After seeing each food, they were asked to judge first their desire to eat it, and second, where they felt the accompanying sound came from (i.e., from the computer they were doing the task on versus from themselves or the environment). Playing a stomach rumble sound while viewing pictures of food enhanced participants' desire for the foods, *but* only in those who mistakenly attributed the stomach rumbling sound to their own stomach. This effect is illustrated in Figure 3.4, where greater desire to consume the depicted food (i.e., hunger) is associated with greater attribution of the stomach rumble sound to self (Stevenson et al., 2025). This suggests that when the participant experiences an illusory feeling that it is their stomach that is rumbling while they view the food, the excitation generated by the stomach rumble transfers to the episodic memory that is retrieved by seeing the food picture. This finding not only points to the psychological nature of general hunger – that is, the effect was a psychological induction of an interoceptive state and nothing about the person's physiological state was manipulated – but this effect could also be obtained irrespective of when the participant had last eaten.

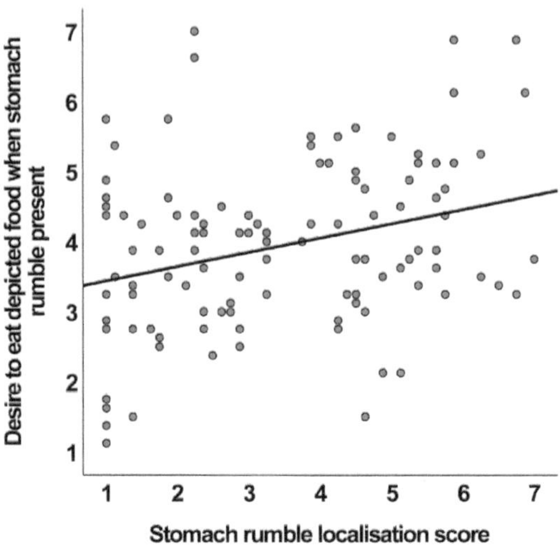

Figure 3.4 In this study, participants viewed pictures of food while listening to stomach-rumbling sounds. Ratings for desire to eat (i.e., specific hunger) the depicted foods were consistently higher (i.e., greater specific hunger) when participants misattributed the stomach-rumbling sound to their own stomach (higher localisation score = greater misattribution to self).

Source: Data adapted from Stevenson, R. J., Saluja, S., Forsyth, J., Rodgers, S., Brasher, S., Ho, V., & Francis, H. M. (2025). Psychological induction of interoceptive hunger cues and their effect on food desire. *Appetite*, *206*, 107855. https://doi.org/10.1016/j.appet.2025.107855

A further test of the capacity of psychologically generated interoceptive states to induce general hunger was recently completed. Stevenson et al. (unpublished data) had participants listen to either stomach-rumble sounds or control sounds, while judging non-food pictures for both liking and for where they felt the sound was coming from (as described earlier). Snack food was available throughout testing. Participants who heard stomach rumbling *and* mislocalised this sound to their own stomach (i.e., they experienced the illusion that it was their stomach that was rumbling) were both hungrier and consumed around 50 per cent more food – see Figure 3.5 – than those who did not experience illusory mislocalisation of the stomach-rumble sound, or those who heard the control sound. There was no difference between these groups in terms of when they last ate. These findings suggest that interoceptive cues such as a stomach rumble can cause hunger and eating via a purely psychological pathway.

In terms of the basis of interoceptive hunger cues in semantic memory, the only pertinent data come from people with semantic dementia (and see

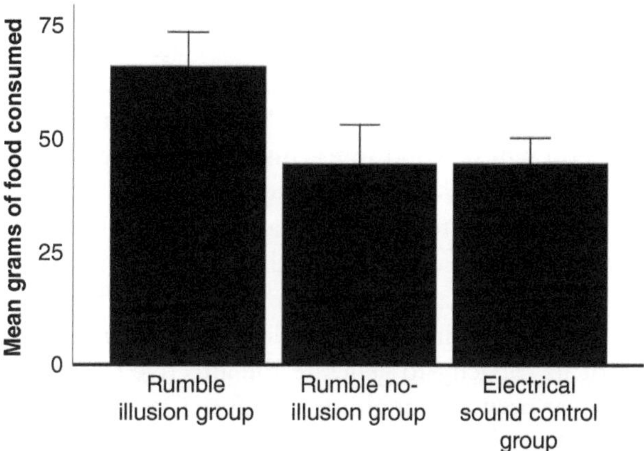

Figure 3.5 In this study, participants viewed pictures of neutral objects while listening to stomach-rumbling or control sounds. Food was incidentally available, and the amount consumed by each of the three groups is illustrated.

Chapter 9 for further discussion), in which a major manifestation of this illness is a loss of conceptual knowledge (i.e., semantic memory). Semantic dementia particularly affects brain structures in the anterior (notably the temporal pole) and medial (notably the perirhinal, entorhinal and parahippocampal cortices, amygdala, and hippocampus) temporal lobes (see Figure 3.2), which not surprisingly reflect the brain structures supporting semantic memory (Davies et al., 2009; Squire et al., 2004). People with semantic dementia often no longer understand what their internal bodily sensations *mean*, and this includes interoceptive hunger cues (Gan et al., 2016). This suggests that the meaning of these cues is held in semantic memory. It is also worth noting that transient damage to the anterior temporal lobe can produce intense general hunger, suggesting again the relevance of this brain area (Fisher, 1994).

3.4.2.3 *Temporal Cues for General Hunger*

Human food intake often has temporal patterning – mealtimes. In many developed countries this manifests as a small breakfast, a moderate-sized lunch, and a larger evening meal, plus snacks (Kant, 2018). It is possible to conceptualise routine mealtimes in much the same way as interoceptive hunger cues. If a meal is typically eaten at around a certain time, this time can then become a cue to indicate that food consumed now will be good to eat. The initial presumption is that this resembles the key features of interoceptive cues listed earlier. Namely, that parents teach their children to eat at certain times, and those times are associated with a large range of different foods. As the time interval between meals is usually sufficient for the stomach to empty (i.e., 3–4 hours), then mealtimes should be a good predictor that food will be good to eat now. In just the same way that an interoceptive hunger cue is hypothesised to generate an affective state that connotes it is a good time to eat, and relatedly can transfer this excitation to other food memories, the same is predicted here. Finally, this too may be supported by the semantic memory system, in that temporal cues acquire a particular meaning. Thus, a loss of meaning should rob the temporal cue of its capacity to generate the affective state connoting that food is good to eat now (although see Chapter 2, as time-based cues may involve additional mechanisms).

One of the interesting findings to come out of the literature on time-related feeding in animals is food anticipatory activity. This is a highly robust effect, in which animals that are only given access to food in a limited time window (e.g., two hours per day), demonstrate increased activity – such as wheel running, lever pressing, approaching a feeder, pacing, and drinking – in the period immediately before food is due (Mistlberger, 1994). That this behaviour is a prelude to feeding seems to be suggested by another finding. Here, animals that have been trained to feed at a particular time are then *not fed* at that time. Instead, their food is presented a couple of hours later. Interestingly, these animals eat *less* than they normally would at their earlier scheduled feeding time (e.g., Bousfield & Elliott, 1934). One interpretation of this finding is that the animals are not so hungry, because of the absence of the excitation normally generated by the scheduled feeding time. From this same perspective, the anticipatory activity observed prior to a scheduled feeding time represents another manifestation of this excitation.

Apart from the observation that many people eat at fixed times, which suggests that feeding time may serve as a general hunger cue, there is some additional evidence. Van den Akker et al. (2017) had participants consume a chocolate at one consistent time each day, but not at another (even though chocolate was available). As can be seen in Figure 3.6, desire to consume chocolate progressively increased at the scheduled feeding time and decreased for the non-scheduled feeding time. While this study used just one food, it does illustrate the broader principle that people can use time as a cue to hunger, albeit in this case just for chocolate.

It was suggested earlier that the semantic memory system may be important for supporting temporal cues, in the same way it appears to

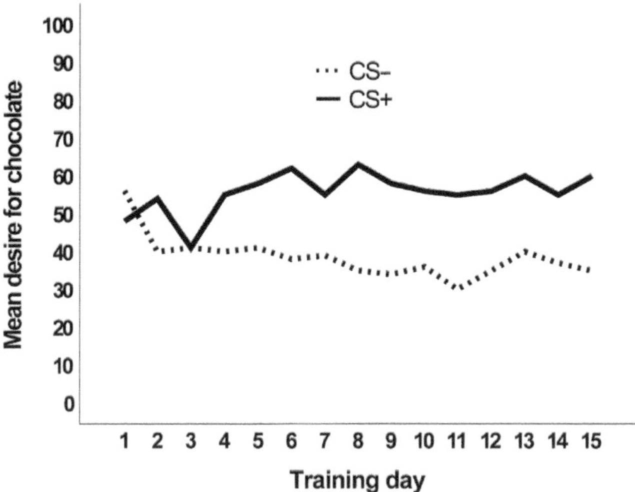

Figure 3.6 An experimental demonstration with time of day serving as the CS, either being paired with chocolate (CS+) or no food (CS−) over the fifteen-day acquisition period. Participants rated desire for chocolate (i.e., hunger for chocolate) as the scheduled time of day approached.

Source: Data adapted from van den Akker, K., Havermans, R. C., & Jansen, A. (2017). Appetitive conditioning to specific times of day. *Appetite*, *116*, 232–238. https://doi.org/10.1016/j.appet.2017.05.014

be (albeit based on limited evidence) for interoceptive hunger cues. While understanding of temporal magnitude (i.e., $4 < 7$; $2 > 1$) seems to be uniquely preserved in semantic dementia (it may rely on the parietal cortex), linkages of time-to-eating are abnormal. Nonaka et al. (2014) studied a man with semantic dementia. He could no longer comprehend the difference between the hour and minute hand of an analogue clock, so that every time the minute hand approached the 8, which he could recognise, he went in search of his breakfast. As the disease progressed further, this association was lost and he no longer reacted in this way. Assuming this interpretation is correct – and again there is little data to go on – time–food associations may be preserved quite late in semantic dementia, but they too succumb as the disease progresses. This would be consistent with a basis in semantic memory.

3.4.2.4 General Hunger: Conclusion

General hunger occurs when certain interoceptive or temporal cues are encountered. Each cue generates a mental state of positive anticipation that food in general will be good to eat now. This excitatory affective state (i.e., general hunger) can also be transferred to other food memories, generating a greater specific hunger for a particular food. For both interoceptive and temporal cues, it is assumed that their meanings are learned during childhood, and there is some evidence favourable to this view. General hunger relies upon an intact semantic memory system, which depends upon structures in the anterior and medial temporal lobes. The meaning of interoceptive hunger cues is lost in semantic dementia, and this disease also seems to affect the meaning of temporal hunger cues – but there is little data as yet.

3.4.3 *Interactions between Hungers*

There has been a deliberate attempt, so far, to segregate the components of hunger. This is useful in trying to understand what a highly complex system is. However, they are often intertwined. One way in which they are concerns the boundaries between specific and general hunger, which may not be as clear as text or diagrams make them appear. There are several reasons for this blurring. An individual brand logo can often encompass multiple foods and drinks (think McDonald's). All these foods and drinks may be palatable. The brand logo may then be associated with a semantic memory, an abstracted form of affect covering all their foods and drinks. Alternatively, it could reflect an individual favourite, in which case it is more of an episodic food memory. It is also possible that the occurrence of general hunger results in the deliberative search for a particular food class ('yum cha'), and then individual foods ('crispy fried silver fish'), thereby inducing a specific hunger (i.e., a form of elaboration). This would seem to follow a specific directional path, always going from general hunger to specific hunger (the reverse seems less probable). A further example of interaction within the model is excitation transfer from an interoceptive general hunger cue to an episodic food memory (i.e., a specific hunger; see Figure 3.4) and the use of temporal cues for a specific food, with the chocolate experiment illustrated in Figure 3.6 reflecting this.

One place where interaction is likely to be particularly important is between temporal and interoceptive hunger cues. Stomach growls at lunchtime *may* be better at inducing general hunger than those occurring following a meal or at times of day not normally associated with eating. Indeed, one of the intriguing aspects of the experiment illustrated in Figure 3.6 was that desire to eat chocolate reduced at a time that was not predictive of its arrival, hinting at an inhibitory process (i.e., excitation from a stomach rumble outside mealtimes may be inhibited).

Whether interoceptive and temporal hunger cues act additively or synergistically, or whether one serves as an occasion setter for the other (i.e., the interoceptive cue only means hunger in the context of 'lunch-time') is not known. Such contextual factors may also be important in the acquisition of interoceptive hunger cues during development. If a parent hears a child's tummy rumble, or they see the child is irritable or fatigued, and it is around a mealtime, this may be interpreted and acted upon in a different manner than if it is closer to bedtime. In this case, rather than suggesting to the child that they may be hungry the parent may instead tell them they are tired and need to rest (see Stevenson, Serebro, et al., 2024 for some evidence of this).

3.4.4 *Turning Hunger Off*

There are several things that can eliminate hunger before eating has started: nausea, disgust, high levels of stress in some people, physical and mental illness, self-control, and many other things as well (see Chapter 8). At this juncture the focus is on how hunger is diminished following eating. There may be three routine factors that supress hunger after eating – alliesthesia, sensory specific satiety, and memory inhibition. Each is discussed in turn.

Alliesthesia (Cabanac, 1971) refers to the change in pleasantness (liking) of a sensation, which occurs as a function of 'bodily needs'. In the context of eating, food after a meal is reported to taste less pleasant than before. Bodily needs was put in single quotes because in the light of Chapter 2, it should be clear that bodily needs (i.e., for energy) may only have a limited role in day-to-day feeding behaviour. If bodily needs are instead considered to reflect the organism's ability to *utilise* a reward, then signals indicative of a full stomach or gut that indicate food cannot be utilised now, would seem a better fit. As alliesthesia impacts sensory-induced pleasure, then it would be expected to also reduce the affect generated by looking at or thinking about a food and remembering/imagining what it tastes like. So, this would predict an impact on specific hunger, by reducing the positive affect it might otherwise induce. For general hunger the situation is less clear. First, a full stomach and gut would preclude the occurrence of certain interoceptive hunger cues (e.g., the rumbling of an empty stomach), thus preventing general hunger occurring. Second, alliesthesia *may* not be able to impact semantic affective memories generated by temporal or interoceptive hunger cues, because these memories are not presumed to have any direct sensory component (i.e., they are an affective abstraction).

What data there are do indeed suggest that interoceptive general hunger cues are not sensitive to internal state (Stevenson et al., 2025).

Sensory specific satiety refers to the decline in pleasantness that occurs as a particular food is eaten (Rolls et al., 1981). This reduction in liking is presumed to have its basis in habituation. It seems reasonable to presume that it would affect specific hunger. If one palatable snack food has been eaten to satiety, it is difficult to imagine that one could still feel a specific hunger for that food. If this intuition is correct, then the habituation process would also affect memories specific to that food. The limiting effect of sensory-specific satiety on food intake can easily be lifted by providing a different food, which then increases intake (Rolls et al., 1981). This would suggest that sensory specific satiety has less influence on general hunger. If it did, presumably, a person would not eat more when variety was increased. There is a further conceptual reason why sensory-specific satiety should not affect general hunger. General hunger relies on an abstracted affective semantic memory, which *probably* does not have a sensory component. As the name implies, *sensory*-specific satiety leads to the habituation of affect to that particular sensation (i.e., flavour). This would suggest that sensory-specific satiety should not be able to impact general hunger.

The third process is memory inhibition (Davidson et al., 2005; Parent et al., 2016). The idea here is that feedback signals resulting from eating a meal serve as feature-negative occasion setters (Fraser & Holland, 2019). That is, people learn, probably during infancy and/or childhood, that eating when these feedback signals are present is unrewarding. The consequence of this is the inhibition of food-related memories when these feedback signals are present. As this mechanism serves to inhibit memory, it may function for both episodic and semantic forms. Consequently, retrieval of both food-related episodic and semantic memories should be inhibited after a meal. On this basis, memory inhibition would result in a reduction of both specific and general hunger, as the memories necessary to support both forms of hunger would be inhibited (noting this does not seem to be the case for interoceptive general hunger (Stevenson et al., 2025) – clearly something that needs further examination). A further implication concerns the impacts of prolonged periods of time without food (i.e., day/s), where memory inhibition may cease altogether (i.e., in day-to-day life, some degree of memory inhibition may operate all the time). In this case, any cue that has food-related associations, however tangential, will become activated when that cue is encountered, resulting in many food-related thoughts and images, manifesting as a preoccupation with food (see Chapter 4.1), or 'food noise'.

Interestingly, the same brain areas that are involved in supporting episodic and semantic memory seem to be also involved in memory inhibition. Animal and human experimental work suggest that the hippocampus, a key part of the medial temporal lobe memory system, is instrumental in supporting memory inhibition (Davidson et al., 2019; Davidson et al., 2010). While there are likely to be other processes that play a role in reducing specific and general hunger after a meal, memory inhibition may be especially important as it could serve as a conduit for the multiple psychological (e.g., knowing you have eaten) and physiological (e.g., gut hormones) signals that comprise satiation/satiety. And the hippocampus has exactly such inputs (Kanoski & Grill, 2017).

3.4.5 Linking a Declarative Memory Account to Biological Models of Hunger

Three types of linkage are examined in this section. These are: (1) the cephalic phase response, namely the body's learned ability to prepare for food intake; (2) the biological agent, excitation–inhibition, and circadian accounts of hunger; and (3) how some of the other physiological moderators identified in Chapter 2 might link to a declarative memory account.

3.4.5.1 Cephalic Phase Response

The consumption of a meal represents a significant physiological challenge for the body (Woods, 1991). Ingested nutrients have to be transported and stored, and this must be done with minimal disruption to the body's metabolic systems (e.g., maintaining euglycaemia; Teff, 2011). One way that the body copes with food intake is to anticipate its arrival. This has a learned basis, with cues that signal the imminent arrival of food (e.g., a mealtime or the sight of food), or of food entering the gut (e.g., a taste in the mouth) both able to stimulate release of hormones that aid the digestive and absorptive phases of ingestion (Skvortsova et al., 2021).

The importance of these processes is illustrated by people who must receive their nutrition via enteral (e.g., feeding tube) or parenteral (intravenously) means. They are at much higher risk of developing metabolic abnormalities, especially of glucose metabolism (Btaiche & Khalidi, 2004a, 2004b). This may arise in part because of the absence of anticipatory feeding cues (i.e., cephalic phase response). The interesting point of convergence here is between the biological utility of being able to learn cues that anticipate food intake, and the learned cues described in this chapter that are argued to signal hunger. They seem to be one and the same. One distressing illustration of this convergence is seen in both parenteral and enteral feeding. People can get very hungry even though their nutritional needs are being fully met (e.g., Stratton & Elia, 1999). This is presumably because hunger cues are not followed by eating.

3.4.5.2 Biological Accounts of Hunger

It was suggested in the closing part of Chapter 2 that learning could serve as the interface between excitatory and inhibitory processes in the brain on the one hand, and the internal (i.e., bodily) and external environment on the other. This basic idea can be used to draw together the declarative account proposed in this chapter and some of the biological approaches of Chapter 2. First, for interoceptive cues that evoke general hunger, it was suggested that these are learned during childhood. There may be several physiological events that correlate with food tasting good now (e.g., release of orexigenic peptides). The way these physiological events make the body *feel* could become associated with the discovery that food is enjoyable if eating occurs when this feeling is present. The reverse argument has also been made to explain how different sets of bodily events that signal that food will *not* be good to eat now (i.e., satiety) also come to be learned (e.g., Woods et al., 2018). The learning processes that support both these feature-positive (i.e., hunger) and feature-negative (i.e., satiety) occasion setters (these being the biological events accompanying being unfed or fed) are arguably *more crucial* than the biological events themselves. This is because there seems to be a lot of redundancy among the biological events, so that if, say, a particular hormone is missing, there will be other physiological events that co-occur with it that can also serve as cues. It may be for these reasons that knocking out particular peptides has a much smaller impact on rodent feeding than would be expected (i.e., reliance on a replacement event), and relatedly why eliminating these agents in adulthood can be so devastating (i.e., harder to learn replacements or insufficient time to learn them) – other biological events have not acquired meaning.

Second, the brain has multiple excitatory and inhibitory feeding networks. Triggering an excitatory node nudges the system towards feeding and an inhibitory one away. Learning can serve as the link between these internal processes and events in the environment. Learned cues that signal palatable food and evoke an episodic memory generate specific hunger and its neural corollary excitation of the brain's feeding systems. This can be extended to interoceptive signals that indicate that the gut is empty (or other bodily events that correlate with having gone without food) and which then trigger semantic affective memories that are experienced as general hunger. And, again, the neural corollary is excitation of the brain's feeding systems. The same argument can be extended to time-based cues. Thus, it is these internal (bodily) and external environmental events that serve as the cause of hunger, with this mediated via learning and memory processes, and enacted by the brain systems discussed in Chapter 2.

Third, there is an important link that needs to be made between time-based feeding cues described in this chapter and the circadian model in Chapter 2. It seems likely that animals have: (1) a circadian-entrained feeding clock; and (2) a range of learning-based mechanisms to establish connections between regular feeding events and preparation to feed. Humans too probably have the same range of time-related mechanisms, and the declarative memory model of hunger does not preclude this possibility. Instead, what the declarative model adds is a mechanism for turning a signalled feeding time into hunger via an affective semantic memory. It is possible that anticipatory activity, as seen in animals just before a scheduled feeding, is quite different to the emergence of hunger at around a typical feeding time in humans. Indeed, whether humans demonstrate similar increase in activity around a scheduled feeding time and how this correlates with hunger has not been established. What is apparent, though, is that a declarative learning model can work with a circadian model.

3.4.5.3 Other Physiological Influences

There are at least three physiological influences that seem important to link to the declarative memory model of hunger. The first is the finding in Chapter 2 that lean body mass – effectively an index of total energy requirements as muscle mass contributes much to basal metabolic rate – is a correlate of reported hunger. This relationship could emerge in several ways. Lean body mass could cause a tonic-level increase in *any* experience of hunger, a greater likelihood that any hunger cue will elicit an excitatory response in the brain (after all, many things are associated with food, but typically do not make one hungry – such as a chef's hat) or perhaps augment retrieval of protein-related episodic food memories. Equally, there are pathways that do not directly involve hunger, and that instead affect satiation/satiety with this being reduced in strength, which would have then the same effect of generally increasing hunger.

A further influence on hunger is temperature, with cold being correlated with greater food intake (de Castro, 1991). Just as in the same way that greater lean body mass reflects a need for more energy to meet the needs of metabolically active tissue, cold temperatures also require increased metabolic activity to maintain stable body temperature. There may then be a common mechanistic convergence between these two variables in how they induce hunger. A final influence, and one that is discussed in some depth in Chapters 4–8 is starvation, where there really is a significant depletion of bodily energy stores.

3.5 Conclusion

This chapter presents a declarative memory model of hunger. The model proposes two forms of hunger (see Figure 3.1). Specific hunger can occur for a particular palatable food (or food category) when a cue to that food is encountered in the environment. This process draws upon episodic memory and produces a brief re-experiencing of the sensory and affective properties of that food. General hunger occurs when interoceptive or temporal cues occur, which in the past have signalled that food will be good (rewarding) to eat now. This process draws upon semantic memory and the retrieval of an affective state connoting that food will be good to eat now. This state of affective excitation can be transferred to episodic memories of specific foods, boosting their desirability. Following a meal, several processes can serve to supress specific hunger – alliesthesia, sensory-specific satiety, and memory inhibition – but how these apply to general hunger is often less clear. During development, interoceptive and temporal general hunger cues are acquired, providing one means of linking biological mechanisms of feeding to hunger. Specific hungers, which are also learned, provide another link to biology, via excitatory feeding mechanisms. In the remainder of the book, this declarative memory approach serves – where useful – as the lens for thinking about hunger-related phenomena.

CHAPTER 4

Hungry Minds

4.0 Introduction

As described in Chapter 3, hunger is a consequence of the acquired meaning of various internal and external cues. These cues are often transitory, and so too are the episodes of hunger that follow (Cannon & Washburn, 1912; Murray & Vickers, 2009). If a person has not eaten for several hours, then interoceptive hunger cues arising from stomach and gut emptiness, and from metabolic and hormonal changes, should occur with greater frequency and salience, than if only a few hours have passed since the last meal. In addition, as the digestion of the last meal completes, and satiety's inhibitory effects on memory wane, any environmental cue to food will arouse more affectively positive memories (i.e., greater salience). If the length of time without food increases further, then any inhibitory effect of satiety on food memory may be lost altogether, and more remote associations between an object/event and food will result in food-memory-related retrieval (e.g., seeing a picture of Adam and Eve would lead to the recall of fruit (i.e., from the tree of knowledge; Genesis, 2:4–3:24)). This would serve to make food-related thoughts, and hunger, more frequent. Not only then should a longer period without food increase the probability of an episode of hunger, but each episode should also increase the likelihood that a person will think about food and vice versa. This may result in preoccupation with food, particularly with longer periods without it. The first part of this chapter considers this issue.

While increasing length of time since the last meal may result in more frequent episodes of hunger and preoccupation with food, other aspects of cognition seem largely unaffected, as with mood. After longer periods without food – days – cognition again seems largely intact, but low mood and irritability may become a more consistent feature (e.g., Accurso et al., 2014; Keys et al., 1950; Stevenson & Francis, 2023). A more critical change, and one that may relate to low mood and irritability, is the capacity for extended periods without food or with food shortage to adversely affect moral decision-making – at least in some people. The second part of this chapter focuses on this aspect of hunger-related behaviour, with its implications for survival, and more broadly for society.

4.1 Hunger and Preoccupation with Food

Preoccupation with food emerges following both shorter- (several hours) and longer-term (days) periods without food or with reduced food intake. Most laboratory studies have used short-term manipulations, typically overnight fasts. These are referred to as hunger/fasts, as they serve to increase the *probability* of an episode or episodes of hunger. Note that the participant also knows they have not eaten when they normally do, invoking whatever beliefs they may hold about the consequences of not doing so. Studies employing short-term fasts suggest that food cues become more salient the longer the person has gone without food. For example, people who have experienced sixteen hours without food (in contrast to one or four hours) are more likely to identify a need for food, and how to get food (i.e., cook, shop, forage, etc.), when asked to describe ambiguous pictures from the thematic apperception test (Atkinson & McClelland, 1948). Several hours without food also results in subtle perceptual changes, which may also reflect greater food cue salience. People become better at detecting food cues and food words (e.g., Radel & Clément-Guillotin, 2012), they perceive food objects as brighter, and objects in their mouth as larger (e.g., Crutchfield et al., 2018).

Food stimuli are also better able to capture attention following six hours without food than after a meal (e.g., Piech et al., 2010). If food-related stimuli are presented incidentally during a cognitive task, there is an attentional bias towards them, which is greater when participants have not eaten for a longer period of time, an effect that has been confirmed meta-analytically (Pool et al., 2016). Whether the effects on attention occur subliminally is less clear (but see Radel & Clément-Guillotin, 2012), as where this has been tested, suprathreshold food stimuli are found to be more distracting (e.g., Mogg et al., 1998). Relatedly, memory for food stimuli also improves when a significant period of time has elapsed since last eating, when contrasted with performance following a meal (e.g., Morris & Dolan, 2001). These effects on memory may extend into related domains, with more vivid imagery for food accompanying hunger, following ghrelin administration (Schmid et al., 2005).

The effects of several hours without food do not appear to exert any systematic effects on cognition or mood, and several studies have carefully explored this (e.g., Lieberman et al., 2008; and see Benau et al., 2014, and Stevenson & Francis, 2023, for reviews). Even with more hypothesis-driven tests, such as searching for cognitive deficits akin to those seen in people with anorexia nervosa (e.g., set shifting), the evidence is at best inconsistent (see Stevenson & Francis, 2023, p. 260). A further related question that has received attention is whether dieting may impair cognition via preoccupation with food. These results are also inconsistent (e.g., Green et al., 2000), but there is some evidence of interference with aspects of executive function (e.g., Kemps & Tiggemann, 2005). It is, though, less clear if these executive function effects reflect the impact of periods without food, or periods without *specific* foods (i.e., the ones the dieter is consciously avoiding).

Observations of people following much longer periods without food also suggest that preoccupation with it occurs. Brožek et al. (1951) describes a dream of the Danish explorer Ejnar Mikkelsen, who had to overwinter for two seasons in the north of Greenland, with very limited food. Mikkelsen's dream was suffused with food, containing in his words 'mountains of bread and butter' and 'huge smoking joints of meat'. The best documented report on food preoccupation comes from the Minnesota Starvation Study, which is discussed in detail in Chapter 7. Following a semi-starvation period the participants' food preoccupations emerged in several ways. They daydreamed extensively about food – although they did not tend to dream about it at night. In any film they watched they were not interested in the love scene or plot, but *just* at what the cast were eating. Any conversation tended to veer towards the topic of food, and especially so before meals, where lengthy discussions on how it would be eaten occurred (Franklin et al., 1948). Many of the participants started to collect recipes from newspapers, buy cookbooks (e.g., one diary entry notes 'stayed up until 5am studying cook books – so absorbing I can't stay away') and developed new interests in food production statistics, agriculture, gardening, dietetics, gastronomy, and the rural economy (Keys et al., 1945; Keys et al., 1950). Similar preoccupations with food have also been observed in people with anorexia nervosa with significant body weight loss, including the collection of recipes, buying food, preparing food, and ensuring those around them are well fed (see Chapter 8 for discussion).

Together, these findings suggest a graded response to periods without food, which is characterised by progressively more attention towards food cues (i.e., greater salience). As described earlier, one way to view this effect is to see it in relation to the memory inhibition mechanism described in Chapter 3. Here, food-related memories are inhibited by hippocampal-dependent processes that are modulated by neurohormonal satiety cues (e.g., Davidson et al., 2005; Parent, 2016). As satiety diminishes and memory inhibition eases, more environmental cues can serve to bring pleasant food-related memories to mind. As the period of time without food lengthens, memory inhibition may be wound back altogether, to the point where even remotely food-associated objects or events can serve as cues to bring food to mind (Stevenson, Yeomans, & Francis, 2024). This may combine with other mechanisms that serve to enhance the detection of food-related cues in the environment (e.g., selective low-level filtering of information) – although these too may be regulated by the same inhibitory feedback. In all cases, and indeed for any mechanism that serves to promote the detection of food cues in the environment, these will depend upon learned associations between the cue (this typically being a visual or auditory stimulus) and its meaning.

4.2 The Historical Basis for Linking Hunger and Immorality

Pitirim Sorokin, a pioneering sociologist, visited the Volga region of Russia during its 1920–1921 famine that killed around five million people. The spectacle of devastation that greeted him – and his experience of hunger – was so severe (see, for example, Figure 4.1, which does appear to be a genuine image as it concurs with written accounts such as Sorokin's) that it prompted him to write a book (Sorokin, 1975) about the impacts of famine on human society and behaviour (see Vågerö et al., 2013). In this book, Sorokin proposed, as have several others since (e.g., Dirks et al., 1980; Morell-Hart, 2012), that famine leads to a breakdown in networks of obligation – societal and familial – and to all normal standards of morality.

Dirks et al. (1980) proposed that people's behaviour in famines could be categorised into three stages. The first is 'Alarm', characterised by anxiety, hyperactivity, irritability, and hostility, with these fuelled by the knowledge that others are competing for the same limited resource as oneself – food. At the societal level, these characteristics manifest as increases in crime, political unrest, and rioting. For example, in the Madras famine of 1876–1878, which caused between six and ten million deaths, its early stages were marked by rioting over rising grain prices, widespread theft, and a documented increase in the prison population (Arnold, 1993). Similar occurrences in the early stages of famines in other countries, and at other times, have been reported (e.g., Scrimshaw, 1987), although how

Figure 4.1 A man and woman sell human remains for food during the 1921 Russian famine. Purchased from Album 25/6/25 with extended publication rights.

Figure 4.2 The famine stela located on Sehel Island, Egypt.
Source: Picryl; https://picryl.com/media/famine-stela-5e54db

rapidly such behaviours may emerge will depend on the initial nutrition status of the population.

Dirks et al. (1980) termed the second phase of famine behaviour 'Resistance'. This has a rather different set of characteristics. These include reduced activity, greater egocentricity, and food hiding. In addition, there is sharing of food supplies only in the close family circle and active prevention against food theft (e.g., guarding livestock and vegetable patches at night). At its most extreme, food guarding can result in murder, with Dirks giving an example from a famine in the Trobriand islands. Here, people driven by famine from their inland homes, came down to the coast to obtain food from the sea, only to be murdered as 'plunderers' by locals trying to eke out an existence from 'their' ocean. There are also many historical examples. One is from the famine stela (see Figure 4.2), carved on a rock on Sehel Island in the Nile. It describes an ancient Egyptian famine in which 'each man has become a thief to his neighbour' (Prentice, 2005).

The third stage of famine, according to Dirks et al. (1980), involves intense egocentricity, and social and familial collapse, with *everyone* now regarded as a competitor. Under these extreme conditions, there are reports of cannibalism, both passive (i.e., consuming people who have died) and active (i.e., murder for the purpose of eating the body). Overcoming the revulsion that people have for eating another human being forms part of a broader change in eating behaviour that occurs during a famine, namely consuming anything potentially nutritious – weeds, earth, leather, skin, roots, pits, seeds, and so on (Boggiano et al., 2013).

Famine-related cannibalism has been widely documented. Prentice (2005) provides several examples. During the 1319 European famine, it was reported in Flanders that 'parents killed their children and children killed their parents, and the bodies of executed criminals were eagerly snatched from the gallows'. The Donner party provides a more contemporary example among a group of people travelling to California in 1846, who became stranded and ran out of food due to bad decisions, bad luck, and bad weather. Not only did they engage in passive cannibalism but one subgroup who set out to seek assistance also appear to have murdered and eaten their native American guides (McCurdy, 1994).

Many instances of cannibalism are recorded in Jisheng's (2008/2012) history of the Great Chinese Famine of 1959–1961. Both of the following quotations come from contemporary observers, who were interviewed by Jisheng as part of the preparations for his book. The first is from Li Lei, who was a party committee secretary at the time. She described (p. 135):

> In some cases individuals barbarously consumed their own parents, children, spouses and siblings. Some ate corpses of people who just died, while others dug up bodies that had been dead for a week or even a month. In Qiezang, Ma Xishun ate the corpse of a diseased person and then died himself along with the rest of his eleven-member family. A commune member Bai Yinu ate a total of eight dead bodies, including his father, wife and daughter. A poor peasant from Qiezang Commune, Ma Abudu, near death, enjoined her daughter 'there's no meat left on my body but after I die cut out my heart and eat it'. Her daughter followed this instruction. In Qiezang, a poor peasant couple, Ma Yibulu and his wife, killed and ate their 14 year old daughter, and after Ma died, his wife ate him. Li Galiu ate two of his dead children. After Li died, he was eaten by a fellow commune member, Hu Ba, who in turn was eaten by Xiao Zhenzhi.

A second set of observations come from Yu Wenhai, who was an accountant for Huabin county's township. He described (p. 41):

> It was not unusual for people to eat corpses, I myself did so at Yaozhuang. I had gone to see the production team head Yao Dengju, and in the production team office I smelled the fragrance of cooked meat. He said 'Have some meat'. I asked 'What kind of meat?' He said 'Meat from a dead pig'. I opened the pot and took out a piece. It was tender in my mouth. I said 'This isn't pork'. He said it was the flesh of a dead person that someone else had cut away, that it had been cut from a buried corpse, and

Table 4.1 *Changes in criminal activity in Moscow during the severe food shortages in 1918 relative to 1914 (adapted from Sorokin, 1975, p. 231)*

Crime	Increase relative to 1914
Theft	3 times higher
Fraud	4 times higher
Prostitution	8 times higher
Armed robbery and burglary	285 times higher
Attempted murder	16 times higher
Murder	11 times higher

> that he taken a piece and cooked it. At this point my driver Xiao Chen asked 'Did the human flesh taste good?' Yo Wenhai replied 'It was pretty good, just a bit spongy'.

There are many similar instances recorded in Jisheng's book.

In a somewhat less extreme vein, Morell-Hart (2012) describes how in many famines 'elders appropriated the rations of children' and that infants, children and the elderly were abandoned as 'burdens'. It was exactly these sorts of observations that led to Sorokin's (1975) book, where he recounts many similarly disturbing acts (e.g., patrolling of cemeteries to stop theft of the bodies for food (p. 112); documented cases of older children murdering younger siblings for their food (p. 115); etc.) and the increase in crime, and especially violent crime (see Table 4.1).

A rather different but equally compelling set of narratives emerges from the Second World War. Many of these accounts were made by doctors who were either inmates of Nazi concentration camps (e.g., Adelsberger, 1946), of prisoners of war (POW) camps (e.g., Leyton, 1946), or who were involved in the care of the people who remained alive after their liberation (e.g., Lipscomb, 1945). Adelsberger (1946) assisted Nazi 'doctors' in the camp hospital at Auschwitz. In her description of life in the camp she noted that 'full amounts of rations were rarely received, owing to theft and dishonesty among the prisoners themselves' (p. 317). Leyton (1946), who was in a Nazi POW camp, described in some detail the effects of chronic starvation on standards of behaviour and these are presented in Box 4.1. It is noteworthy that the impacts that Leyton described were on young healthy men who were under British military discipline during their period of their incarceration, so presumably the effects on 'moral character' would have been worse among people with no *esprit de corps*.

Box 4.1 Leyton's (1946) Observations on the Response of British Prisoners of War to Chronic Starvation

Observation

'Half-starved men would go to the greatest lengths of ingenuity and dishonesty to obtain small amounts of extra nourishment' (p. 74)

'Moral standards were in complete abeyance, for a man would steal his best friend's rations or sell his overcoat for food or tobacco' (p. 75)

'The whole attitude [of the men] was strongly reminiscent of hungry animals waiting for food. Standards of cleanliness were below normal and any pride in personal appearance was entirely lost' (p. 75)

'It is certain that persistent hunger, which is of a different intensity from that felt normally before meals, completely alters the character and outlook of the starving man and is perhaps the chief cause of his moral degeneration' (p. 75)

'None of the hardships suffered by fighting men observed by me brought about such a rapid or complete degeneration of character as chronic starvation, and it seems that the silent areas of the brain that control character suffer very early from deficient nutrition' (p. 76)

'Once the first barriers are broken down, deterioration proceeds very rapidly, especially when he sees other behave like him' (p. 76)

Lipscomb (1945) was a senior Royal Army Medical Corp doctor in the Belsen concentration camp refeeding centre. As with all the examples described so far, it is very important not to forget the high levels of trauma that people experienced *independent* of any effects of starvation. Belsen is a case in point. When the British Army first entered this camp, there were over 13,000 corpses lying unburied (see Figure 4.3). Lipscomb made several pertinent observations, gleaned from his own experiences at the refeeding hospital and from talking to survivors. He noted: 'The most conspicuous psychological abnormality [of the survivors] was a degradation of moral standards characterised by increased selfishness, and it was proportional to the degree of undernutrition' (p. 315). In describing the psychological impact of starvation, he wrote: 'In the first stage consideration for others was limited to personal friends, then the circle contracted to child or parents, and finally only the instinct to survive remained' (p. 315). He also described how all self-respect disappeared, there was a blunting of sensitivity, and there was a focus on finding *any* food even if it was human flesh.

Figure 4.3 Lorries were required to transfer the 13,000 corpses for burial that were found in Belsen concentration camp following its liberation by the British Army in April 1945. *Source*: US Holocaust Museum

These instances of selfishness, theft, murder, and cannibalism characterise description after description of severe food shortage and famine. It was these observations that first led to the idea that significant shortages of food may drive behaviour that would ordinarily be regarded as immoral, delinquent, and criminal.

4.3 Hunger, Crime, and Delinquency

One proponent of a relationship between food shortage, crime, and delinquency has been Nettle (2017). His argument is based on a series of premises. First, there is a well-established socio-economic gradient to crime and delinquency, with these acts being more common in people with less education, less wealth, and lower social status (i.e., people of low socio-economic status (SES)). Second, impulsivity, irritability, and aggression are also more frequently observed in people with low SES. Third, impulsivity, irritability, and aggression are known risk factors for crime and delinquency. Fourth, based on historical reports of starvation (see earlier) and observational and experimental evidence (see later), Nettle (2017) suggests that prolonged periods of no food or reduced food intake ('hunger' in Nettle's theory) can cause impulsivity, irritability, and aggression. Fifth, periods of food shortage are also associated with lower SES, even in developed countries. In sum, Nettle's core argument is that one contributor to the SES crime and delinquency link is periods where food is unavailable or in short supply, because this makes people impulsive, irritable, and aggressive.

Before evaluating this theory, it is important to consider two of its components. First, what is meant by 'hunger' in the context of Nettle's theory? Second, is lack of food, and hence more frequent episodes of hunger, a serious issue in the developed world? The answers are interrelated. Two types of food supply problem have been identified in the developed world. One is *food insufficiency* where a person or family sometimes (or often) does not have enough to eat (Alaimo et al., 2002). The other is *food insecurity*, which refers to a person's or family's limited or uncertain ability to acquire food (Nettle, 2017). Typically, people who are food insufficient will also be food insecure. This will manifest as periods of time when people have no food, skip meals, or cut down portion size to get by. Hunger will manifest here in both the forms described in Chapter 3. For example, any screen media will expose a person to adverts and pictures of food, generating specific hunger. Similarly, knowing it is a mealtime, or feeling one's stomach rumble, and so on, will generate general hunger. As food insufficiency and insecurity are periodic phenomena, there will also be times when food is available, and often in ample quantities, sufficient indeed to explain the association between food insufficiency, food insecurity, and obesity (e.g., Smith & Richards, 2008). Food insufficiency and insecurity will then serve to increase the frequency and intensity with which a person/family experiences both specific and general hunger.

Many families in developed countries experience food insufficiency and insecurity. Data from 2010 to 2020 suggest that rates of food insecurity vary from 10 per cent of the population (European Union) to 20 per cent (Australia), with the US and Japan falling in between (Pollard & Booth, 2019). Food insufficiency and insecurity are strongly related to SES. Nettle (2017) reports that, in the US, for food insufficiency, 21 per cent of low-income families were classified as 'Hungry' and a further 50 per cent as 'At risk of hunger'. For food insecurity in the US, 20 per cent were classified as 'Very low food security' and 40 per cent as 'Food insecure'. Similar statistics can be found for other countries, all linking low SES to greater levels of food insecurity and insufficiency, and hence greater experience of specific and general hunger.

To recap, Nettle (2017) claims that the more intense and frequent experience of hunger by people of low SES contributes to higher rates of impulsivity, irritability, and aggression, which in turn disposes to crime and delinquency. Two specific variants of this model have been advanced by Nettle (2017). The first is that at any point of assessment (i.e., by a survey, interviewer, etc.) a person of lower SES is *more likely to be hungry* and hence more likely to be impulsive, irritable, and aggressive. The second is that experience of more frequent hunger during development leads to permanent changes in behaviour, characterised by greater impulsivity, irritability, and aggression in adulthood. In this second case, even if a person went on to live their life in a high-SES environment, they would still exhibit the psychological scars from their childhood hunger. The following section examines the observational and experimental evidence for these models and, more generally, the evidence for (and against) an association between hunger and impulsivity, irritability, aggression – and criminal proclivities.

4.4 Evidence Linking Hunger to Impulsivity, Irritability, and Aggression

4.4.1 Observational Evidence

Healthy people who are asked to describe what it would be like to be very hungry (i.e., they are imaging this state) report they would feel greater irritability, nervousness, and tension (Monello & Mayer, 1967). Presumably then people who are subject to real and more significant episodes without food might evidence exaggerated forms of these changes. Several pieces of evidence bear on this.

The Minnesota Starvation Study (see Chapter 7 for more discussion) provides some evidence for the type of psychological changes that accompany severe reduction in food intake. This study was conducted during the latter part of the Second World War and involved a period of six months of supervised semi-starvation (the target was a 25 per cent loss of initial body weight), followed by three months of refeeding. The refeeding component was the key focus of the study, to identify the best way of restoring body weight in people subjected to starvation (i.e., such as those in war-torn Europe). Thirty-six highly motivated male conscientious objectors volunteered to assist this worthy goal. Psychological changes were measured in several ways, but the best summary is provided by one of the participants, Samuel Legg. He wrote:

> The psychological effects of starvation are unbelievable. We went there because we were concerned about people abroad and wanted to do what we could to help those less fortunate than ourselves, and I think that feeling was lost after about 2 months. At the end of 5 months of starvation our attitude was 'to heck with the people abroad: I'm hungry!'. That was all that was important. The only important thing left was whether I was ever going to get food. I was only interested in myself.

Samuel Legg's description echoes the changes the investigators observed (Keys et al., 1950). The dynamics of the participant group, who lived, worked, and dined together for the duration of the study, shifted from friendly and supportive to irritable, sombre, sarcastic, and stilted during the starvation period. The participants became increasingly egocentric, with outbursts of temper over trivial things, but particularly for anything construed as wasting food. Recalling how motivated these participants were to take part, four engaged in 'serious dietary violations' (i.e., cheating), secretly eating food outside of the experiment. In addition, four participants required psychiatric treatment during the starvation phase, with two becoming violent, and one self-mutilating (he cut off a finger) to escape the study.

There have been few experiments like the Minnesota study. Two situations that approximated it are Biosphere 2 and medically supervised fasting. Biosphere 2 was a supposedly self-contained set of environments, in which a four-person medical and scientifically trained crew could subsist without outside input for two years. Due to various exigencies, food was in short supply, which led to weight loss among the crew (around 10 per cent of initial body weight; Weyer et al., 2000). The consequences of this were food theft, irritability, and the formation of factions within the group.

A more controlled environment to examine the psychological effects of starvation is medically supervised fasting as a treatment for obesity. This was popular during the 1960s and 1970s and involved voluntary *total* starvation to lose weight in a hospital setting (i.e., ensuring adequate hydration and vitamin intake; Silverstone et al., 1966). This literature is interesting because several reports suggest that these obese participants had few problems even with total fasts of 100+ days (e.g., Drenick et al., 1964; Thomson et al., 1966). The complete absence of *any* reported adverse outcomes is surprising in the light of two further studies that included psychiatric observations. Rowland (1968) studied six people with obesity undergoing a total fast. All six manifested symptoms of depression – a commonly noted aspect of starvation – as well as outbursts of anger and aggression. Rowland (1968) felt that these aggressive outbursts were augmented forms of their normal behaviour. Swanson and Dinello (1970) reported on a larger series of obese patients, who averaged thirty-eight days of starvation with a 21 per cent loss of initial body weight. Seventeen out of the twenty-five obese people studied had some form of adverse psychological outcome, which included paranoia, impulsivity, aggression (including verbal abuse of staff), depression, and anxiety. Swanson and Dinello (1970) also noted that these reactions may have reflected pre-existing dispositions.

A further group that has been studied are people with restrictive anorexia nervosa (see Chapter 8 for extended discussion). Fessler (2002) reviewed the evidence, addressing, if in their semi-starved state, they exhibited more impulsive, irritable, and aggressive behaviour. While it takes a high degree of self-control to starve oneself, other aspects of restrictive anorexic behaviour suggest poor impulse control, such as anger attacks, aggressive outbursts, suicide attempts, stealing, and robbery (Fava et al., 1995; Fessler, 2002; Thompson et al., 1999). Fessler (2002) suggests these changes reflect psychological adaptations to starvation that feature enhanced risk taking to secure food, with a focus on current (i.e., the need to feed) rather than longer-term goals.

In sum, while there is favourable evidence from observational studies that starvation can enhance irritability, aggression, and impulsivity – and so dispose to crime – experimental tests of this idea are needed. These are examined next.

4.4.2 *Experimental Evidence*

4.4.2.1 *Cheating*

If periods of limited or intermittent food promotes crime, via an increase in impulsivity, aggression, and irritability, then it would also be expected to increase cheating to obtain food (i.e., a petty crime). Two studies have examined this. Yam et al. (2014) split participants by time since their last meal into hungrier and fuller groups. Each completed two quizzes in counterbalanced order, one for a bottle of water and one for a palatable snack. Each quiz contained five questions. Four questions in each quiz were simple but one was unsolvable, and so the only truthful answer would be either 'don't know' or this is 'unsolvable'. Participants were told they would be given the palatable snack (or water) if they provided an answer to *every* question. Rates of cheating were highest in the hungrier group when they were completing the quiz for the palatable snack.

Yam et al. (2014) then undertook a second study using the quiz task. Participants were assigned to receive either hunger cues (i.e., hunger-related words) or neutral words, before undertaking the same quiz task for food and drink. Hunger cues led to more cheating on the quiz for the palatable snack. A third and a fourth study used a different cheating task, with participants asked either to complete a maths quiz before or after lunch, for either a food or a non-food prize. Participants were told they had one minute to complete the maths quiz, but the browser window did not close at the one-minute mark and instead the actual length of time they took was recorded. In both studies, cheating (i.e., spending longer than one minute on the task) was more frequent in hungry participants undertaking the quiz for a food reward. A further finding arising from Yam et al.'s (2014) studies was that rates of cheating for prizes that were not desirable (i.e., a bottle of water when hungry) were *lower* than for the comparison state (i.e., a bottle of water when sated). In sum, hunger-related conditions exerted a food-specific cheating effect.

A study by E. F. Williams et al. (2016) used a different type of cheating task. People were approached at lunchtime and asked if they would take part in a marketing study for 'snack packs'. The snack packs were ostentatiously displayed and contained salted potato chips, a granola bar, a chocolate bar, and a mint. Participants were told they would be given a chance to win a snack pack as there were not enough for everyone. As part of the mock marketing exercise participants undertook several ratings, including hunger, how attractive they found the snack pack, and its likely cost. This was followed by a game to win the snack pack, with participants given a die in a clear-topped box. To win they had to roll an even number, and they were instructed to have a few practices before their 'prize roll'. The experimenter then feigned interest in another task while the participant rolled the die. This task can only detect cheating at the aggregate level. Cheating clearly occurred, as 76.5 per cent of the 136 participants reported an even number on the prize roll, thereby winning a snack pack. Chance would, of course, expect only around 50 per cent to win! Moreover, the hungrier a person reported being, the more likely they were to report rolling an even number on the prize roll. Overall, both the Williams et al. (2016) and the Yam et al. (2014) study suggest that people will be more inclined to cheat for food under hunger-related conditions.

4.4.2.2 Impulsivity

Greater trait impulsivity is a risk factor for many things – obesity, certain eating disorders, poorer sexual decision-making, greater drug and alcohol use, and for crime and delinquency – among other maladaptive behaviours (Bari & Robbins, 2013). Impulsivity is not a monolithic entity and there is uncertainty as to what its core components might be. Nonetheless, one form of measurement that has been widely used to assess it, and the dominant one reported here, is delayed discounting. On this task, participants must make binary choices of the form 'would you prefer $5 now or $20 tomorrow?'. In essence, this task determines a person's preference for smaller immediate rewards (i.e., the impulsive choice) over larger delayed rewards (i.e., the self-controlled choice).

For studies exploring the impact of hunger/fasting on delayed discounting, an influential meta-analysis of pre-2014 studies was published by Orquin and Kurzban (2016). In these studies, hunger was manipulated by asking participants in one group to fast while the other received glucose or high glycaemic index foods (many were testing a once popular theory of self-control based on blood glucose levels). The studies in the meta-analysis were fractionated into those where food was used as the reward (e.g., one chip now or several in five minutes' time) or where a non-food reward was used instead (typically money). Irrespective of reward, hunger/fasting was associated with more impulsive choices. Hungry/fasted participants preferred smaller more immediate rewards over larger delayed ones. The magnitude of this effect was somewhat larger for food but not significantly so.

Several studies have emerged since this meta-analysis. Some have explored the effect of specific hunger, by exposing participants to palatable food cues and then determining the impact of this manipulation on delayed discounting or related tasks. Yeomans and Brace (2015), using a female sample, reported that exposure to food cues increased impulsivity on a delayed discounting task (for money) and a risk-taking task (bursting a balloon), but only in participants with higher levels of disinhibited eating. Rao et al. (2015) exposed participants to either palatable food images, control images, or romantic pictures, and then examined preference for immediate or delayed financial rewards. Viewing palatable foods enhanced preference for immediate rewards, when compared to viewing romantic pictures; however, the effect of viewing palatable foods did not differ from that of the control image condition. Neither study provides clear-cut outcomes.

A further study manipulated hunger using fasting, and then examined the impact of this, separately, on delayed discounting for food, money, and music, so allowing a more direct comparison of the effects of different rewards (Skrynka & Vincent, 2019). Consistent with Orquin and

Kurzban's (2016) meta-analysis, they found a general increase in impulsive choices across all domains in hungry/fasted participants. However, the effect was significantly larger for food.

Otterbring (2019) also addressed the question of different types of reward, but used another approach. Based on self-report of hunger, participants were split into two groups that both rated their preference for 'vice' or 'virtue' foods and 'vice' or 'virtue' non-food items (e.g., an attractive colleague vs a competent colleague). Overall, hungry participants made more 'vice' choices than sated participants; however, the effect was significantly smaller for the non-food items (see Figure 4.4). These findings suggest that hunger increases impulsivity generally but especially so for food.

Two studies have explored Nettle's (2017) second model, namely that the experience of hunger during development leads to greater impulsivity in adulthood. Both studies tested his idea indirectly by examining if childhood adversity in general – which might include periods of food scarcity and hunger – influences impulsive choice in adulthood. Allen and Nettle (2021) studied the impact of self-report current hunger, and

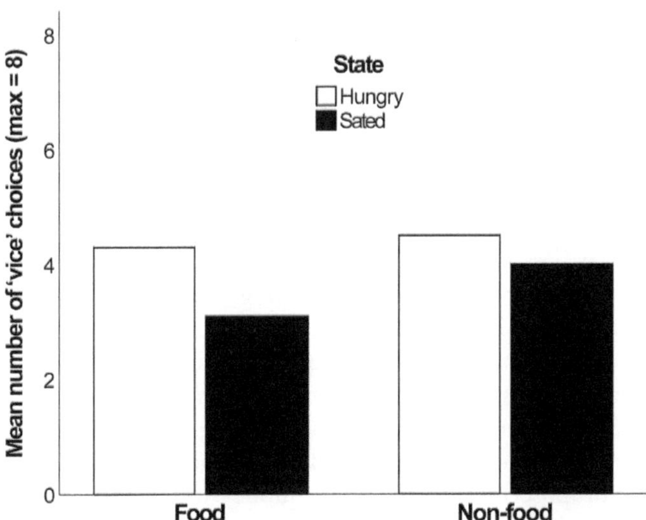

Figure 4.4 Mean number of 'vice' choices for foods (e.g., choosing chocolate over carrots) and non-foods (e.g., choosing an apartment with beautiful views over one close to work), selected when hungry and sated.

Source: Data from Otterbring T. (2019). Time orientation mediates the link between hunger and hedonic choices across domains. *Food Research International*, *120*, 124–129. https://doi.org/10.1016/j.foodres.2019.02.032

experience of childhood adversity (or not), on delayed discounting. While they obtained some weak evidence linking childhood SES and adult impulsivity, current reported hunger did not impact delayed discounting. A second study by Elbaek et al. (2022), which was a registered report, found no evidence for an impact of childhood adversity. In addition, it used a cheating task for money and did not find any impact of hunger/fasting on this task either – but noted that the positive findings for cheating reported earlier all used food rewards. These results do not support Nettle's (2017) second model.

A final source of data comes from animals. In both Nettle's (2017) article and in Fessler's (2002) review examining the link between restrictive anorexia nervosa and impulsivity, both make the claim that hunger/fasting increases impulsivity in animals. However, more recent evidence is not supportive. In pigeons, delayed discounting is not affected by periods without food (Oliviera et al., 2013). In rats, periods without food seem to make them *less impulsive.* Rats were more willing to wait for a larger delayed reward than for a smaller immediate reward, when hungry (Prince et al., 2020). Whether these findings reflect some peculiarity of the methods used to assess delayed discounting in rats or imply a different response to periods without food, is not clear. What is clear is that animal findings do not offer unambiguous support for increased impulsivity during hunger/fasting. This contrasts with most human studies reviewed in this section, which do.

4.4.2.3 Egocentricity and Resource Sharing

Several studies have explored if hungry people are more egocentric, and hence greedier, less willing to share, and less cooperative. Findings have been mixed, with some suggesting that hunger/fasting makes people more altruistic, others that it makes them greedier, and others finding nothing at all. Recent attempts to address these questions are examined here.

S. Fraser and Nettle (2019) undertook two experiments, where the hunger manipulation involved either eating or skipping breakfast. In experiment 1, participants played the ultimatum game, where one person (the proposer) is given a sum of money which they must split with another person (the respondent). The respondent then decides whether to accept or reject the proposed split. If they reject it, neither player gets a thing. Hunger/fasting had no effect on the behaviour of either proposers or respondents. In experiment 2, participants played the public goods game, where each player is given a sum of money, and they must decide how much to put into a common pot. At the end of each round all the money in the common pot is multiplied by 1.4 and this cash is then *equally* distributed among the players. In this game, it is possible to freeload by not putting any money in the pot, as everyone receives a share irrespective of what they put in. In the variant of the game used here participants were allowed to punish freeloaders. Contrary to expectations, hungry/fasted players put *more* money into the pot on the first round of the game – suggesting greater generosity – but after the first round, there were no differences between hungry/fasted and sated players. An additional finding was that punishment was less effective in changing behaviour in hungry/fasted participants.

The most extensive set of investigations have been conducted by Häusser et al. (2019). An outcome summary is presented in Table 4.2. The findings provide little support for the idea that *brief periods* of fasting make people less cooperative and more egotistical. Häusser et al. (2019) used multiple tasks, including the ultimatum and public good games (see earlier) as well as the dictator and stag hunt games. In the dictator game, the player just allocates money or food between themselves and another person (hence *dictating* their gain). In the stag hunt game, players get to choose cooperation, which results in a higher pay-off, or they can go it alone, netting a lower pay-off. Across studies, which either manipulated (fasting/feeding) or used self-reported hunger, hungry/fasted participants evidenced: somewhat greater cooperation on the stag hunt game (unexpected finding); less propensity to volunteer (expected but not replicated); and less self-rated self-control (expected). Notably, most predicted effects were not significant even though the study was well powered.

Table 4.2 *Summary of findings from Häusser et al.'s (2019) studies*

Study (sample size) and design	Outcome
Study 1 (62): Fasted vs not fasted; PGG[1], SHG[2]	PGG no effect, SHG somewhat more cooperation in fasted group
Study 2 (103): Fasted vs not fasted; PGG, UG,[3] VT[4]	PGG no effect, UG no effect, less volunteering in fasted group
Study 3 (267): Cross-sectional, hunger at that time; VT	VT no effect
Study 4 (363): Before vs after lunch; VT, DG,[5] S-RS-C[6]	VT no effect, DG no effect irrespective of reward type, less self-control reported in before lunch group
Study 5 (197): Lay theories about fasted people	People thought that fasting made them and other people more selfish, less helpful, and less cooperative

Notes: [1] Public good game; [2] Stag hunt game; [3] Ultimatum game; [4] Volunteering task; [5] Dictator game played using money or food; [6] Self-report self-control.

A further feature of the Häusser et al. (2019) study is that it measured lay beliefs about the impact of hunger/fasting on selfishness, helpfulness, and cooperativeness in self and others. Participants reported that hunger/fasting would make them and other people more selfish (self 62%, others 79%), less helpful (self 59%, others 68%), and less cooperative (self 68%, others 73%). In addition, participants were asked how they thought people in Study 4 would distribute money in the dictator game, with most believing that hungry/fasted people would allocate little to others relative to sated people – contrary to what was observed.

The findings on enhanced egocentricity, reduced willingness to share, and lack of cooperation are mixed, with few consistent effects for hungry/fasted participants. There are three things to note about these findings. First, they do not generally use food stimuli. It is possible that using real food sharing might reveal something different, as has been observed in hungry children, who are less willing to share food in this state (Huppert et al., 2020). Second, the results suggest that the experience of hunger generated during periods of brief fasting may be insufficient to impact egocentricity, cooperation, and sharing, beyond food. Third, people might behave quite differently if: (1) they had not eaten for several days, if specific hunger was induced (e.g., having to decide how much of a preferred food to share); and (2) if general hunger cues were present during testing (e.g., the participant could see it was lunchtime or their stomach was rumbling, etc.). The impact of manipulating these sorts of variables remain to be explored.

4.5 Mechanism and Function

4.5.1 Evidence Summary

Reports of behaviour during famines suggest that some people engage in immoral acts ranging from minor deception, such as cheating people out of food, to murder. These observations parallel those made under more controlled settings, which indicate that people can become more irritable, aggressive, and selfish under conditions of reduced food intake (i.e., involving loss of initial body weight of greater than 10 per cent). These types of changes have also been tested for experimentally, but under far less onerous conditions, with most studies utilising overnight fasts or the skipping of a single meal. Even under these limited conditions, evidence of a greater willingness to cheat to obtain food has been documented. There is also generally favourable evidence for an increase in impulsivity when hungry/fasted – typically general hunger, but some limited evidence for specific hunger too. However, animal data is not consistent with the human hunger–impulsivity findings. Finally, the weakest line of evidence is for greater egocentricity and a reduced willingness to share, but the major issues here are not using food rewards and the magnitude of the hunger induction (i.e., brief fasting).

4.5.2 Theory and Function

Nettle (2017) argued: (1) low SES is linked to greater impulsivity, irritability, and aggression; (2) low SES is linked to crime and delinquency; (3) low SES is linked to the experience of periods of no food or reduced food intake, which in the developed world manifests as food insufficiency and insecurity; (4) periods of no food or reduced food intake – more frequent hunger – can yield greater impulsivity, irritability, and aggression; and so (5) periods of no food/reduced food intake (and hunger) may explain variance in (1) and (2).

Fessler (2002) offers a functional explanation as to why periods of hunger/fasting may exert some of these effects on behaviour. He argues that hunger/fasting should result in behaviours that maximise obtaining food. Thus, hungry/fasted people and animals should be more active to enable greater foraging range, less risk averse so they can explore novel environments (i.e., they risk encounters with predators and competitors), and more focussed on their immediate needs than those of others (e.g., feeding offspring). Fessler's (2002) functional perspective would suggest greater activity, greater impulsivity, less cooperation, more egocentricity, and more aggression, the last mentioned due to more interactions with competitors and predators.

There are some interesting parallels between the behaviour of people who experience food shortage and the behaviour of people with drug dependence, something also alluded to by Nettle (2017). Drug dependence has a well-documented association with criminal activity, particularly when people want to buy drugs *now* but lack the means to do so. In this situation they turn to prostitution, fraud, and property crime, to generate cash. This is why, for example, when people with opiate dependency are put on methadone programs, their frequency of offending is significantly reduced (e.g., Ward et al., 1999). Moreover, the neural reward systems that are hijacked by addictive drugs such as amphetamines, cocaine, and opiates are largely the same systems that support desire for food, and consummatory pleasure on eating it. Indeed, animals that have not been fed are far more willing to work for drugs of addiction than sated animals (Carr, 1996). There seems then an important nexus between the effects on behaviour of hunger/fasting, especially where there have been longer periods without food, and the effects on behaviour of drug dependency. Both may dispose to crime.

While these theoretical perspectives provide some insights into why hunger might produce impulsivity, irritability, aggression, and ultimately criminal behaviour – perhaps to facilitate obtaining food – the actual mechanism/s by which this takes place are less clear, and they are the focus of the final part of this chapter.

4.5.3 Mechanistic Perspective

Periods of hunger/fasting could adversely impact brain function and hence impair certain aspects of cognition in this way. This seems an unlikely explanation because, as described earlier, brief or even longer episodes of fasting/starvation have little impact on tests of cognitive function (e.g., Keys et al., 1950; Kretsch et al., 1997; Shukitt-Hale et al., 1997).

Another possibility is that diet may be the problem rather than hunger/fasting per se. This type of explanation may be most applicable to people who are food insufficient or insecure – that is, those in developed countries who experience periodic hunger, and periods of food availability, but where food quality/variety/healthiness may be inferior. In Benton's (2007) review of links between diet and crime, the most well-supported link was between micronutrient deficiency and delinquent behaviour. Benton (2007) described two clinical trials that compared micronutrient supplementation versus placebo, finding that the active treatment reduced aggression. While micronutrient deficiency (and there are other possible dietary causes too) cannot account for all the effects described in this chapter (e.g., cheating following a brief fast; aggressive behaviour during a medically supervised fast with micronutrient supplementation), it does offer a plausible mechanism for some effects (i.e., impacts of food insufficiency and insecurity).

Any effect that co-occurs with hunger/fasting (e.g., a nutritionally poor diet) can also potentially serve as a causal explanation. Hunger may often be a correlate of situations that produce very adverse psychological states. As noted earlier (and see Keys et al., 1950), trauma surrounds many instances of starvation and could potentially explain people's behaviour. A further possibility, as Nettle (2017) points out, is reverse causality, where certain dispositions, such as impulsivity, irritability, aggression, and so on result in a person having little money and hence food. Thus, hunger/fasting becomes a consequence rather than a cause. Indeed, some of the researchers overseeing medically supervised fasts suggested exactly this possibility, and dispositional variables may explain why not everyone murders their family for food when starving. While these confounds are likely to play a role, they cannot explain all the findings, especially the experimental data.

A final possibility, and the one that seems to garner much support, is to consider hunger/fasting as a source of stress. Stress induces a response in the hypothalamic-pituitary-adrenal (HPA) axis, leading to the release of cortisol. Elevated cortisol has been observed in healthy participants undergoing prolonged experimental fasts (e.g., Fichter et al., 1986). Similarly, animal models of starvation also consistently show elevated levels of glucocorticoids, with the HPA axis response serving in part to maintain a euglycemic state (e.g., Makimura et al., 2003).

Putting the role of hunger/fasting as a stressor into a broader perspective, a characteristic feature of poverty (i.e., low SES) is that it causes multiple forms of stress, many of which result from financial pressures. Consistent with this idea is the finding of elevated cortisol levels in people of low SES. Cortisol has the effect of making immediate rewards more salient than delayed ones (Haushofer & Fehr, 2014). In other words, it can enhance impulsivity. Psychological stress can also contribute to low mood, irritability, and depression, with elevated cortisol offering one mechanistic pathway by which these adverse psychological changes can occur. Hunger/fasting then represents one further source of stress that people commonly experience when they are poor, adding to all the others, and contributing to behaviours that dispose to crime and delinquency (see Felson et al., 2012).

4.6 Conclusion and Implications

Observational and experimental evidence suggests that periods without food increase people's preoccupation with it. In addition, hungry/fasted people are more likely to cheat, lie, and steal, and to prefer a small reward now rather than a larger reward later. Some of these effects may be beneficial in fostering behaviours that promote the acquisition of food. Hunger/fasting is a stressor, which results in activation of the HPA axis and the release of cortisol. Elevated cortisol can result in more impulsive behaviour and, longer term, in irritability, low mood, and depression – all of these can be observed in hungry people, especially during prolonged fasting or starvation. Poverty is stressful, and hunger adds yet another source of stress, contributing to the elevated cortisol levels observed in people of low SES. Hunger/fasting may contribute to crime and delinquency by being a further source of stress. Food insecurity and insufficiency occurs in many people. It is preventable, and its resolution would benefit everyone, via reduced crime and delinquency.

CHAPTER 5

Famine

5.0 Introduction

Any examination of hunger is incomplete without an exploration of its most extreme manifestation, namely famine and starvation. Famine is the condition under which a group of people in a particular locale or group starve because they cannot access enough food. The first part of the chapter concerns definitions and the epidemiology of famines (and starvation), including over evolutionary timescales, and into modern times. Two famines are then examined in more detail, namely the 1845–1849 Irish potato famine and the Great Chinese Famine of 1959–1961, as a way of illustrating the causal factors that give rise to widespread starvation. The latter part of the chapter describes the biopsychosocial impacts of acute and chronic starvation, especially in children, how these may be remediated, and the link between overabundance in developed countries and starvation in developing countries.

5.1 Epidemiology of Hunger

Inadequate supply of nutrients has its own terminology, and so to understand the statistics one must start with definitions. Malnutrition covers both the consequences of too much food and too little. Only the latter is of interest here. A subtype of malnutrition is undernutrition, which has four subsidiary categories. First, wasting, which is normally used in reference to children (typically five years and under) who are too thin for their height. Wasting is usually considered an acute phenomenon and hence a manifestation of recent food shortage (and/or from diarrhoea, a related cause). In 2022, there were forty-five million children categorised as 'wasted' (World Health Organization (WHO), 2024). Second, stunting, which is associated with a more chronic shortage of nutrients and refers to being too short for one's age (again, typically in children five years and under).

In 2022, there were 149 million children aged under five who were stunted. Third are micronutrient deficiencies, the principal ones being iodine, iron, and A group vitamins, which, respectively, affected 2,200 million adults/children, 1,000 million adults/children, and 140 million children in 2022. The fourth category is underweight (and see NCD Risk Factor Collaboration, 2024, for very concise and informative graphical representations of these data for all nation states), which is low weight for age, and is usually used to describe whole populations or just adults. In 2022, 462 million adults were categorised as underweight.

Two further measures are important. The first is food insecurity, which is an index of the extent to which people do not have access to food. Food insecurity is a concern even in developed countries (see Chapter 4). In the US, the USDA (US Department of Agriculture, 2022) estimates 44 million people were food insecure during 2022 – defined as periods of time where food supply was uncertain or unavailable. In Australia, 3.7 million people were reported as having periods of time during 2022 with no food (Foodbank Australia, 2024). A more stringent use of the term is employed by the World Food Program (WFP), namely: 'When a person's inability to consume enough food puts their lives or livelihoods in immediate danger'. In 2022, the WFP estimated there were 258 million people who met this definition across fifty-eight different countries. Forty per cent of these people were in just five countries – Afghanistan, the Democratic Republic of the Congo (DRC), Ethiopia, Nigeria, and Yemen (World Food Program, 2023).

The second measure is a composite score, made up of stunting, wasting, child mortality in under-fives (noting that around 50 per cent of all deaths in this category are linked to undernutrition) and the per cent of the population that is not receiving an adequate intake of energy. These data have been used to calculate a Global Hunger Index (Global Hunger Index, 2024), which has scores that can vary from 0 to 100, with scores more than 50 categorised as 'extremely alarming', 35–49.9 'alarming', 20–34.9 'serious', 10–19.9 'moderate', and anything under 10 as 'low'. In 2023, no country's score fell into the 'extremely alarming' category, but nine had scores in the 'alarming' category. The highest score of 42 was for the Central African Republic (CAR), which has had a troubled history of political instability, civil war, and that continues to be affected by the HIV/AIDS epidemic. Nearly half of the CAR's population experience some form of undernutrition, one in ten children do not live to their fifth birthday, 40 per cent of children are stunted, and 5 per cent wasted.

The second highest score of 41 was from Madagascar, which had similar statistics to the CAR, with nearly 50 per cent of the population undernourished, 40 per cent of children stunted, and 7 per cent wasted. Madagascar's food supply issues have been attributed to climate change. In contrast, the third highest score was for Yemen, which has been engulfed in armed conflict, leaving 49 per cent of children stunted and 14 per cent wasted. The remaining six countries to score in the 'alarming' range were Niger (armed conflict), Lesotho (drought), the DRC (civil war), Somalia (drought), South Sudan (flooding and armed conflict), and Burundi (extreme poverty). The last mentioned had the highest rate of child stunting in the world (51 per cent).

While African countries feature consistently in these statistics, it is not the only region experiencing undernourishment and its consequences. Table 5.1 outlines several of the statistics described earlier but organised on a regional basis. Proportionally, Africa has the highest rates of undernutrition, food insecurity, and proportion of the population unable to afford a healthy diet. However, Asia had the highest number of people who were experiencing undernutrition and the highest proportion of wasted children. Oceania had the highest rates of stunting. Figure 5.1 and 5.2, respectively, illustrate some of these data at the country level, namely prevalence of undernutrition across the world and stunting in under-fives – revealing how widespread this is as a problem, and how unlikely it is that the world will meet the second United Nations sustainable development goal of 'zero hunger' by 2030. Indeed, since the Covid epidemic and its economic consequences, and with the war in Ukraine impacting agricultural supplies (i.e., Russian fertiliser and Ukrainian grain), nearly all these hunger measures have gone backwards. This has reversed an otherwise positive trend of improvement over the last fifty years.

5.2 Famine History

5.2.1 *Famine in Prehistory and Its Evolutionary Impacts on Human Feeding/Hunger*

According to the WHO, in 2022, 19,000 million people were overweight (in adults a body mass index 25+) and of these 650 million were obese (in adults a body mass index 30+). After the Second World War and until the early 1970s the proportion of overweight and obese people was not substantial. However, since the 1970s the numbers have increased steadily, especially in developed countries, suggesting that some change has occurred in the environment to promote excess weight gain. There is agreement that this environmental change reflects the availability of cheap, ubiquitous, highly

Table 5.1 *Region-specific hunger statistics for 2022 (data from WHO annual report, 2023)*

Region	Prevalence of under-nutrition	Number of people under-nourished	Prevalence of stunting	Prevalence of wasting	Prevalence of severe food	Prevalence of inability to access a healthy diet
Africa	19.7%	282,000,000	30.0%	5.8%	24.0%	77.5%
Asia	8.5%	402,000,000	22.3%	9.3%	9.7%	44.2%
Latin America & Caribbean	6.5%	43,000,000	11.5%	1.4%	12.6%	22.7%
Oceania	7.0%	3,200,000	44.0%	8.3%	3.4%	2.9%
North America & Europe	<2.5%	*	3.8%	*	1.5%	1.4%

Note: * No data available.

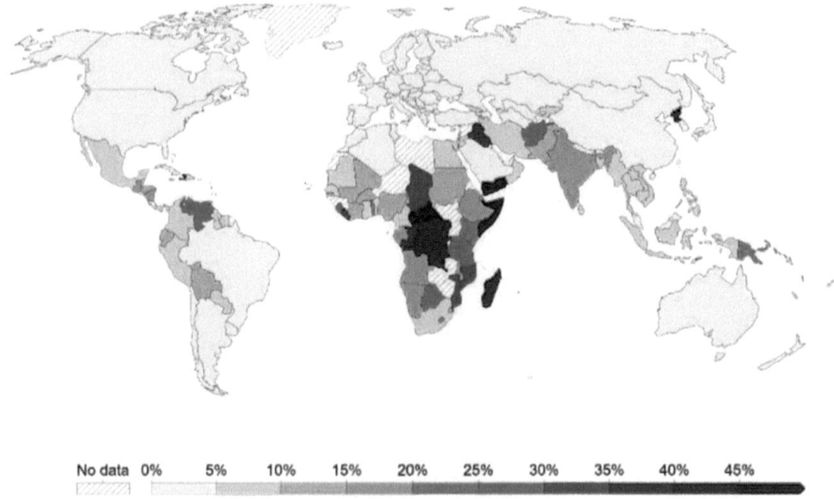

Figure 5.1 Percentage of the population undernourished across the world in 2019.
Source: Figure 1 in Arigbede, O., Kilanko, O., Arigbede, O. J., & Matthew, O. (2023). Hunger, food security, and sovereignty: A need for evidence-based public health approaches to meet sustainable development goals. *International Journal of Public Health, 68*, 1605956. https://doi.org/10.3389/ijph.2023.1605956

palatable food that is energy dense. Importantly, not everyone is equally susceptible to this obesogenic environment, and much of the variance (some 40–70 per cent) in who does and does not gain excess weight can be explained by genetic factors (e.g., Locke et al., 2015; Visscher et al., 2012).

It has been suggested that one reason for a propensity to gain excess weight could be a history of famine and starvation in either our 'recent' evolutionary past (i.e., the last 10,000 years – since the advent of farming) or back in more distant times (i.e., last 1–2 million years – as hunter-gatherers). Periods of famine and starvation could arise in several ways. Variations in climate (e.g., El Niño), seasonal variation, climatic catastrophes (e.g., floods, drought), and other natural disasters could lead to extended periods without food, with this being more likely once farming began (Prentice, 2001). This is because farming typically relies on fewer varieties of food than are available to hunger-gatherers, and so increases vulnerability to disease. In addition, the advent of farming meant that food could be stolen. Finally, the impact of any crop loss would be amplified by its effect on people who were not primary producers but town-dwelling dependents.

Shorter-term cyclic or seasonal variations in food availability have been observed. In a study of people in the Gambia (Prentice, 2001), cyclic

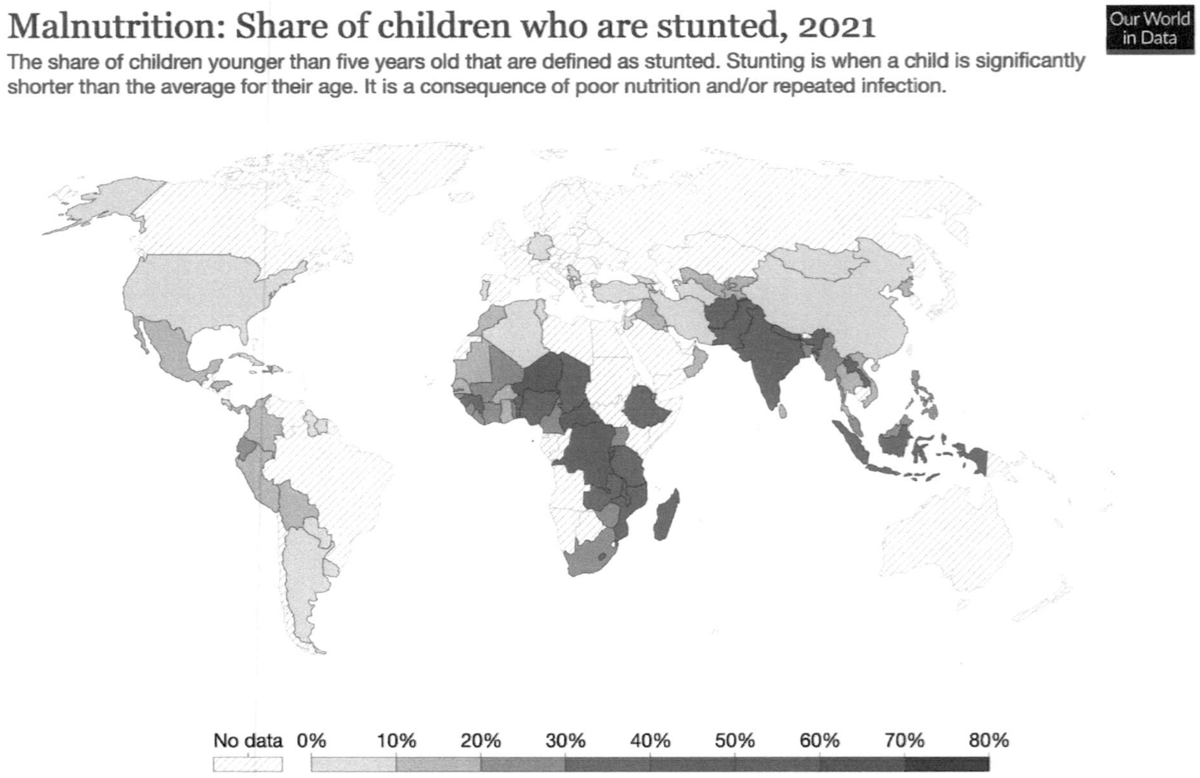
Malnutrition: Share of children who are stunted, 2021
The share of children younger than five years old that are defined as stunted. Stunting is when a child is significantly shorter than the average for their age. It is a consequence of poor nutrition and/or repeated infection.
Our World in Data
No data
0%
10%
20%
30%
40%
50%
60%
70%
80%

Figure 5.2 Percentage of children under five who were stunted in 2021.
Source: Our World in Data. https://ourworldindata.org/grapher/share-of-children-younger-than-5-who-suffer-from-stunting

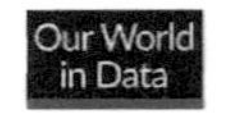

availability of food was found to correlate with body weight. In a bad year, this might mean a person losing 5–6 kg of body fat. It seems probable that, at various periods in our history, we have been subjected to periods of famine and seasonal food shortage. Those able to survive these periods by perhaps being better able to store excess energy as fat when food was plentiful, would then have: (1) survived to have more children; (2) enhanced the survival of their infants by being able to breastfeed them through a famine; and (3) be able to maintain fertility for longer during a famine. All these benefits would aid the propagation of genetic variants favouring excess weight gain. This type of model was first described by Neel (1962) as the 'thrifty genotype' hypothesis. It has been developed by several other theorists (e.g., Higginson et al., 2016; Prentice, 2005; Sellayah et al., 2014; Speakman et al., 2011; and see discussion in Chapter 2).

One variant of this evolutionary approach to body weight has been to suggest that any species-wide 'thrifty genes' (i.e., gene variants favouring conversion of food to body fat) would be unlikely, and that it would depend on more local environmental factors, especially climate (Sellayah et al., 2014). The key factor in this model is the presumption that groups living in colder regions would select for burning excess calories to keep warm, while those in warmer regions would not be under such selection pressure. There is some evidence favouring this model, in that people with different ancestral geographic origins have different rates of obesity (e.g., higher in Americans of African (warmer ancestral climate) vs European descent (colder ancestral climate)). However, it is hard to dismiss the impact of *current* socio-economic differences when evaluating this piece of evidence. This is because there is a potential confounding between ancestral origins (and hence climate) and current socio-economic status (SES). Low SES makes it harder to eat healthily, and both poverty and racism are stressful, all of which are risk factors for excess weight gain. These could explain some or perhaps all the difference in body weight, when comparing African Americans and Americans of European descent. In addition, there is a further criticism of this model, which concerns the best strategy to maintain body temperature under cold conditions. Storing excess fat subcutaneously is an effective means of retaining body heat via insulation. This could be more efficient than just using energy for generating heat.

Another approach has been to consider the major evolutionary forces affecting body weight. One proposal has been the dual threshold model. Here, natural selection operates on the regulatory mechanisms that control the lower and upper thresholds for body weight (e.g., Higginson et al., 2016; Speakman et al., 2011). Selection pressure on the lower threshold arises from the consequences of excess weight loss – such as from a famine – which will either reduce opportunities for reproduction or prevent it permanently because of death. Selection pressure on the upper threshold concerns excess weight gain and its consequences. This will make the person more vulnerable to predation and disease and reduce their sexual attractiveness. All these consequences would reduce transmission of genes to the next generation.

Genetic modelling suggests that even a small risk from starvation exerts selection pressure on mechanisms regulating the lower threshold of body weight (Higginson et al., 2016). This would imply that ancestral exposure to famine would favour gene variants associated with storing excess calories as fat. For the upper threshold of body weight, it has been argued that some of the selection pressure has been relaxed – that is, weight can increase with little consequence for fitness. The advent of fire, cooperation between individuals, safe shelter, and weapons makes selection pressure from predation much less important than it once was. This has led to another model called the 'drifty gene hypothesis' (G. Wang & Speakman, 2016), where a propensity for higher body weight is no longer under strict selection pressure, thus allowing excess weight gain to occur when food is readily available.

There have been two major studies testing for an evolutionary signature of these theories in the human genome. The first was Wang and Speakman's (2016), which examined for evidence among protein coding genes. If there was selection pressure for thrifty genes, then one should find an association between certain protein coding gene variants and higher body weight – that is, evidence that some genes favour accumulation of fat. It would also be possible to tell, should such variants exist, whether they were recent (i.e., linked to farming lifestyle) or more distant (i.e., linked to hunter-gatherer lifestyle) in evolutionary terms. However, no evidence was found for the existence of such gene variants, and so Wang and Speakman (2016) concluded that these findings favoured the 'drifty gene' account.

The second major study was reported by L. Wang et al. (2020) and reached a different conclusion. Rather than focus on protein coding gene variants, it studied small pieces of RNA (microRNA) that exert an influence over a group of genes. MicroRNAs are heritable through the same basic pathway as protein coding genes – via DNA. The microRNA under study was 128-1 and it is involved in metabolic regulation. Elimination of this microRNA in animal models results in reductions in body fat and blood glucose, consistent with it functioning as a thrifty gene. The area of the human genome that codes for this microRNA is also linked to the ability to tolerate lactose into adulthood, which likely confers a survival advantage in human groups that keep ruminants. Consistent with animal data, the presence of microRNA 128-1 in humans favours fat deposition and higher blood glucose. This variant is also of recent emergence, suggesting that it was periods of shortage, starvation, and famine when farming first started that favoured its selection.

5.2.2 *Famine in Recorded History*

While there has been considerable speculation about the frequency and nature of food shortages and famines in the deep past (i.e., 5,000 years+), recorded history offers a more concrete guide and one that improves in accuracy as more recent times are approached. Ancient civilisations endured famines. Egypt is one example, with evidence of a seven-year famine and drought recorded in hieroglyphics carved on to a rock face on Sehel island (see Chapter 4). This 'famine stela' has been dated to 200 BC. For the United Kingdom, Keys et al. (1950) estimated that there have been 190 famines in the period starting from 1 AD, with the last major one being the Irish potato famine of 1845–1849. China has also provided a comprehensive record of famines over the same period. From 1 AD there have been over 1,800 famines (Prentice, 2001), but the last one from 1959 to 1961 eclipsed all others in terms of its scale and brutality (see Figure 5.3). In the last hundred years or so (see Figure 5.3), there have been around seventy major famines (i.e., with 50,000+ deaths), with these occurring on every continent except Antarctica. To illustrate the factors that contribute to the genesis and maintenance of a famine, the following section focusses on two important examples, the Irish potato famine (1845–1849), which was the UK's last, and the Great Chinese Famine of 1959–1961, which was the worst in recorded history.

5.2.3 *Famines and Their Causes*

5.2.3.1 *The Irish Potato Famine*

The Irish potato famine (1845–1849) was caused by a combination of colonial history, British politics, fungal biology, and wet climate. Ireland (the whole of it) had a population of 3.2 million people in 1754. Just prior to the famine (1841), this had increased to 8.2 million people. Some three decades after the famine ended, Ireland's population had still not recovered, standing at 5.2 million in 1881, and it continued to fall right into the middle of the twentieth century (4.3 million in 1946). Today (2025), its population – now 7.1 million – has still not surpassed that of 1841. It is estimated that the famine caused the death of around one in four of Ireland's population over its most active period (1845–1849) and led to the migration of another 1.2 million people to North America and a further 1.2 million to

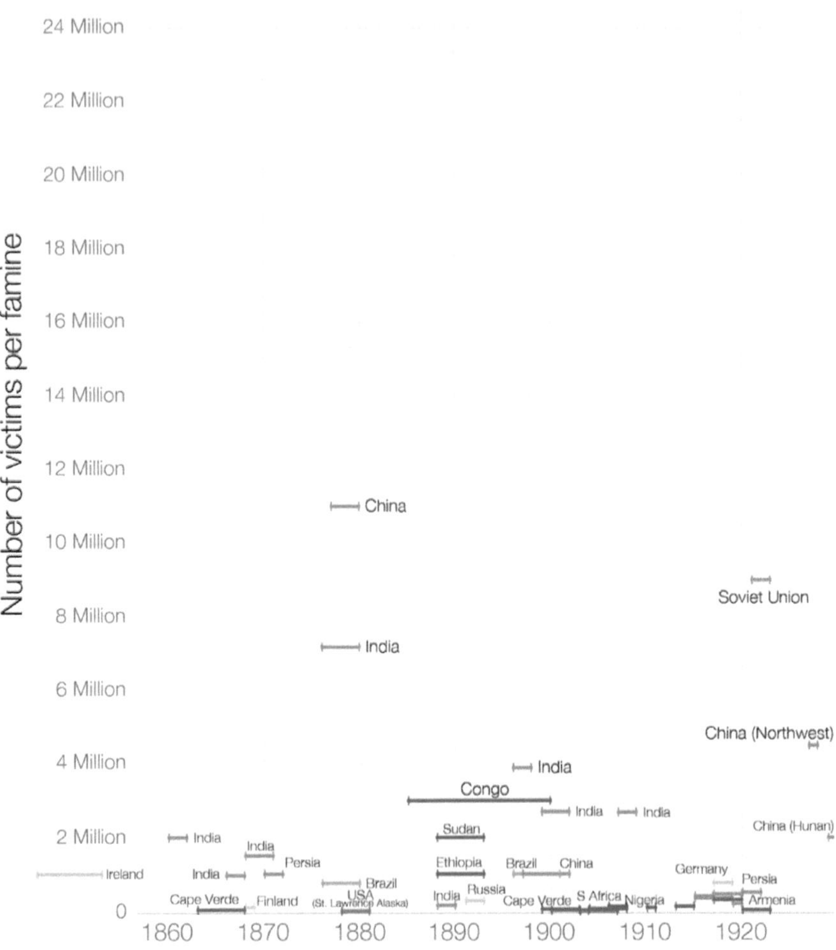

Figure 5.3 Global famines across the last 150 years.
Source: Our World in Data. https://ourworldindata.org/famines

the UK (Woodham-Smith, 1962). This catastrophe (the 'Great Hunger' or *An Gorta Mór*) has cast a long shadow over its people, their relationship with Britain, and Britain's reputation as an enlightened colonial power.

Ireland experienced multiple invasions by British forces from 1169 onwards. It was formally brought into the United Kingdom in 1801 by the Act of Union, which was viewed more as 'a rape than a marriage' as it conferred little benefit to Ireland but much to the UK. Large parts of Ireland were owned by absentee landlords, often wealthy English aristocrats, many of whom never ventured to see their Irish estates. Much estate management

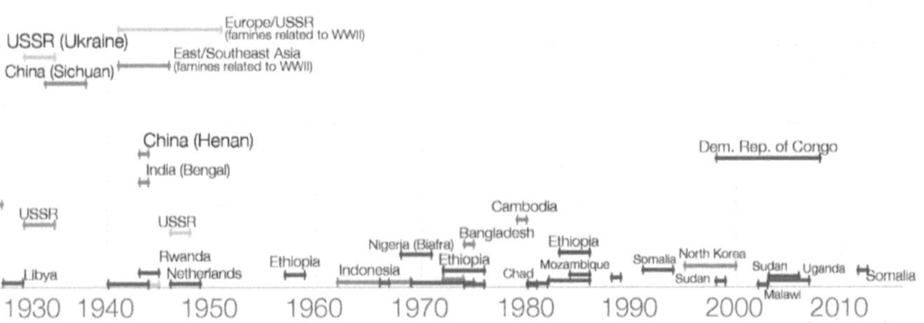

fell to local agents, who sublet small plots of land and an accompanying shack to families. Each of these families then engaged in subsistence farming, raising just enough food to feed themselves and pay the rent. Because plot sizes were small, and little money was available to develop the land, families relied upon a single crop, the potato. All it needed was a spade to sow and it provided a rich source of food. A typical small plot of 1.5 acres (about 6,000 m^2) could provide enough potatoes for a family of six for a year. The most important thing to note is how fragile this whole system was. A series of bad harvests meant penury and eviction. The reliance on one crop was risky from the perspective of disease. The failure to educate the populace or to aid them in developing the land and enlarging single plots into bigger enterprises, meant in turn there were few opportunities for work in the countryside. And, importantly, all these systemic weaknesses were well known and appreciated by the UK government in London, as *prior* to the famine there had been 175 reports on these issues (Woodham-Smith, 1962).

Disaster struck in the form of a fungal infection called potato blight (*phytophthora infestans*). This may have come from North America, but its origins remain unclear. The weather in Ireland is well disposed to fungal plant infections, as it is mild and wet. Indeed, conditions were ideal in 1845 – very wet. The fungus largely wiped out the Irish potato crop. Each potato rotted (see Figure 5.4) and eventually turned into an inedible black sludge. Potato blight struck again in 1846, less so in 1847, and then returned in full force in 1848. Given the reliance on the potato, the absence of other work, and the need to pay rent, many people were evicted from the land and shack they rented. The consequences of eviction were made worse by the severe winter of 1846/1847, and by outbreaks of typhus and dysentery in 1846 and cholera in 1849. The land stunk of rotting potatoes, people died of disease, starvation, and exposure – with much of this being reported in the English press, and graphically in the *Illustrated London News*. A particularly well-known and tragic image depicted a mother with her dead baby and two starving children (see Figure 5.5).

London greeted the unfolding events in Ireland with consternation, especially the likely cost to the exchequer. The British government's initial relief efforts were partially effective, in that without them it is likely that many more people would have died. A major architect of the relief schemes enacted in Ireland was a senior treasury official Charles Trevelyan (see Figure 5.6). He was an evangelical Christian, an economic rationalist, and

Figure 5.4 Potato blight.
Source: © Feb 14, 2022 OpenStax. Textbook content produced by OpenStax is licensed under a Creative Commons Attribution License

Figure 5.5 A graphic illustration of the Irish potato famine: a starving homeless family with the mother carrying her dead infant.
Source: Picryl.

a disciple of Malthus, and was described by Woodham-Smith (1962) thus: '[H]e disliked both new expenditure and new taxes and was a firm believer in laissez faire, preferring to let matters take their course and allow problems to be solved by "natural means"' (p. 87). Natural means in the context of the Irish potato famine meant starving to death.

London's relief efforts initially consisted of secretly imported American corn. The secrecy was believed to be necessary – first so as not to disturb food prices in Ireland, and second to avoid inflated costs on international food markets. This limited food aid was supplemented by local relief committees that could levy landlords for funds to pay for food. This was combined with a public works scheme to try to employ those who had been made destitute by the famine. Many of these schemes were only

Figure 5.6 Charles Trevelyan, a key architect of the British relief efforts in Ireland. Courtesy of the National Trust, UK.

partially effective. The food relief was insufficient. Many landowners were themselves either unwilling or unable to contribute funds to local relief committees, and the make-work schemes became bogged in a sea of paperwork. As the famine worsened with successive crop failures, these approaches were supplemented by soup kitchens and, with a touch of the twenty-first century, a Victorian celebrity chef (Alexis Sayer) provided recipes for cheap and nutritious soups. None of these efforts, nor the workhouses, were able to mitigate the enormous suffering that ensued. From an academic perspective, the principal lesson from this famine is how a series of events, notably involving politics and biology, combined to cause this disaster.

5.2.3.2 The Great Chinese Famine of 1959–1961

The Irish potato famine is a typical one, in having a combined political-biological cause. However, the Great Chinese Famine of 1959–1961 is unusual in two regards, first in having an entirely political cause, and second in its sheer scale. Over its span, the lower bound for deaths is fifteen million; however, most demographic estimates place it in the range of thirty-six to forty-five million, with an upper bound of fifty-five million deaths (Dikötter, 2010; Jisheng, 2008/2012). As with all famines, birth rates plummeted due to starvation-related infertility and death. This is estimated to have led to at least fifty million forgone births.

It is impossible to comprehend such a number of deaths, but one description from a survivor provides some sense of its enormity:

> I went back twice to my village in Fanghu. Just before the Lunar New Year I saw 6 corpses along several km of roadway. Five km from my home there were dead bodies everywhere, at least 100 corpses lying out in the open with nobody to bury them. Among the reed ponds along the river bank, I saw another 100 corpses. It was said that dogs had eaten so many of the corpses that their eyes glowed with bloodlust. But this was inconsistent with the facts. People had already eaten all the dogs, so where would there be dogs to eat the corpses? (Yu Dehong, quoted in Jisheng, 2008/2012, pp. 39–40)

The primary architect of this famine was the chairman of the Chinese communist party, Mao Zedong. The cause of the famine was a policy decision to rapidly convert what was an agrarian society into an industrial one, the so-called Great Leap Forward. One component of this was the decision to collectivise farming. This aimed to advance communism in China but more importantly to improve agricultural efficiency and production. Collectivisation would involve moving every single Chinese farmer into one of 26,000 communes. There would be no private property, no private homes, no ownership of farming tools, land, or animals, not even cooking implements or pans. As each commune was established everyone was forced to join and to yield *all* their property. A communal kitchen was also built to feed commune members, and initially a large amount of food was available because of the forced collectivisation. Mao himself encouraged people to eat all they wanted – 'seven meals a day!' – and they did. When the available food ran out the collectives shifted to 'performance feeding', allocating food based on how important one's labour was to the commune. Perhaps not surprisingly, the rapidly burgeoning bureaucracy necessary to run each commune – a staggering 7 per cent of the rural workforce – appeared to fare best in terms of rations.

The peasant farmers were not particularly motivated to work for the commune. The sense of unfairness at seeing all their property confiscated doubtless led many to hide food, steal, cheat, and avoid communal labour. In addition, large numbers of farmers were moved to the cities to aid industrialisation, and millions more in the countryside were co-opted to work on infrastructure projects. These included massive irrigation schemes – all done with manual labour – and the insane scheme to industrialise the countryside by building thousands of small-blast furnaces and ball-bearing works. The upshot of this was the mass siphoning away of agricultural labour, which, rather than growing food, needed feeding. To further the processes of industrialisation all 'surplus' food had to be exported to raise cash to import overseas machinery and equipment to aid industrial development. As only exaggerated outcomes or ridiculously high targets could be presented to leaders – due to the pervasive climate of fear, with its 'struggle sessions', public beatings, executions, and disappearances – provinces exported far more food than they could afford, contributing to the starvation of their own populations.

As if all these forces were not enough, pseudoscientific ideas also gained traction. A whole slew of bizarre agricultural practices were promoted. Deep ploughing involved turning the soil over in some cases to the depth of several metres. Not only was this very time and labour intensive, but at best all it accomplished was to bury the most fertile top-soil layer. Another practice that was encouraged was close planting to boost yields, but all this did was reduce yields as the growing plants crowded each other out in a competition to survive. Perhaps the most devastating idea was the 'four pests' campaign (Figure 5.7). While the move to kill mosquitos, flies, and rats was well motivated, the decision to also include sparrows was not. Millions of birds were killed, rendering much of the countryside silent of birdsong. Unfortunately, it also allowed insect pests, particularly locusts, to flourish. While sparrows may have stolen some food, unchecked plagues of locusts stole far more. All these factors contributed to starvation through reduction in crop yields.

There was considerable variation between provinces in deaths, with Sichuan perhaps the worst affected (around ten million deaths), and then Anhui (six million), with many escaping with far less (i.e., less than one million). Much of this variation could be accounted for by the level of adherence to the policies emanating from Mao in Beijing. People's response to the famine was initially to adapt their diet (see Table 5.2). As food and pseudo-food sources failed and deaths mounted, people started eating corpses to stay alive (see Chapter 4). As the dead were often emaciated, they had little to offer in the way of meat, and so just temporarily delayed the inevitable. As news of what was happening in the countryside percolated slowly back to the leadership in Beijing, Liu

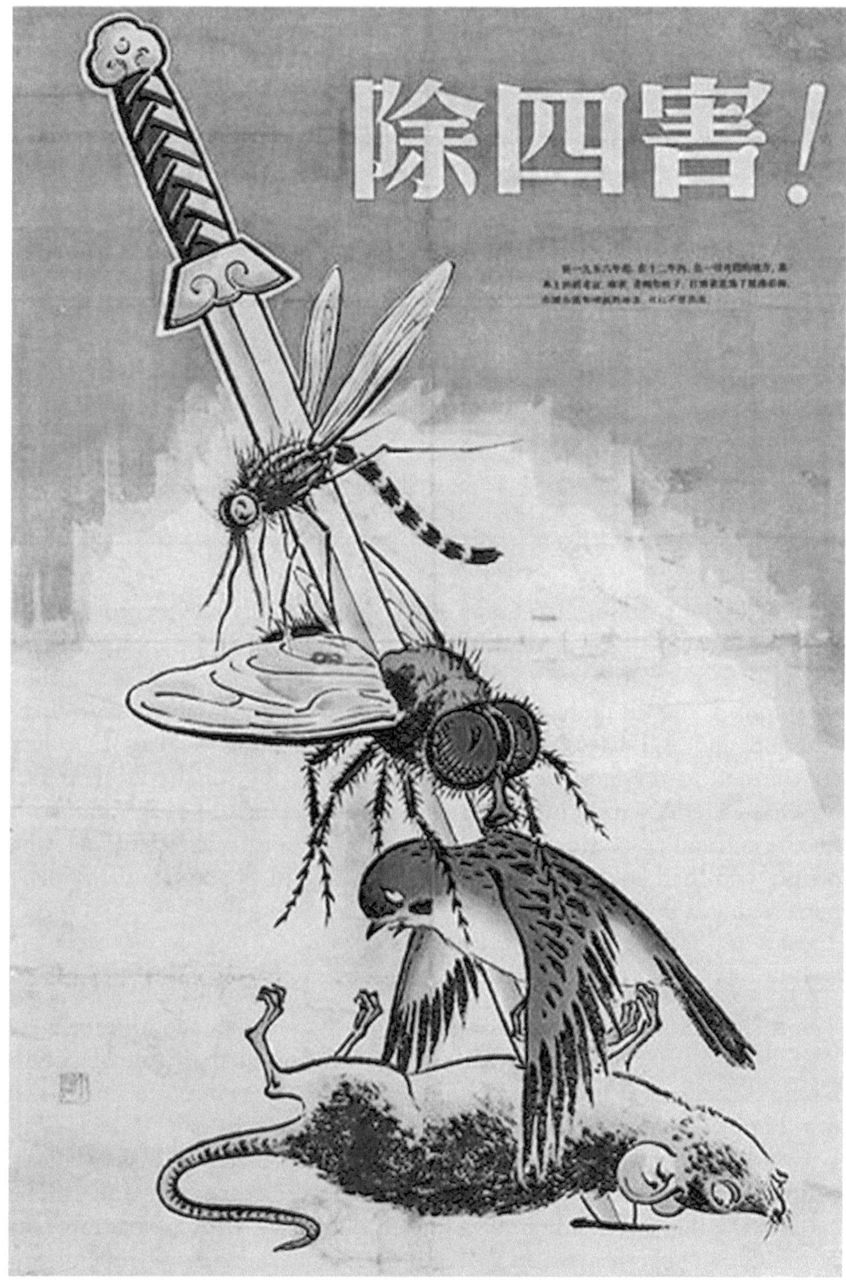

Figure 5.7 Chinese poster promoting the four pests campaign. Courtesy of Chineseposters.net

Table 5.2 *Famine foods described by Jisheng (2008/2012) and as used in the Great Chinese Famine of 1959–1961*

Name	Preparation/food
Rice straw	Normally livestock feed, chopped, cooked, and ground, mixed with sweet potato flour and made into steamed buns
Corn stalks	Normally livestock feed. Same process as for rice straw
Egret droppings	Composed of remnants of their fish diet; these do not smell and are washed and steamed
Acorn flour	Ground, crushed, powdered, and soaked in bicarbonate of soda to remove tannins
Leaf protein	Grass and leaves minced and reduced by boiling to a protein sediment, dried, and powdered
Man-made meat essence	Fermented vegetable waste, with scum harvested and cooked to produce a meat-like essence
Miscellaneous	Dried algae, insect protein, aged bones, double-cooked rice (to increase volume and fillingness), wild herbs, peanut sprouts, rats, sparrows, roots, tree bark, clam shells, cotton batting

Shaoqi, a senior communist leader, told Mao: 'History will record the role you and I played in the starvation of so many people, and the cannibalism will also be memorialised' (Jisheng, 2008/2012, p. 15). Mao was ultimately forced into an embarrassing climbdown, having to abandon collectivisation and roll back many of his other signature policies that had contributed to the famine. Mao's pride was hurt by this backdown, and he sensed a reduction in his power and standing. This laid the groundwork for the cultural revolution, which served both as a vehicle to eliminate the people who had told him the truth (such as Liu Shaoqi) and those he perceived as a threat to his power.

5.2.3.3 Conclusion

The Irish potato famine was a disaster waiting to happen, combining a set of politico-historical factors with a biological one in the form of potato blight. The Chinese famine was unique in two ways. First, it is one of the few famines that have a sole cause in politics (i.e., the 'Great Leap Forward'). Second, it exceeds all known famines in terms of how many people died. While climate, disease, and other misfortunes of nature can be calamitous, they tend only to be so when they occur with an incompetent or indifferent government. As the Chinese famine shows, governments can be far more dangerous than the environment.

5.3 The Impacts of Famine

5.3.1 Acute

There has been a focus on child over adult starvation, as children are more vulnerable to both its immediate and delayed effects. The reasons for this vulnerability relate to children's lower fat stores, greater nutritional needs to support growth (especially for protein), less developed immune response to common pathogens, an inability to fend for themselves, and, as is often the case, being underweight at birth due to their mother experiencing starvation during pregnancy. In addition, children who exhibit signs of wasting (i.e., underweight for height) or other nutritional deficits typically have other adverse circumstances that contribute to their malnourished state. These include poor maternal education and health, multiple siblings, limited opportunity for breastfeeding, familial poverty, female gender, and a lack of immunisation (e.g., Batool et al., 2015; Sarkar et al., 2019). While lack of food represents the proximal cause of a wasted or underweight child, the distal causes are more complex.

Children can manifest two extremes of nutritional deficiency, although they are often encountered together. One extreme results from a diet that provides sufficient energy but contains inadequate amounts of protein (note that micronutrient deficiencies may also be relevant here as well). This is known as kwashiorkor ('the sickness of weaning' in the Ga language of Ghana), which often occurs when a child swaps from breast milk to solids. The process of weaning can result in a large reduction in protein intake if the food being offered is carbohydrate rich, such as cassava. The risk to the child increases further if it is difficult for the family to obtain sufficient water to wash the cassava properly prior to cooking. This exposes the child to toxic cyanogenic glucosides, which can lead to the crippling neurological disease konzo. Indeed, many bush foods eaten when a family is under food stress carry such risks (e.g., grass pea and lathyrism), and young children are especially vulnerable as they are less able to process toxins as effectively as adults.

Kwashiorkor (see Figure 5.8) has a distinctive manifestation that allows its ready discrimination from the effects of an energy-poor diet (the other extreme). The child will have significant oedema (often as a pot belly), noticeable abnormalities of skin and hair, and an enlarged liver, while not necessarily being that underweight. In contrast, children who are fed a diet that is insufficient in energy content develop a disease called marasmus (see Figure 5.9). Such children have no subcutaneous fat, appear emaciated and

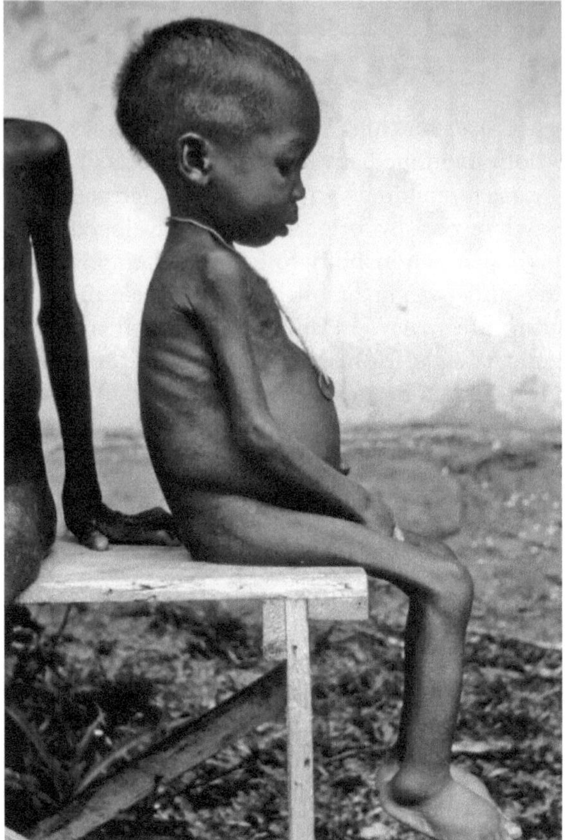

Figure 5.8 A child suffering from kwashiorkor.
Source: Public Health Image Library, CDC

apathetic, and are significantly underweight for age (Grover & Ee, 2009). The loss of skeletal muscle in marasmus follows a particular pattern as the starvation period lengthens, starting with muscles in the groin and axillary region, then affecting the thighs/buttocks, the chest/abdomen, and finally the face. It is the loss of facial musculature that gives a child with marasmus the look of an elderly person.

Kwashiorkor and marasmus are extremes of a spectrum disease termed either protein-energy malnutrition (PEM) or severe acute malnutrition (SAM). Most children who experience PEM or SAM have diets that are deficient in both protein and energy, in addition to multiple micronutrients, especially iodine, iron, and A group vitamins (Batool et al., 2015). Irrespective of whether the person is an adult or child, the body has a

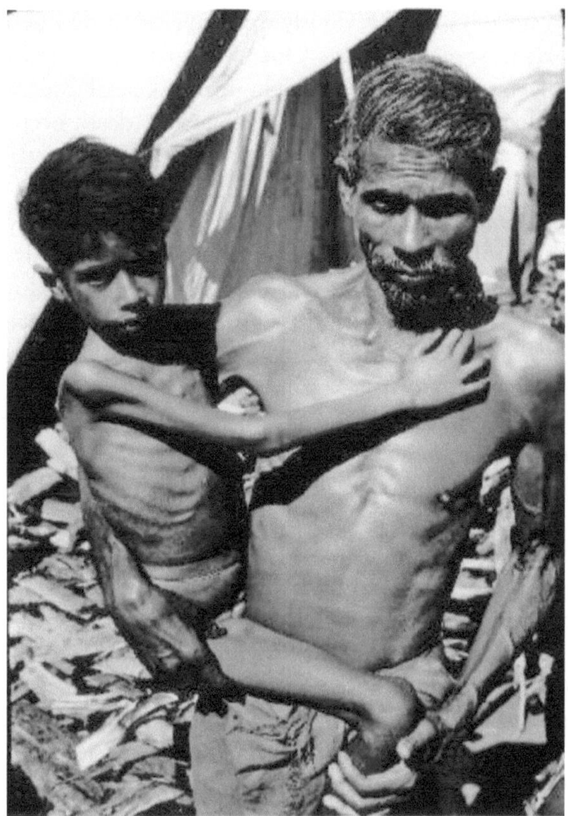

Figure 5.9 A child suffering from marasmus.
Source: Public Health Image Library, CDC

sequence of physiological responses to starvation. This has often been divided into three phases. The first is brief, spanning the time since the last meal until all the body's glycogen stores are depleted – a period of a day or so without food. During this period the body subsists on its glucose reserves (i.e., stored as glycogen in the liver), by digesting any residual food left in the gut, and from metabolising circulating fatty acids (T. Wang et al., 2006). The second phase is termed 'adaptive starvation', as it is truly a biological adaptation to survive periods of food deprivation (McCue, 2010). The body initially utilises skeletal muscle-derived protein as fuel (generating glucose), but as the switch to starvation physiology kicks in, it uses accumulated fat stores instead. These allow for some limited glucose manufacture, but the main brain and bodily fuel becomes ketone bodies (Cahill, 2006). The length of this second adaptive phase lasts as long as the body's supply of fat. In a child this may be several days, in a previously well-fed adult it may be a month, and in an obese person several months. Once these fat stores are exhausted, the third phase of starvation starts. Protein from skeletal muscle is used to generate fuel (glucose) and, when this is exhausted, death occurs.

During the second and third phases of starvation, a variety of other physiological changes occur (e.g., McCue, 2010). There is a reduction in basal metabolic rate to conserve energy, which is accompanied by a persistent feeling of being cold. The immune system, which is energetically costly to maintain and a significant user of protein, is downregulated, especially cellular immunity, with this controlled by the reduction in leptin that follows lack of food (Lord et al., 1998). Again, to conserve energy and protein, menstruation stops, resulting in temporary loss of fertility (T. Wang et al., 2006). Similarly, it takes a considerable amount of energy and protein to maintain an active digestive system, both in terms of the mucosal barrier of the gut wall and to produce digestive enzymes. Consequently, this system is also downregulated (McCue, 2010). It is stressful to experience starvation, resulting in elevated cortisol levels. This has impacts on the brain, notably the hippocampus, resulting in impaired learning and memory, which includes a loss of memory inhibition, and hence more persistent hunger and thoughts of food (Nagura et al., 2003).

The cumulative effect of these physiological changes depends on who is being starved. For a child, the effects may be rapidly fatal, but less so for adults. The less developed immune protection of a child, the absence of immunisation, and the weakened immune system from starvation-related changes leave them open to disease. In particular, because of starvation-related changes to the digestive system, the gut wall becomes more vulnerable to pathogens. If faecal contaminated water is drunk – a likely event under conditions of social stress, forced migration, or a refugee camp – this will be more likely to result in parasite infestation or diarrhoea.

Pregnant women are also vulnerable if they are subjected to starvation after conceiving, as the foetus will not receive sufficient nutrients, and so will be born underweight, and with an abnormally small brain. Finally, adults are at much greater risk of succumbing to disease, and especially the elderly who may have weakened immunity. While adults may make a good physical recovery from starvation, this is not generally the case with children because of their developmental need for nutrients and nurture, both of which are restricted during a famine.

5.3.2 *Chronic*

In children, a chronic lack of nutritious food is associated with stunting, namely abnormally low height for age. The risk factors for stunting are identical to those for wasting, although many more children evidence stunting. Developmentally, longitudinal studies reveal that wasting is a risk factor for later stunting. However, most infants who later become stunted do not experience wasting during development (Wright et al., 2021). Rather, a combination of a diet inadequate in protein, calories, and micronutrients, combined with all the ills of poverty – disease, maternal and paternal deprivation, and lack of stimulation – result in impaired growth (Grantham-McGregor et al., 2007). While there is some uncertainty about the extent to which stunting results primarily from nutritional deficiency or, as is more likely, an interaction between malnutrition, poverty, and disease, the consequences of stunting for development are very clear. Adults who were stunted as a child – and assuming they live to adulthood, as stunting is a risk factor for an early death – suffer life-long adverse consequences. They have a lower IQ, lower educational attainment, reduced capacity for manual labour, earn less as adults, and are likely to have children who will also experience stunting – perpetrating intergenerational poverty (Perkins et al., 2017).

5.3.3 Remediation

There has been some study of how best to remediate the acute and chronic effects of starvation. The acute effects in both children and adults, wherever they may fall on the PEM/SAM spectrum, are quite well understood. If disease does not intervene, and the intervention is not too late, a good recovery can be made. For protein deficiency, milk or other high-protein foods are used for nutritional recovery. For energy deficiency, this too may involve milk or high-protein and carbohydrate feeds. Refeeding must be pursued carefully. First, because of downregulation of the digestive system resulting from starvation-related changes. Second, due to 'refeeding syndrome', a disorder of electrolyte balance caused by their depletion during starvation (Corsello et al., 2023). Refeeding syndrome can be fatal.

For chronic starvation, how to enact effective remediation is less clear. If stunting were just a nutritional disease, then treating this cause would ameliorate its adverse effects. However, it is complicated because, as described earlier, stunting arises from an interaction of nutritional deficits, poverty, and disease. Not surprisingly then, systematic reviews and meta-analyses of nutritional interventions in stunted children find only a *very* small benefit (Cohen's d = 0.08), even if adequate micro- and macronutrient supplementation is provided (L. M. Larson & Yousafzai, 2017). Avoiding the detrimental consequences of stunting clearly requires a broader interventional agenda, aimed at improving family health, education, and the elimination of poverty. These are far harder to fix than a nutritional deficit.

5.3.4 *The Relationship with Overabundance*

The food system in industrialised nations gradually developed from the mid 1800s. By the end of the Second World War it was so successful that most people in developed countries received an adequate level of nutrition for the first time in human history. However, the continued pressure for profit growth among food producers led to an overabundance of cheap palatable energy-dense food, causing an epidemic of obesity in developed countries that started in the 1970s (Fogel, 2004). One component of this food system is farm subsidies, which protect the income of farmers in developed nations against the vagarics of price fluctuations in agricultural staples. This has had adverse consequences for developing nations, who may be reliant on purchasing staples from developed countries at below cost prices. This then precludes developed countries from growing these staples as they cannot compete on price. This in turn pushes local agriculture towards cash crops – tobacco, oil palm, coffee, cocoa, and so on – both to raise foreign currency to pay for imported agricultural staples and to repay external debt that many developed countries first accrued in the 1970s and 1980s – money that could be far better spent on poverty alleviation. Cash crops require agricultural labourers, whose wages need to be as low as possible to maximise the export income earned from the crop. As most of the labour force in developing countries work in the agricultural sector – some 60 per cent in Africa – this means that many people have a subsistence income that can be insufficient to purchase enough food. It also places local populations at risk of price collapses from cash crops. These are just some of the ways in which the economics of food supply in developed countries impacts food availability in developing countries – keeping people in poverty, hungry, and at risk of premature death (Lang & Heasman, 2004).

5.4 Conclusion

The good news is that the number of people who are hungry has been progressively declining over the last fifty years. The bad news is that there are too many hungry adults and children, with this still being measured in the *hundreds of millions*. A simple and incorrect view of famine and starvation is that they arise from lack of food. The literature suggests a more complex set of causes. Famines require bad government. Starvation, especially as it manifests in children as stunting, results from a complex interaction of disease, poor diet, and poverty. Eliminating hunger is not as simple as providing food.

CHAPTER 6

Fasting

6.0 Introduction

Fasting refers to the voluntary restriction of food intake, varying from some degree to complete abstinence. This chapter examines various manifestations of fasting, namely its use as a tool of persuasion, to reduce body weight for health or other goals, and ways this may be assisted (drugs/surgery). It also covers fasting as entertainment, fasting for spiritual and religious purposes, and fasting for longevity.

6.1 Hunger Strikes

A hunger strike is a type of protest in which food is refused for varying lengths of time and, in the most tragic cases, until death intervenes. For most hunger strikers, water is still consumed. If it were not, death would be rapid (i.e., in the order of several days), which in the brutal calculus of political persuasion is too fast to let pressure build on those in power. Some hunger strikers also consume salts, sugar, and vitamin pills (Crosby et al., 2007). These can eke out the length of the hunger strike by, respectively, preventing electrolyte loss, slowing muscle loss, and preventing micronutrient deficiencies that can compromise health post-recovery.

6.1.1 History

Examples of hunger strikes can be found throughout recorded history, with the earliest being attributed to the mythical Spartan lawmaker Lycurgus (Vandereycken & van Deth, 1994). The Roman historian Aulus Cremutius Cordus undertook a hunger strike to death in 25 AD to protest the destruction and banning of his works, which were considered seditious. In India, until the mid nineteenth century and its outlawing by the British, Hindus had a tradition of hunger striking on a debtor's doorstep to shame them into paying. Medieval Ireland had a similar tradition, again using a hunger strike on the doorstep of someone who had wronged them, to shame that person into doing the right thing. Both India's and especially Ireland's modern history has been heavily influenced by the use of hunger strikes.

Hunger strikes have been widely used by Irish republicans as a political tool. Starting with the war of independence in the 1920s, many Irish republicans were arrested and imprisoned by the British. It is estimated that, between 1916 and 1923, over 10,000 such prisoners undertook hunger strikes. Three were tragically notable, with Terrence MacSwiney – who was the Lord Mayor of Cork – Michael Fitzgerald, and Joseph Murphy starving themselves to death (Miller, 2016). Aware that the publicity surrounding these deaths was not favourable to British rule in Ireland, threats of, or actual force feeding, were used to ensure that nobody else died. Force feeding in the manner employed in British prisons amounted to torture, because there was no consent for this assault on the body and, critically, the procedure was often used after only a few days of hunger striking, when there could be little risk of the person dying. So, rather than being a lifesaving act by the authorities, it served as a tool to threaten and coerce prisoners into eating.

Force-feeding techniques were first used on another group of English political prisoners, the suffragettes. They engaged in multiple acts of civil disobedience prior to the First World War, which landed many in jail. Once in jail, hunger strikes were common. This panicked the Home Office and led it to instigate force feeding. The unwilling prisoner was pinned down by at least five people. The next step was to open the mouth, by inserting a metal jack between the teeth to crank the jaw open after which a wooden gag with a hole in it was placed in the mouth. A prison doctor then inserted a stiff tube through this hole, down the oesophagus and into the stomach. Milk, with an egg mixed in, was then poured down the tube. The tube induced a potent gag reflex, and a sensation akin to drowning. As insertion depended on the skill of the prison doctor, errors could be made. These could be fatal if the milk and eggs were delivered to the lungs or if there was an oesophageal tear.

A second wave of Irish republican activism emerged in the 1970s in Northern Ireland. A campaign of mainland bombing led to an explosion outside the Old Bailey, and the later arrest of the instigators including two women from a prominent republican family – Dolours and Marian Price. Following their conviction in 1973, both were imprisoned in the UK, and they undertook a hunger strike with the goal of relocating to an Irish prison. They were ultimately successful in this regard, but both endured forced feeding and, for one of the sisters, it appears to have initiated an eating disorder. This was to be the last of the episodes of force feeding in the UK, as in 1975 the World Medical Association pronounced it a form of torture, a view echoed by many Western medical associations. This made it unethical for a doctor to undertake this procedure.

A third wave of Irish republican hunger strikes started in Northern Ireland in the early 1980s to reinstate the special category status originally given to prisoners convicted of political offences. This was led by Brendan Hughes, along with seven other republican prisoners in the Maze jail, Northern Ireland, who started their hunger strike together. It was called off after several weeks when it appeared the British would reinstate special category status. Brendan Hughes was to later lose his sight because of this hunger strike, and all to no avail as the British reneged on their apparent concessions. This action formed the prelude to the most politically successful hunger strike of the whole period. Bobby Sands and several other republican prisoners, again in the Maze jail, started a staggered hunger strike, to maximise publicity. Around thirty days into the Bobby Sands hunger strike, the opportunity arose for him to stand for the parliamentary seat of Fermanagh and South Tyrone, for which he was duly elected, becoming a British parliamentarian.

After sixty-six days of hunger striking the 27-year-old MP Bobby Sands died. His funeral attracted over 100,000 people and there was international condemnation, especially from the United States, over his death. This focussed on the refusal of the Thatcher government to enter negotiations to end the hunger strike. Mrs Thatcher made her views very clear: 'Crime is crime is crime: It is not political!' But, of course, it was and is political and her unbending stance was gradually eroded by the subsequent deaths of nine other men – Hughes, McCreesh, O'Hara, Doherty, McDonnell, Hurson, Lynch, Mcllwee, and Deane – before, finally, partial concessions were offered in public, but full in private, and the hunger strike ended. As the *Starry Plough* newspaper reported, the British government's approach to the hunger strikers was the 'best recruiting sergeant' the republican movement could have ever had. It led to a wave of violence, and the eventual desire on the part of the British for a lasting settlement in Northern Ireland, and one that had to involve the Irish republican movement. It is for these reasons that Bobby Sands is memorialised in republican circles (see Figure 6.1).

Miller (2016) examined British prison records from 1913 to 1940, for all recorded instances of hunger strikes. Over this period there were over a thousand hunger strikes, many involving ordinary convicts protesting conditions or their innocence, alongside a notable number of First

Figure 6.1 Bobby Sands mural in Belfast.
Source: FlickR (The Meat Case)

World War conscientious objectors, who refused any form of participation in the war. Many of these individuals were force fed. British Indian and South African authorities also faced repeated hunger strikes from Mahatma Gandhi. He termed these 'fasts', to focus on their non-violent nature. They formed an important part of his protests against racism in South Africa and British rule in India. In total, he undertook eighteen fasts, the longest of which were three weeks – a considerable feat considering how lean he was and that the last of these was undertaken in his seventies. In more recent times, and especially during the apartheid era, South Africa has been the site of multiple hunger strikes. Political prisoners on Robben Island undertook repeated strikes to end indefinite detention without trial, prison conditions, the food, and their treatment as convicts. In 1966, over a thousand were on hunger strike (Machin, 2016). Ironically, they were then joined by some of the white prison guards who were also protesting, but about their food (Shah, 2022).

Hunger strikes continue due to their success as a political weapon. Turkey, which has had a history of political repression, was the site of rolling hunger strikes in the early 2000s, with over a hundred deaths. The US off-shore prison located at Guantánamo Bay has seen several bouts of hunger striking, often with little public awareness. In 2005, some

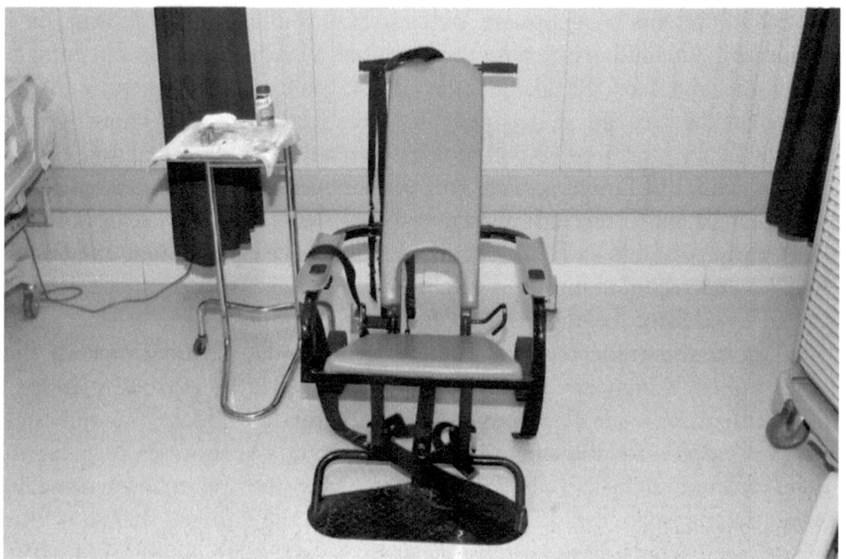

Figure 6.2 Restraint chair used for enteral feeding.
Source: Dvids. https://www.dvidshub.net/image/920530/joint-medical-group The appearance of U.S. Department of Defense (DoW) visual information does not imply or constitute DoW endorsement.

200 prisoners undertook a hunger strike, with the US military force feeding those who persisted. Further rounds of hunger strikes took place in 2008, resulting in eighty prisoners weighing less than 45 kg. Another wave in 2013 involved 166 hunger strikers, with 45 being force fed – including by rectal infusion for those who refused fluids. Unlike many Western countries, the US continues to use force feeding. The procedure is to strap prisoners into a restraint chair (see Figure 6.2), insert the tube, and feed. Beyond these examples, there are many other individuals and groups who have engaged in hunger strikes (see Fessler, 2002), from well-known political activists (e.g., César Chávez), to refugees (e.g., Australian asylum seekers), US detainees (e.g., Japanese Americans held in the Second World War; Shah, 2022) and many others who wished to press their cause. Prison food has been a persistent complaint and, in the 1970s, some British prisons were spending more per capita on feeding each guard dog than each inmate!

6.1.2 Potency

There are several features that combine to make a hunger strike a potent form of political protest. For the authority being challenged by the hunger striker, it presents a nightmare public-relations dilemma – at least in a democracy. The authorities have three options available. First, let the hunger striker die and face the likely unfavourable political consequences (think Bobby Sands). Second, if it is possible, force feed them, but knowing that this is a form of torture that will have its own adverse political fallout. Third, bargain with the hunger striker and appear weak and willing to yield to blackmail (or bargain secretly and lie to the public). None of these options are particularly palatable and, in Britain, which has perhaps the best and seemingly longest recorded history of dealing with hunger strikers, the choice has tended to be force feeding or secret bargaining – to avoid loss of face.

In more autocratic regimes, hunger strikers may be unknown to the wider public, which can rob the protest of some of its persuasive power. This is because it ideally needs an audience for full effect. The audience can well appreciate the dilemma that democratic authorities find themselves in, and many people are likely to enjoy the spectacle of those in power facing such 'heat'. More importantly, the hunger striker is one person against an often monolithic entity – the state. Public sympathy will typically favour the person over the state, especially if the human aspects of the struggle are carefully choreographed in the media (i.e., crippling nature of starvation, heart rendering effects on family, etc.).

In addition, many people know well the feeling of powerlessness when faced with state authority and so a person battling this force will attract further sympathy. Indeed, Waismel-Manor (2005) has argued that certain political structures are more favourable to hunger strikers' demands than others (noting their greater use in Israel relative to the US), especially where there are not effective conduits for resolving complaints. Finally, the spectacle of watching (or hearing about) someone slowly dying from starvation, by their own hand, with the authorities seemingly powerless to do anything about it, compels attention in the same way that many drivers slow to see a road accident (e.g., Andersson & Sundin, 2021).

6.1.3 Impacts

The physical and physiological impacts of the hunger strike are akin to the effects discussed in Chapter 5 for famine victims. The difference is the totality of the fast, in that while famine victims are usually still eating *something* for as long as they can, hunger strikers avoid all food. Some hunger strikers report that after several days they no longer have any general hunger (Peel, 1997). This is illustrated by a quote from Frank Gallagher, an Irish republican hunger striker:

> I noticed in yesterday's papers that some French journalists spoke of our 'pangs of hunger'. Nobody would ever believe that there are none. There is revulsion at death, a wild longing to live, but no physical call for food. That ceased on the second day. Now tastes and smells are pleasant to think of but mean nothing. If the mind took the fast as quietly as the body does, the whole thing would seem like a joke, there would be so little suffering in it. If our friends would believe this! But it is true, and they never will. (Miller, 2016, p. 104)

Yet other hunger strikers have reported being preoccupied with thoughts of food (Miller, 2016, p. 104) and Bobby Sands, in his diary, remarked on his daily struggle against the temptation to eat (Shah, 2022). This divergent pattern of reaction to starvation has been commented on before (Stevenson & Francis, 2023, p. 298) but why it occurs remains unclear. It may relate to the types of hunger and the habitual diet that a person has prior to starting the hunger strike. The contention here is that different types of hunger may extinguish at different rates – and perhaps less so if the fast is intermittently broken – which would produce divergent patterns of hunger in different people.

Crosby et al. (2007) and Peel (1997) both outline a timeline of reactions to hunger striking, which is illustrated in Table 6.1. Both these papers also note that the critical turning point in the hunger striker's health occurs at around forty days or when the person has lost around 20 per cent of their initial body weight (for a healthy adult). This represents the point at which

Table 6.1 *Symptom evolution across the course of a hunger strike*

Time	Event (ordered by approximate time of emergence)
Start	Euphoria
	Weakness and dizziness
	Feeling cold
	Abdominal pain
	Absence of hunger or thirst (in some cases)
	Emotional lability
	Lethargy, apathy, irritability
	Vomiting on drinking
40 days	Physical weakness
	Confusion
	Somnolence
	Impaired hearing and sight
	Organ failure, heart problems
60–70 days	Death

serious medical problems start to emerge, such as vitamin deficiencies (e.g., Wernicke's encephalopathy; scurvy), sensory impairments, and depression, for example. At around 30 per cent loss of initial body weight (for a healthy adult) death becomes imminent and may result from heart failure, immune dysfunction, small bowel obstruction, and multiple organ failure (Crosby et al., 2007).

Attending doctors are caught between their professional responsibility to preserve life versus the right of the person to bodily autonomy, which includes choosing not to eat. However, this is all premised on the person being mentally competent to make the decision to fast. While this may be obvious at the start of the hunger strike (discounting peer pressure, which may be substantial), as time passes and the adverse health consequences of the fast emerge, it becomes less clear. As Fessler (2002) describes, the mind is affected in several ways by starvation. Depression and low mood are common, as is irritability and heightened impulsivity (see Chapter 4). Psychosis and hallucinations are less frequent occurrences, as with suicidal thoughts. All or any of these are not conducive to mental competence and may impair decision-making. They may also impact advance care directives, notably what is to happen when the person becomes unresponsive – can refeeding then occur? Or not? If refeeding is an option, then all the same issues apply to self-starvation as they do famine survivors, with risks concerning refeeding syndrome and the capacity of the gut to absorb food (Crosby et al., 2007; Peel, 1997).

6.2 Dieting

Dieting refers to the practice of intentionally following a specified feeding programme to either lose, maintain, or gain weight. While gaining weight was a concern in the past (see Figure 6.3), losing weight is now synonymous with contemporary usage of the word 'diet' – and is the focus here.

6.2.1 Types of Diet

Diets to lose weight can be classified into four kinds: adjusting the amount of food eaten, altering the type of food eaten either in terms of nutrients or whole diets, and changing meal timing (J. Y. Kim, 2021). As Hall and Kahan (2018) so aptly observe, 'a calorie is a calorie is a calorie', and all any successful diet does is to reduce energy intake, leading to negative energy balance and weight loss. While it really is that simple, you would not be left with that impression from reading contemporary diet books. And

ROUTINE FOR PUTTING ON WEIGHT

Plenty of rest and exercise, a good diet of fattening foods and no worries—those are the essentials

PUTTING on weight is very much more difficult than taking it off. Even those few extra pounds which can make all the difference to the appearance, comfort and, no doubt, general health, can be quite a problem.

Before embarking on a diet, it is always advisable to seek the advice of your own doctor. This is particularly important if there has been a sudden or prolonged loss of weight for no good reason and without affecting normal appetite. Where loss of weight is the result of an illness or operation, it is usually quite quickly and easily regained after recovery. The routine to be described in this chapter will help in such cases, subject to the approval of your own doctor.

We are concerned here chiefly with that large army of men and women who are anxious to put on weight but who are the thin type by nature. Such people are born worriers, with excitable and energetic natures and over-active bowels, whose food does not remain in the intestines long enough to be properly absorbed.

Essential in the fattening process are:

Italian actress Pier Angeli gets through a huge plate of ice cream—an excellent fattening food

(1) **Keep calm and stop worrying.** That is obviously a counsel of perfection to those who easily get worked up, but it *can* be achieved by cultivating outside interests that take your mind away from the source of anxiety (it may be professional, domestic, financial, or all three).

(2) **Take plenty of rest.** A minimum of between 8 and 9 hours in bed at night, plus between 10 and 30 minutes after every meal.

(3) **Avoid rushing about but take regular**

(4) **Eat well and regularly, and concentrate on the fattening foods** (list follows). But be careful not to stuff between meals or you will defeat the whole object and be unable to eat your main meals, which are far more important. You must also avoid *over*-eating, with the inevitable danger of indigestion and biliousness. Aim at three good meals a day, plus any extras (such as sweets, etc.) which you really fancy and a hot, preferably milk, drink last thing at night. The housewife should take as

Figure 6.3 A section from the *Women's Own Cook Book* (1964) for putting on weight.
Source: Photograph by the author of the page from the *Woman's Own Cook Book*, hardcover, 1964 published by George Newnes, currently an imprint of Elsevier, with their permission

although there may well be a diet plan that makes weight loss easier, and perhaps faster too, escaping the first law of thermodynamics is not a lifestyle choice.

For adjusting the amount of food eaten (i.e., hypoenergetic diets), the aim is to keep the ratio of macronutrients (fats, carbohydrates, and protein) within their typical ranges, but to decrease quantity, so that energy intake is reduced anywhere between 25 per cent and 60 per cent below the typical adult requirement (Abete et al., 2006). Rather than adjusting quantity, a more popular approach has been to: (1) selectively reduce dietary fat (so <25 per cent of energy comes from this source); (2) selectively reduce dietary carbohydrate (so <30 per cent of energy from this source); (3) selectively increase dietary protein. All of these have advantages and disadvantages. Low-fat diets can be low energy but still have a high volume of food, as fat has almost twice the energy gram for gram as carbohydrates and proteins. Low-carbohydrate and high-protein diets allow one to consume lots of fatty foods that are often highly palatable, but you do not get much bread, pasta, or rice, or sweet desserts. As noted earlier, weight loss is simply contingent on reducing energy intake.

Another strategy is to adopt a whole-diet approach, focussing on the types of food being eaten rather than on the macronutrients (Tahreem et al., 2022). Several whole diets have been explored (see Table 6.2) – and there are many others (e.g., the Daniel fast, Okinawa, ketogenic, DASH, low GI, etc.). All the diets listed in Table 6.2 are associated with weight loss, but typically less than those considered earlier, and many of them are also linked to improved metabolic function (see Kim, 2021; an effect resulting to some degree from weight loss and some from reduced salt, saturated fat, and added sugar). Notice how these whole diets vary in the

Table 6.2 *Whole-diet approaches for weight loss and improving cardio-metabolic profile*

Whole diet	Characteristic foods or characteristic exclusions
Mediterranean	Whole grains, legumes, fruit, vegetables, olive oil, fish, nuts
Palaeolithic	Lean meat, eggs, fruit, vegetables (not starchy), nuts
Nordic	Whole grains, lean meat, fish, vegetables, berries, dense bread
Vegetarian	No meat, meat products, seafood, or poultry
Vegan	No animal-derived products (i.e., eggs, dairy, honey)
Vegan whole food	As for vegan, plus no processed food or refined oils
Raw vegan	As for vegan, plus no processed food, no refined oils, no legumes, no cooking

level of restriction they require, with the Mediterranean diet being the most flexible to a raw vegan one being the most prescriptive. They also vary in the cost burden they impose, with healthier foods typically more expensive to buy. A final strategy is to alter meal timing. Three main approaches exist: alternate day fasting (cutting energy intake to <25 per cent of normal on a fast day), periodic fasting (e.g., five days *ad libitum* intake and two days fasting), and time-restricted feeding (e.g., eating only between 8am and 5pm). All these methods result in some weight loss and, relatedly, improvement in metabolic function (Kim, 2021; Tahreem et al., 2022).

6.2.2 Biopsychological Impacts

During dieting some consistent psychological effects have emerged (Stevenson & Francis, 2023). Food cues becomes more salient, with an attentional bias for food-related words and images. There is improved memory for food-related stimuli, and memories of food are more affectively positive than after hunger is sated (e.g., Stevenson, Francis, et al., 2023). People are more willing to work for food, and the brain shows greater activation (i.e., cerebral blood flow) to food-related pictures (e.g., Piech et al., 2010). Beyond these effects, more general impacts on cognition do not seem to occur, except to the extent that food-specific effects can be distracting ('food noise'). In this case there is evidence that executive functions (e.g., working memory) can become disrupted by intrusive thoughts about food (e.g., Kemps & Tiggemann, 2005; and see Section 4.1). Whether dieting also generates immoral-related behaviour, as Chapter 4 would suggest, has not been well explored.

In the earlier discussion of hunger strikers, it was noted that some did not report feeling hungry while others did. The same range of claims has been made for dieting. In clinical trials, with typically obese participants undergoing 15–20 per cent energy-reduction diets, reports have been obtained of either significant and protracted increases in hunger, some increases, or no changes in hunger at all. Indeed, no consistent picture emerges for hunger (Stubbs & Turicchi, 2021). Perhaps the most striking example of 'no hunger' comes from a series of weight loss studies in people with obesity, who were put on total fasts in a hospital setting, as discussed in Section 4.4.1. In some cases these lasted several weeks, and purportedly participants did not claim to be hungry when asked (e.g., Silverstone et al., 1966). It could, of course, be a peculiarity of a total fast, as some have argued (e.g., Franklin et al., 1948). Alternatively, it might reflect the demand characteristics of the situation (i.e., being asked by your physician), because increased desire to eat, and especially for foods typically avoided during a diet, can be one reason that diets fail (Contreras et al., 2019). Beyond hunger, investigators have also examined if dieting affects mood and fatigue, but no consistent findings have emerged. Finally, when people who are obese lose weight, this is linked to significant improvements in cognition, notably in attention, executive function, and memory (e.g., Veronese et al., 2017).

6.2.3 Does Dieting 'Work'?

With high rates of excess body weight in Western countries, alongside heightened concerns in women and men about their appearance, many people (66 per cent of US adults; Gudzune et al., 2015) report dieting to lose weight. Since the 1970s there have been three major concerns about the biopsychological consequences of dieting: (1) it *causes* excess weight gain; (2) it *causes* disordered eating; and (3) it does not work (i.e., there is no lasting weight loss). While there is still much to learn, it is now possible to provide tentative answers to each question.

The claim that dieting may cause weight gain is based on the premise that once weight has been lost and the diet stops, changes to brain and metabolic systems lead to an 'overshooting' of the pre-dieting body weight. The literature suggests that this may be the case for people of normal body weight who diet (Jacquet et al., 2020). Observational data indicate that normal weight dieters typically have higher BMIs than non-dieters, but of course this does not indicate that dieting caused this (Pélissier et al., 2023). A better test comes from interventional studies. While some of these are equivocal, others do suggest that normal weight people who diet will in the longer term gain more weight than those who do not (Pélissier et al., 2023). The suggestion has been made that lean people may be more susceptible to weight 'overshooting' than people who are overweight or obese.

A second claim is that dieting can result in disordered eating, and especially binge eating. This now seems unlikely. One source of evidence against this idea came from the CALERIE 2 trial, where lean to overweight participants were either asked to maintain their usual diet or to engage in 25 per cent reduction in energy intake for two years (Stewart et al., 2022). Participants were very carefully screened for psychiatric disorders before being recruited into the trial and were randomised to group, so any emergent disordered eating, in the treatment arm, would likely be caused by dieting. The study found no evidence for any difference in the incidence of disordered eating between groups at the end of the study,

Table 6.3 *Weight regain following dietary intervention (data from Anderson et al., 2001)*

Time point	Months (years)	Mean body weight in kg	
		Low energy diet	Very low energy diet
Baseline	0 (0)	93.0	106.0
End of intervention	3 (0.25)	84.2	–
	6 (0.5)	–	81.9
Follow-up	54 (4.5)	91.0	99.0

suggesting that dieting *alone* is unlikely to cause an eating disorder (Stewart et al., 2022).

The third claim concerns the effectiveness of dieting in people who are obese. Data from a key meta-analysis are summarised in Table 6.3, where it can be seen that most participants in the various diet clinical trials regained (on average) much – *but not all* – their lost body weight over the 4.5 year follow-up period (Anderson et al., 2001). This seems to be the rule with dieting, namely that weight loss plateaus (often at 5–15 per cent of initial body weight) and then there is progressive weight regain over the following four to five years post-intervention. More recent data do not contradict this picture (e.g. LeBlanc et al., 2018; Perreault et al., 2023). While the rate of weight regain can be slowed, by for example combining dieting with exercise and increasing the length of the initial intervention (Machado et al., 2022), weight regain is still the norm. There are two important points here. First, this average weight loss, which may only be a few kilos after five years, is still beneficial to health (and animal data suggest this is the case even if weight 'yo-yo's' up and down; Di Germanio et al., 2018). Second, while some people may have regained all their lost weight, a subset, typically around 20 per cent, manage to maintain their new weight. This subset has been studied in some depth (e.g., Wing & Phelan, 2005), and they manage this by continuing with their diet, exercising, eating breakfast daily, and continuously monitoring their weight.

The biology of weight regain following dieting has also been studied and involves three main processes. The first, which seems to make the smallest contribution to weight regain, is the reduction in basal metabolic rate that accompanies weight loss. Thus, even if less food is eaten after a successful diet, the downward reduction in basal metabolic rate may mean that this lower food intake is still sufficient to create a positive energy balance and weight gain (e.g., Contreras et al., 2019; Koliaki et al., 2018). A second factor, which is deemed to be more influential, is increased hunger (Hall & Kahan, 2018). This may make it difficult to maintain a neutral or negative energy balance. The causes of this increased hunger are not fully understood but have been attributed to the upregulation of orexigenic hormones and the downregulation of anorexigenic ones – but the evidence for this is equivocal (Contreras et al., 2019). The final factor is motivational, and whether the person has the capacity to maintain a long-term programme of continued dieting and exercise.

6.3 Fasting as Entertainment

With the advent of print media in the sixteenth century, people would visit and leave gifts of food and money at the homes of 'miraculous maidens', typically adolescent girls who claimed to have not eaten for months or even years. As the public became less credulous, doubting that such feats of starvation could be survived through the 'providence of God', they came instead to fairs and circuses to see giants, dwarfs, and other 'freaks' of nature. Among these natural wonders, which *The Lancet* sniffily termed 'exhibits to the vulgar gaze at two pence a head' (Vandereycken & van Deth, 1994), were the thin men. Among these the most famous, exhibited across the US and Europe – and to royalty too – was Claude Ambroise Seurat (see Figure 6.4). He was a French national whose BMI was (reportedly) as low as 11.3 at the height of his fame. He could be seen in his booth for 7–8 cents a view, where he sat naked except for a loincloth for thirteen hours a day. He was reportedly so thin that people could see his heart beating, and that in the dark a lighted candle could be seen through his stomach. Whatever the cause of his extreme thinness (purportedly a tapeworm. . .), his food intake was limited to around 200 g per day. There were many other such thin men, with the last being Glen Pulley, who performed at Ringling Brothers Circus in the US right into the 1950s.

The public were also avid fans of hunger sports – namely watching people who claimed to be undergoing a prolonged fast. The initiator of this new entertainment was Dr Henry Tanner, a US doctor of homeopathic medicine and a big fan of therapeutic baths and fasting. In 1880 he decided to perform a public fast in New York, under medical supervision, which by the time it ended, at forty days, was watched by over 6,000 people per day. There were many subsequent imitators, all of whom had to endure (and rightly so in many cases) accusations of cheating, and

Figure 6.4 Claude Ambroise Seurat, the very thin man.
Source: Wellcome collection, public domain

questions about their state of mind (Vandereycken & van Deth, 1994). Similar public spectacles have continued right into the present (and perhaps the TV show *The Biggest Loser* should also be counted among these). David Blaine's 2003, forty-four-day *Above the Below* fast was undertaken in a transparent box suspended above the Thames in London. His BMI dropped from 29.0 to 21.6 by the end of this show, which attracted crowds of viewers, and much media attention, with special interest in whether he was secretly being fed in the box. In the history of fasting for entertainment there have been several deaths, and the danger was made clear when David Blaine developed a potentially life-threatening refeeding syndrome after his fast ended. This should not be tried at home!

6.4 The Dieting Assistants

When people fast to lose weight, they may be assisted by drugs and surgical interventions. Historically, drug-assisted weight loss started with amphetamines, which purportedly lead to weight loss via a reduction in hunger (Bett, 1946). What a reduction of hunger means is difficult to ascertain, as simply reporting/rating 'I do not feel hungry' offers little insight into the psychological mechanisms at play (e.g., memory inhibition, blanket positive affect caused by the drug that cannot be displaced by positive affect linked to food, etc., etc.). This issue is poorly explored for all drugs in humans, as clinical trials focus on weight loss not psychological mechanisms. Returning to amphetamines, they had a range of unfortunate side effects – notably addiction and a propensity for abuse – making them unsuitable as a weight loss treatment. Since then, many amphetamine derivatives have seen regulatory approval, only to be later disallowed due to their side-effect profile or addiction potential. Phentermine is the only survivor – and only in the US – as it is not available in the EU, where it is deemed unsafe.

The major approved weight-loss medicines are listed in Table 6.4. All these agents can induce greater than 5 per cent weight loss in clinical trials, relative to placebo (Aaseth et al., 2021). However, with continued use weight loss seems to plateau and, in all cases, weight regain occurs on cessation of the medicine. These drugs also improve the metabolic profile of patients, with this being most marked for the GLP-1 agonists, which were originally developed as treatments for type II diabetes. While the pharmacological mechanisms of action and their metabolic consequences vary across the different drug types, their psychological effect on food intake is usually attributed to either a reduction in hunger and/or an increase in satiety/satiation (D. M. Williams et al., 2020) – but, as noted earlier, this does not offer much mechanistic insight.

Every decade has its new weight-loss wonder drug. Currently, this distinction goes to the GLP-1 agonists. In the small intestine, and

Table 6.4 *Major weight-loss drugs*

Drug	Weight loss*	Mode of action and comments
GLP-1 agonists		
liraglutide	5%	Reduced appetite, enhanced satiety, nausea inducing, with significant metabolic benefits
semaglutide	10%	As for liraglutide
tirzepatide	10%+	As for liraglutide
Orlistat	3%	Pancreatic lipase inhibitor, thereby preventing fat being digested
Bupropion/naltrexone	5%	Centrally acting appetite suppressant and opioid antagonist that reduces food craving
Phentermine/ topiramate	7%	Centrally acting appetite suppressant and anti-epilepsy drug with unknown mode of action

Note: *Advantage over placebo.

especially at its distal end, are enteroendocrine cells that have receptors sensitive to glucose and fat. When stimulated these release GLP-1, which in turn triggers the production of insulin in the pancreas. The production of GLP-1 and other incretins also serves to slow the movement of food out of the stomach, thereby lengthening the period of satiety/satiation (Lenharo, 2023). These agents may also cause nausea, and it may not be possible to feel hungry at the same time as feeling nauseous; they seem mutually incompatible states. Indeed, in animals, at the lowest dose sufficient to produce weight loss, GLP-1 agonists also generate conditioned taste aversions (Airosus et al., 2025). However, nausea does not seem to be a major contributor to their capacity to induce weight loss in humans (Bettadapura et al., 2025), rather it is their effects on hunger, food cravings, thoughts about food (food noise), and increased satiety that seem important (e.g., Blundell et al., 2017). The latest GLP-1 agonist to receive approval for weight loss, tirzepatide, also acts as an agonist for another incretin, and may be even more effective than liraglutide and semaglutide. While these drugs are undoubtedly efficacious, they are expensive, they probably have to be taken for life to maintain weight loss (Wilding et al., 2022), and they have become so popular that a thriving counterfeit market has emerged.

A further adjunct to weight loss is bariatric surgery, which can be loosely divided into three types of procedure – reversible, reducing, and restricting. Reversible procedures include the insertion of temporary objects into the stomach to limit the amount that can be eaten or using some form of barrier to prevent food accessing part of the small intestine. Reducing procedures involve creating a small stomach pouch, again to limit intake. Restricting procedures, which are the most effective at generating significant lasting weight loss, usually involve bypassing part of the small intestine. Interestingly, it is this class of procedures which also produce the most dramatic improvements in type II diabetes. The mechanism for this may overlap with that of the GLP-1 agonists (Aaseth et al., 2021), as nutrients may reach the enteroendocrine receptors faster and in more concentrated form, thereby boosting GLP-1 release, improving diabetic symptoms, and further assisting weight loss.

6.5 Spiritual Fasting

Fasting for spiritual reasons occurs in all organised religions. Outside of the mainstream, the traditions with the most interesting reputation for fasting are the Eastern mystics and fakirs. Many have claimed to survive extended fasts (up to a year in some cases) without food and water. A well-publicised example in nineteenth-century India was Sadhu Haridas, who was buried alive for forty days under continuous guard, and who was interred in the presence of the Maharaja of Lahore and 'medical experts' (Garbe, 1900). When he was disinterred, Sadhu Haridas was at first thought to be dead, but he slowly revived. Cases such as this exist right into modern times. Several medical scientists studied Prahlad Jani, who claimed to have not eaten for several years. As part of this an MRI was performed when he was 82 years old (with a BMI of 14) to test the claim that certain of his organs were unusually youthful (Raghuprasad & Manivannan, 2019) – a claim that was purportedly supported. Not surprisingly, claims of not eating or drinking for several years have been met with considerable scepticism.

Some modern fakirs have been caught eating burger and fries (e.g., Shira Raten Manek), and the new age commodification of extreme fasting into 'breatharianism', the belief that one can exist primarily from utilising sunlight (perhaps the ultimate diet?), has spawned a whole field of proponents. Advocates such as Wiley Brooks and Ellen Greve (aka 'Jasmuheen') stand accused of involvement in several adherents' deaths. In the case of Greve she has been awarded both an Ignoble prize for literature for her book *Living on Light* and a Bent spoon award from the Australian Skeptics. The latter is presented for the 'perpetrator of the most preposterous piece of paranormal or pseudoscientific piffle'.

Figure 6.5 Catherine of Siena.
Source: Image from the Rijksmuseum, Netherlands

Fasting has a long history within organised religion. In the Catholic tradition, Vandereycken and van Deth (1994) outline several female religious from the Middle Ages whose fasting was an integral part of their mystical appeal. Of these, Catherine of Siena (Figure 6.5) is the most famed. She first used fasting as a teenager to avoid marriage to her dead sister's ex-husband, with fasting bouts repeated with increasing severity throughout her short life – she died aged 33 in 1380. Similar accounts can be found for other religious, such as Columba of Rieti (died aged 34) and Marie of Oignie (died aged 35). A spirited debate has taken place as to whether these women suffered from anorexia nervosa or whether their behaviour was peculiar to that time and place. The similarities to anorexia nervosa are so striking, most notably the rigid self-discipline needed for extreme fasting, as is the concern expressed by contemporary Church authorities for these women's health, that it seems hard to avoid the conclusion that they are one and the same – the difference, and it is a subtle one, is the motivation; namely seeking a perfect body (now) or a perfect soul (then).

All major religions include some form of fasting practice, as detailed in Table 6.5. This can range from avoidance of specific foods (e.g., meat, alcohol, and dairy during Lent), to avoidance of food at certain times (e.g.,

Table 6.5 *Religious fasts*

Religion	Fast
Islam	Ramadan, Ashura, Shawwal, Arafah
Judaism	Yom Kippur, Tisha B'Av, 10th of Tevit, 17th of Tammuz, Fast of Esther, Fast of Gedalia
Christianity	Lent, Christmas, Easter, weekly fasts (Wednesday and/or Friday)
Buddhism	Not eating after midday meal, preparation for religious events
Hinduism	Multiple examples, but usually local-specific
Bahai	Nineteen-day fast

sunrise to sunset in Ramadan) or a total fast (e.g., Yom Kippur or Tisha B'Av). There seem to be at least four major spiritual/religious rationales for fasting. The first is self-discipline that comes from not eating when hungry, which presumably trains the adherent to similarly avoid other earthly temptations. The second is penance for sin, typically one's own, so as to atone for these wrongdoings (i.e., self-punishment), thereby cleansing the soul and allowing a return to a purer godlier state. This can also be a rationale if fasting is used in preparation for a special religious occasion. The third is to bring a focus on other people's needs, by highlighting how one's own bodily needs draw attention away from others, and back to the self. The fourth concerns a shared practice between adherents of a particular faith, allowing them to build community and common purpose. While these purported benefits of fasting have not been well explored, there has been some research on whether religious fasting affects cognition. There is little evidence for any consistent effect (Stevenson & Francis, 2023).

6.6 Fasting to Arrest Ageing

In round worms, fruit flies, rats, mice, and hamsters, permanent caloric restriction results in significant increases in longevity. It has been presumed that the evolutionary function of this response to caloric restriction is to allow the animal time for environmental conditions to improve, so benefitting later capacity for reproduction. While this seems reasonable, not all animals demonstrate a longevity benefit from caloric restriction, and so it has been hypothesised that only those that either cannot migrate or cannot sustain extended food deprivation (i.e., those without large fat stores) react in this way (Shanley & Kirkwood, 2006).

Not surprisingly, there has been a lot of interest in whether human lifespan could be similarly extended by a calorie-restricted diet. An obvious question is whether permanently restricting food intake by around 15–20 per cent (as needed in animals) would be sustainable in the longer term. That is, would people feel so hungry that their life would just be depressing and miserable? This is a hard question to answer. Two large studies have explored the biopsychological impacts of 15–20 per cent calorie restriction – the CALERIE 1 and CALERIE 2 trials (Stewart et al., 2022). The CALERIE 1 study only used overweight participants, assigning them to either a 25 per cent calorie-restricted diet or to an *ad libitum* control group for six months. The larger CALERIE 2 trial used the same design, but for twenty-four months, and recruited people who varied from normal weight to overweight. For the CALERIE 1 trial there was little evidence that hunger was bothersome. For the CALERIE 2 trial, the only evidence relating to tolerability (and presumably hunger) came from compliance data, with only around 20 per cent of participants managing this level of energy restriction in the treatment arm. This would suggest that perhaps normal weight participants would struggle to maintain a persistent caloric reduction of this magnitude.

Assuming that this type of regimen could be tolerated, the next question is would it work to extend human life? Theoretically this looks improbable, as humans would, according to Shanley and Kirkwood's (2006) reasoning, be likely to either relocate to another place to find food or survive by drawing upon their significant fat stores. Empirically, one needs long-term data to see if calorie reduction increases human lifespan. However, primate data also suggest the answer would probably be unfavourable. Two studies have examined whether macaques randomised to either a 30 per cent calorie restriction in adulthood versus an *ad libitum* control group, would show an extended lifespan and a later emergence of the diseases of old age. The Wisconsin study (Colman et al., 2009) found exactly that, but the National Institutes of Health (NIH) study did not (Mattison et al., 2012). There may be an important reason why an *apparent* lifespan extension effect was observed in the Wisconsin study but not in the NIH study. The control group in the Wisconsin study had a diet with 30 per cent added sucrose, compared to 4 per cent in the NIH trial. Thus, it may be differences in the control group that account for the different outcome. Indeed, it has been argued more generally that laboratory animals are often overweight compared to their wild relatives, and so placing them on a calorie-restricted diet may just return them to their *potential* natural lifespans. This is, of course, not all there is to the life-extension effect, but the macaques data would suggest that persistent calorie restriction in humans would not be successful.

6.7 Conclusion

This chapter described the ways that fasting has been used as a weapon, to improve physical and spiritual health, and physical attractiveness, as a form of entertainment, and perhaps to delay ageing. In respect of hunger, the most interesting observation is that people differ in how strongly they feel this state when they are fasting. So far, there do not seem any obvious correlates of this individual difference nor any explanation. To examine it, one would need to explore how hunger changes over the course of fasting, its relationship to BMI and other physiological factors, the normal forms of hunger that a person experiences, their habitual diet, and exposure to environmental food cues. It would also be important to establish that demand characteristics did not influence a person's willingness to report (or not) hunger. If people really do vary in their experience of intense hunger, understanding the mechanism would be important to turn this into something medically useful.

CHAPTER 7

Imposed Hunger

7.0 Introduction

This chapter focusses on imposed hunger in animals and humans. The animal literature is divided between laboratory studies, examining the effects of pre- and postnatal starvation, and environmental studies, where seasonal changes in food availability result in striking physiological adaptations – hibernation, torpor, and estivation. The human literature is also divided into two different segments. The first focusses on the relatively limited but highly interesting studies of semi-starvation, covering those of Benedict, Milejkowski, and Keys. The second looks at the use of hunger as a weapon, and especially in the Second World War where this reached its apogee with Operation Hunger, concentration camps, the siege of Leningrad, and the Dutch Hunger Winter. Finally, the delayed and transgenerational effects of hunger on people are examined, both psychological and epigenetic.

7.1 Animals

7.1.1 Impacts of Laboratory-Imposed Starvation

Animals allow controlled study of the effects of starvation on brain and behaviour, something that is not possible in humans. However, animal studies have their limitations. First, for the rat, which is the most widely used lab model of humans, its development is markedly different from people. Rats have greater amounts of brain growth after they are born than do humans, which may mean different impacts of prenatal starvation across species (Rice & Barone Jr, 2000). Second, human infant malnutrition usually co-occurs with an impoverished environment. A poor environment may be as bad for brain/behavioural development as malnutrition – and their interaction may be worse. There has been the assumption that this is not such an issue in animal models, and that the impacts of malnutrition can be observed largely independent of adverse environmental effects. However, this view is probably incorrect, as malnutrition leads to a range of environmental consequences that on their own can be as disruptive as the biochemical effects of malnutrition (Laus et al., 2011).

The general impacts on young animals of diets that do not provide enough energy, protein, fats, and micronutrients are well understood. Animals such as rats, mice, guinea pigs, and pigs have smaller brains than appropriately fed litter mates, and while some of this can be reversed by refeeding, many of the structural abnormalities and their behavioural consequences are retained for life (Levitsky & Strupp, 1995). Two models to explain these effects on the brain have been proposed. The first presumes the brain is most vulnerable during periods of maximal growth. The second presumes the brain is most vulnerable during the early period when its basic architecture is being established – the process of neurulation. Not surprisingly, both are important (Levitsky & Strupp, 1995) and malnutrition during either is costly.

Prenatal malnutrition (i.e., concerning what the pregnant dam is fed) affect both foetal neurulation and brain growth (Barra et al., 2019). This causes the most damage when the dam's diet is highly restricted in terms of protein (<6 per cent). This results in a range of deficits. Apart from the offspring being of abnormally low weight at birth, the pups have fewer neurons and glial cells overall, with abnormalities to the cortex, forebrain, and hippocampus – and poorer learning and memory. A less restrictive low-protein diet (i.e., around 8 per cent) results in normal birth weight, but there are still abnormalities in brain structure, such as a smaller corpus callosum, and again poorer learning and memory. Low-energy diets, with or without adequate protein, impair stress responsiveness, the hippocampus, and learning and memory (Moody et al., 2017). Diets that are adequate in calories and protein but lack key micronutrients (i.e., B vitamins) also impair hippocampal structure and function. The longer-term consequences of prenatal malnutrition into adulthood include a propensity for gaining excess fat and metabolic syndrome. It has been suggested that these changes are a consequence of epigenetic alteration to gene expression caused by prenatal malnutrition (Barra et al., 2019).

Postnatal malnutrition, with diets deficient in protein and energy, also produces multiple impacts on the brain (e.g., at the cellular level reducing dendritic branching and number of synapses) but especially to the hippocampus (Laus et al., 2011; Levitsky & Strupp, 1995). In humans, the negative impacts of malnutrition are amplified if the person is unwell, and especially if they have a gut-related condition, and by adverse environmental circumstances. The same is seen in animal models. Young animals (e.g., piglets) exposed to a low-protein micronutrient-poor diet develop multiple abnormalities in their small intestine (e.g., Lykke et al., 2013), which leave them more vulnerable to gut-related diseases, impairing nutrient absorption and increasing the risk of death (Salamen et al., 2019). This all has consequences for the quality of the environment in which the animal is developing. In rats, malnourishment to the rat dam leads to more time spent in the nest, longer time taken to gather pups, and a change in eating patterns. In pups, it leads to less time spent exploring, less time away from their mother, more ultrasonic calls, and less play (Laus et al., 2011). Many of these effects result in a less stimulating environment, with known adverse consequences for development. Later in life as adults, these animals have poorer learning and memory, hippocampal abnormalities, and altered patterns of social interaction.

In adult animals, low-protein diets impair multiple aspects of hippocampal anatomy (e.g., reducing granule and pyramidal cell numbers; Andrade et al., 1995), with only limited evidence of impairment to other brain areas. Functionally, this manifests as impaired hippocampal-dependent learning and memory. For diets deficient in energy, it is important to focus just on studies that impose a *weight loss* (Mattson, 2005), otherwise they shade into studies examining life extension. Severely energy deficient diets (typically restriction in excess of 50 per cent of energy needs) result in hippocampal abnormalities and dysfunction, again with only limited evidence of effects extending beyond this structure.

Exposing an animal to either a protein- or an energy-deficient diet causes stress (and see Section 4.5.3). This can be adduced by the impact of such diet on the hypothalamic-pituitary-adrenal axis, which results in elevated levels of corticosterone (Heiderstadt et al., 2000). This is characteristic of an animal's stress response. Elevated levels of corticosterone are known to impair hippocampal function (McEwen, 2007), suggesting one mechanistic pathway by which malnutrition could impact the brain, and especially the hippocampus.

7.1.2 Environmentally Driven Deprivation: Hibernation, Torpor, and Estivation

Many animals respond to adverse environmental circumstances – typically extreme cold and/or the absence of food – with metabolic slowing, so that the period of adversity can be survived. This slowing comes in two main forms. The first is torpor, which is typically for a shorter period (days) and often with a less dramatic metabolic reduction. The second is hibernation, which lasts longer – weeks or months – and generally involves significant metabolic slowing. While torpor and hibernation share many commonalities, they are distinct entities (Ruf & Geiser, 2015). An additional process is estivation – metabolic slowing in response to extreme heat and aridity. This was once considered a discrete phenomenon but is now thought to be a form of torpor (Staples, 2016).

Maintenance of a relatively constant body temperature (endothermy) occurs mainly in birds and mammals. Across different bird species body temperatures range between 38 and 44°C and, for monotremes, marsupials, and placental mammals, between 32 and 39°C. While this confers some significant advantages – ability to forage largely independent of environmental temperature, and avoidance of fungal infection – it is energetically costly (Ruf & Geiser, 2015). Having the ability to undertake a controlled downward shift in metabolism and hence body temperature (heterothermy) can deliver significant energy savings from 20–60 per cent of daily energy costs for torpor, to 60–95 per cent for hibernation (Blanco et al., 2018). Thus, having such a capacity would be beneficial when the environment precludes feeding, due to extreme heat or cold.

Torpor has been observed in twelve families of birds and eight orders of mammals (notably rodents and bats, but also primates, hedgehogs, shrews, moles, and marsupials; Ruf & Geiser, 2015). Estivation (i.e., in response to high temperatures) is much commoner among ectotherms, including reptiles, amphibians, and fish, but there are mammalian examples such as the fat-tailed dwarf lemur and the sugar glider. For torpor, this is subdivided into two forms, daily (which may be seasonal and/or cold-induced) and fasting-induced (less common and triggered by negative energy balance). Torpor involves reductions in basal metabolic rate of around 25 per cent and a reduction in body temperature to about 11°C (Staples, 2016). The animal appears to be in a sleep-like state.

Hibernation is an almost exclusively mammalian adaptation, found in monotremes, marsupials, rodents, primates, carnivores, bats, hedgehogs, anteaters, moles, and shrews (Ruf & Geiser, 2015). The capacity to hibernate (and enter torpor) may have been present in the first mammals and *may* just be suppressed in those species that do not normally evidence it now. Indeed, the human response to starvation, with its characteristic metabolic shift to ketogenesis, lowered basal metabolic rate, and reduced body temperature, may represent more than just a superficial resemblance to torpor/hibernation. A human capacity for hibernation/torpor by

Figure 7.1 Male black bear hibernating.
Source: FlickR

induction is being actively explored as an option for prolonged space flight (M. Cerri et al., 2021).

Animals that hibernate are usually categorised into obligate or non-obligate hibernators. Obligate hibernators (e.g., arctic ground squirrels) show a pattern of physiology and behaviour, which is enacted even if the animal is placed in an artificial environment without cues to day length, external temperature, or season, and so on (Staples, 2016). Presumably hibernation here is controlled by some form of internal clock, but the exact mechanism is unclear. In contrast, non-obligate hibernators (e.g., black-footed prairie dogs) depend upon an environmental trigger (e.g., intense cold and season change). There is a lot of variability in the change in basal metabolic rate and body temperature observed in hibernating species. Hibernating black bears (see Figure 7.1) drop their temperature only modestly to around 30°C, in contrast to arctic ground squirrels whose temperature can dip below 0°C. Irrespective of this, the general characteristics are similar. There is increasing hunger, food intake, and body weight as the time to hibernate approaches. This is followed by drops in body weight and basal metabolic rate, and the cessation of eating during hibernation (although some species do wake and snack). After hibernation ends, there is hunger, and an increase in body weight and metabolism (see Figure 7.2).

Once an animal enters hibernation, a variety of changes occur. In the brain, at the cellular level, there can be a reduction in the number of synapses and hyperphosphorylation of tau protein. The latter also occurs in starvation and may reflect a protective response or an energy-saving one,

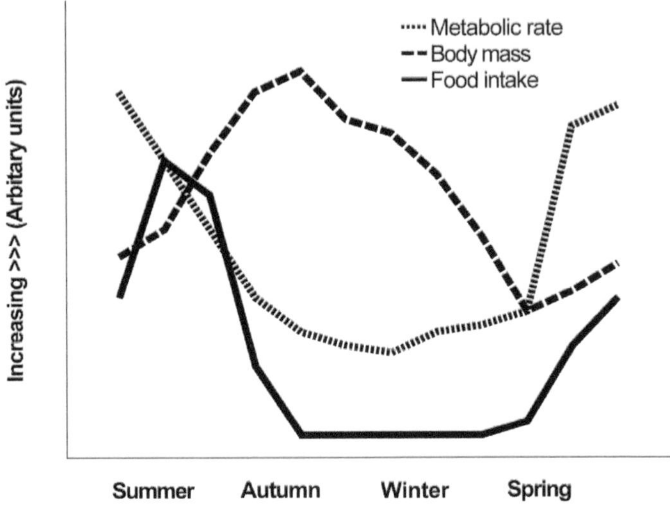

Figure 7.2 Changes in metabolic rate, body mass, and food intake across the seasons, in a hibernator.

reducing axonal transport. E lectroencephalography reveals a brain state different from sleep and more characteristic of 'slow wakefulness'. Changes also occur in the digestive tract (increased leakiness) – defecation ceases during hibernation as with urination – and also in the immune system (reduction in white cells). All these effects are reversed (including synaptic return) on recovery from hibernation (M. Cerri et al., 2021) and most probably reflect energy-saving mechanisms, notably via reducing protein generation.

The big change in hibernation is to basal metabolic rate. Most animals do not eat while hibernating, and so they must actively accumulate fat mass in the months prior. This fat mass is then used as fuel during the hibernation period (Florant & Healy, 2012; Staples, 2016). During starvation, a similar process of ketogenesis occurs, with ketone bodies forming the primary fuel. The process in hibernation seems similar, but here additional features have been observed such as a better ability to move ketone bodies across the blood brain barrier, to fuel the brain.

While suppression of hunger during the hibernation period may just reflect an inability to experience this state due to a reduction in consciousness, there has been interest in the mechanisms driving increased food intake prior to hibernation. One observation is that increasing body fat does not seem to dull hunger (i.e., increasing leptin release). Increases in insulin and ghrelin also occur during the pre-hibernation (fattening) period, and ghrelin is in fact able to induce torpor in some rodents. Not surprisingly, the hypothalamus has been suggested as the brain structure coordinating both the metabolic changes associated with hibernation and the eating-related changes too (Florant & Healy, 2012; Staples, 2016). It may be easier to regard the surge in hunger preceding hibernation as resulting from two indirect physiological processes, rather than consider hunger facilitation as a direct physiological effect. The first would be a winding back of inhibition, such that satiety would not dull desire, as memories of how pleasant it would be to eat would not be inhibited as they normally are post-meal. This would mean a hunger surge, but without any direct effect on the mechanisms that normally induce hunger. The second is rather different and concerns time-based eating cues. This may include a natural widening of the normal diurnal eating period (i.e., at higher latitudes, summer daylength extends significantly).

Not surprisingly, there has been a lot of interest in how the metabolic changes seen in hibernation (and torpor) are enacted (Staples, 2016). These include reduced usage of heat-generating tissue (e.g., muscles), passive thermal effects, and active metabolic suppression. The last mentioned involves both changes to mitochondrial activity and to the production of ATP, as well as a slowing of cellular pumps, and protein synthesis. How this is all initiated, and then reversed, is not well understood.

7.2 People: Laboratory-Imposed Starvation

7.2.1 *Early Studies*

Francis Benedict undertook the first controlled study of starvation in 1912. He originally wanted to employ a hunger artist to serve as the subject, but did not have the funds to pay one. Word of mouth led him to Maltese-born Agostino Levanzin, who was prepared (should he be paid and transported to Boston from Malta) to undertake a total fast for a period of around thirty days. On arrival in the US, Levanzin was housed in the laboratory and constantly observed to ensure he did not eat. Over the thirty-one days of total fast, Levanzin's BMI fell from 21.5 to 16.8, with a loss of 22 per cent of initial body weight (see Figure 7.3). Benedict's primary interest was studying the effects of starvation on basal metabolic rate, and this was found to reduce significantly during this period.

There were also attempts made to examine Levanzin's state of mind across the fast, including a psychiatric interview (Benedict, 1915).

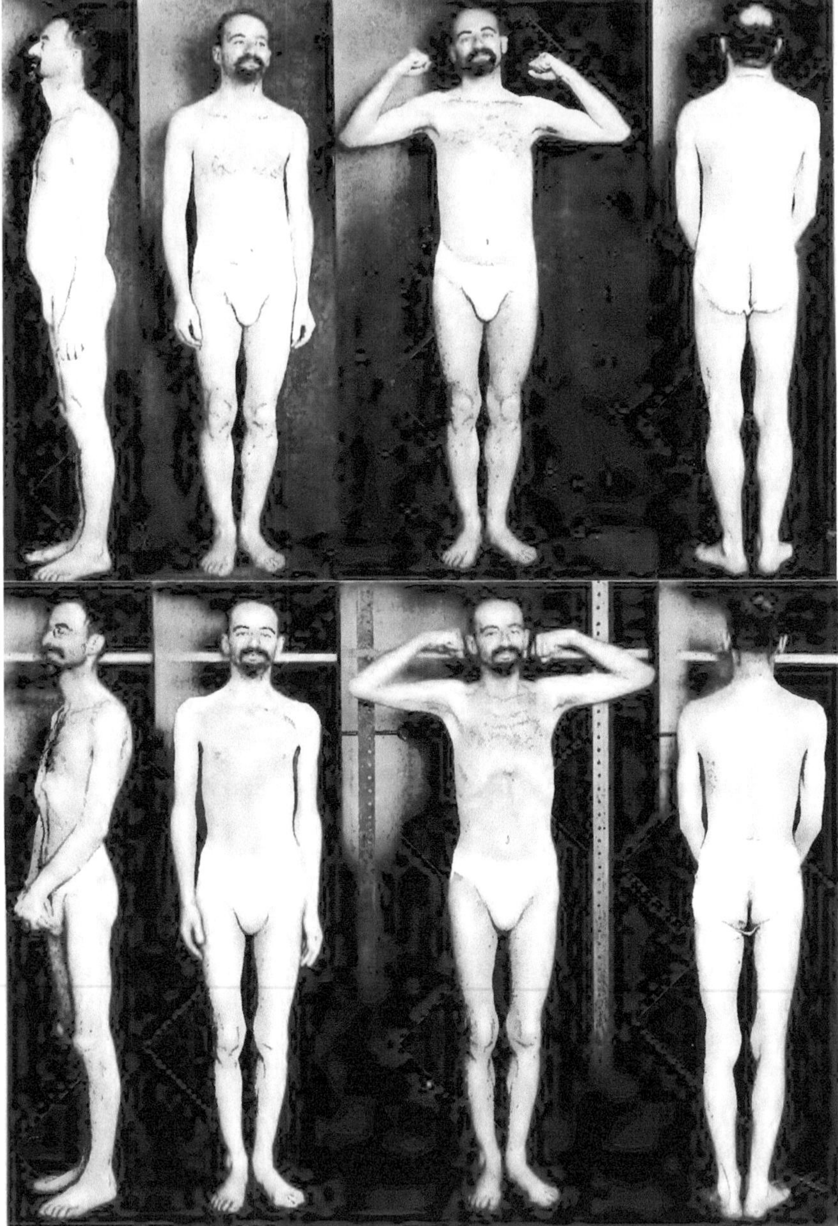

Figure 7.3 Benedict's first study of experimental starvation and its effect on the participant, Levanzin (top before, bottom after).
Source: Image from Carnegie Society Monographs, https://carnegiescience.edu/about/history/publications/monographs

Levanzin did not report being hungry when asked, and Benedict noted: 'Nothing was observed at any time which would lead me to suppose that the subject experienced any sensation of hunger or any feeling of distress in the abdomen throughout the entire fast' (Benedict, 1915, p. 205). Similarly, the psychiatric report indicated no hunger, even when thinking of food. Hunger was reported for the first time five days after breaking the fast. The lab diary entries suggest periods of low mood, irritability, and poor concentration. After several days of refeeding, there was a public falling out between Benedict and Levanzin, with the latter claiming he had been misled about the study and the former refuting such claims (Benedict, 1915).

Benedict then undertook a more elaborate multi-person semi-starvation study funded by the Carnegie Institute (Benedict et al., 1919). The aim was to reduce body weight by around 10 per cent and observe the metabolic and psychological consequences. The all-male participants were recruited from a Christian college, with the first 'squad' of twelve undergoing nine weeks of weight loss, with their BMIs falling from 22.9 to 20.1 (a 12 per cent change). A second squad of twelve was put through a faster and more restrictive procedure (losing 6.5 per cent of body weight in three weeks). Few changes in cognition were seen, but there were reports of lowered libido, reduced strength, fatigue, and irritability. Each participant was asked to keep a diary, and to make reports of hunger in this record. The most notable observation is the variability of these reports. Focussing on the first squad, one participant reported little or no hunger across the nine weeks, while another described persistent and intense hunger (gnawing). The remaining ten participants fell along a continuum between these two extremes. The same pattern was also evident in the second squad. When hunger was reported, it was most common around mealtimes.

The next major report on starvation emerged from the Warsaw ghetto following the end of the Second World War. Warsaw was second only to New York in the size of its Jewish population. After the Nazi invasion, it was decided in November 1940 to concentrate Jewish people in a walled ghetto in inner Warsaw. The non-Jewish Polish population were considered by the Nazis as material for slave labour, and the plan was to feed them accordingly, with a starvation ration of 2,900 kJ per day. In contrast, Jewish prisoners in the ghetto were expected to subsist on 750–1250 kJ per day. While this ration was initially supplemented by black market food, by the end of 1941 little was available, and many starved.

The Nazis were particularly concerned that there might be a typhus outbreak, and so allowed Professor Israel Milejkowski, chief medical officer of the *Judenrat*, to start a 'sanitary course for the prevention of infectious disease' (Weisz et al., 2012). This served as a cover for three Jewish doctors – Emil Apfelbaum, Ludwik Stabholz, and Juliusz Zweibaum – to run a covert medical school, to aid morale and assist in the medical care of ghetto residents. As part of this short-lived medical school, a research study was launched to record the impacts of starvation on the human body.

From the ghetto's inception, until its inhabitants' forcible relocation and murder in Treblinka, around 100,000 Jewish people died, most from starvation. Thus, the Warsaw ghetto hunger study had no shortage of cases to examine and, indeed, around 500 post-mortems were undertaken, and over 100 living patients studied. The study was among the first to identify the three stages of starvation, the consequences of deep starvation on the body's organs, and that as an adult's weight approached 30–40 kg, death would soon follow. It also noted behavioural changes, especially apathy and lethargy, and, in children, the absence of a desire to play, slow movements, insomnia, and a cessation of intellectual development (Grzybowski & Pawlikowska-Łagód, 2023). The study had to be completed before all its components were ready as the Nazis had decided to empty the ghetto. The manuscript was smuggled out and given for safekeeping to a Polish doctor, Witold Orlowski. The manuscript was eventually published after the war, but it did not receive broader attention until its translation into English in 1979 and its publication by John Wiley as *Hunger Disease: Studies by the Jewish Physicians of the Warsaw Ghetto*.

7.2.2 The Minnesota Starvation Study

As the Second World War unfolded there was significant loss of life from starvation. Around 13.8–16.9 million people died from famines in the Soviet Union, India, China, Indonesia, Vietnam, Greece, Austria, and the Netherlands. While rationing in the UK and Germany ensured adequate nutrition for their populations, many other countries, particularly towards the end of the war, were not able to feed theirs. Italy, France, Belgium, Norway, Finland, Japan, and Iran all had per-capita energy allocations well below that needed to maintain stable body weight in an adult. When combined with the malnourished populations in countries that had had wartime famines, it seemed President Truman's concern, that widespread starvation was looming, was prescient.

A major issue, and one that was not well understood, was the impact of starvation on people's behaviour. With the war's end imminent, and the need to rebuild many nations' physical, social, and political structures, would poorly fed people be up to the task? Would they be especially susceptible – as some feared – to the lure of communism or to populist demagogues? And what would be needed, in terms of food (calories, vitamins, etc.), if they were to be re-fed to an adequate level of nutritional health?

To address these questions would require a rather special type of human experiment. People would have to be studied while being deliberately starved on a diet akin to that in war-torn regions, and then re-fed using different regimens, to see which would be most effective at restoring health. Professor Ancel Keys devised such a study in late 1943, and he was ideally placed to execute it (Keys et al., 1945, 1950). He had a good relationship with the US defence establishment because of his work on the K-ration (US Army ration packs used in the Second World War). He had also undertaken interventional human studies on vitamins, he was a physiologist with nutritional experience, and he was used to working across disciplines. With a large team composed of seven academic staff (physiologists, medical doctors, and psychologists), twenty technical and administrative support workers, eighteen civilian public service volunteers (biochemists, biostatisticians, psychologists, administrators, etc.), and eleven external medical consultants, they conducted the Minnesota Starvation Study (Keys et al., 1945, 1950).

To recruit participants, an evocative poster with the tag line '[w]ill you starve that they be better fed?' was sent out to all work camps run by the Civilian Public Service (CPS; Kalm & Semba, 2005). The CPS were tasked with employing the 12,000 US conscientious objectors who had refused military service, with most belonging to religious organisations that did not condone any form of killing. Many of these men were highly motivated to support the war effort in non-combat roles, and Keys and the team received over 400 responses. Of these, 100 were interviewed, and to be selected the individual had to have exemplary personal integrity, an unremarkable medical history, and be emotionally stable (Keys et al., 1945, 1950). The purpose of the study, the methods that would be used, and its rigors and dangers were carefully stressed to each interviewee. While some contemporary commentators have questioned whether the study was ethical (e.g., Sarró, 2018), it seems that Keys was genuinely interested in obtaining informed consent (see Keys et al., 1945, p. 12). There is a good reason for this. If a participant knows exactly what they are getting into, they are more likely to stay the course.

Of the 100 interviewed, 36 were selected to serve as participants, with several others taken on as volunteer support staff. The 36 participants, aged between 20 and 33 years, arrived at the University of Minnesota in November 1944. They were housed inside a football stadium (now demolished) on campus, with meals taken in nearby Shevlin Hall (still standing). The first three months of the study made up the baseline phase, with normal feeding and acclimatisation to the study conditions. This meant being *observed* – there were no toilet or shower stalls, and participants slept in a dormitory. A weekday's routine was made up of breakfast, lunch, and dinner, three hours of housekeeping duties, and five hours of study (a programme drawing on university lectures, etc.). This was augmented by an extensive baseline testing programme, covering their anatomy, anthropometry, histology, biochemistry, physiology, psychology, clinical and other observations. Each participant was also instructed to keep a diary, and to walk around 30 km per week (Keys et al., 1945, 1950).

In February 1945 the six-month semi-starvation period started. The participants were now only given two meals a day – breakfast and dinner – and three meal plans were alternated (see Table 7.1). To ensure consistent weight loss, individual diets were tweaked on a weekly basis, with this information being posted on a Friday evening. The loss or gain of an extra slice of bread became of increasing importance as the semi-starvation phase progressed, with the average energy intake dropping from 13,400 kJ during baseline to 7,500 kJ in this phase. The diet was modelled on that being eaten in Europe, and many participants found it, *initially*, to be too filling and bulky (Schemmel et al., 2001). The reduction in energy intake had its desired effect with the participants' mean BMI falling from 21.6 at baseline, to 17.6 midway through the semi-starvation phase, to a low of 16.4 at the end of this period. The participants by this time looked gaunt and pinched, with sallow complexions and emaciated bodies. Ancel Keys' wife, Margaret, remarked that he was shocked by the physical and psychological impacts of the semi-starvation phase, and she remembered him saying: 'What am I doing to these young men? I had no idea it was going to be this hard' (Kalm & Semba, 2005).

By the end of the semi-starvation phase in late July 1945, participants had not only undergone striking physical changes (see Figure 7.4), they had also become very different people to the highly motivated and virtuous individuals who started the study. Physically, they were enfeebled (a 30 per cent loss of strength), fatigued by day-to-day tasks, highly sensitive to cold (hence the sunbathing in Figure 7.4), they became dizzy on rising, had poor coordination, tinnitus, hair loss, insomnia, night-time urination, and frequent aches and pains (Guetzkow & Bowman, 1946; Kalm & Semba, 2005). A further change was 'famine oedema', with fluid build-up around

Table 7.1 *The semi-starvation menus from the Minnesota Starvation Study*

Meal	Menu 1	Menu 2	Menu 3
Breakfast	Porridge Fried potatoes Jello Bread Jam Milk Sugar	Oatmeal Potatoes Gingerbread Bread Jam Milk Sugar	Pancake Syrup Applesauce Corn bread Bread Jam
Dinner	Fish chowder Spaghetti Meatball Potatoes Peas Carrots Cabbage	Bean and pea soup Macaroni Cheese Swede Potatoes Lettuce salad	Potato soup Stew Potatoes

Note: Note that Menu 1 was the favourite, and that all items contained only token amounts of milk and meat/fish.

Figure 7.4 Participants in the starvation phase of the Minnesota Starvation Study. Courtesy of Hennepin County Library.

the ankles and knees. Body composition was also altered as tissue was used as fuel, with a progressive reduction in both fat mass (amount lost = 6.5 kg) and muscle mass (amount lost = 12.9 kg). Changes to cardiac and metabolic function paralleled the findings of earlier studies, with reductions in heart rate, body temperature, andbasal metabolic rate.

The most striking changes were in the psychological domain (and see Chapter 4 for related discussion). The participants' cognitive and

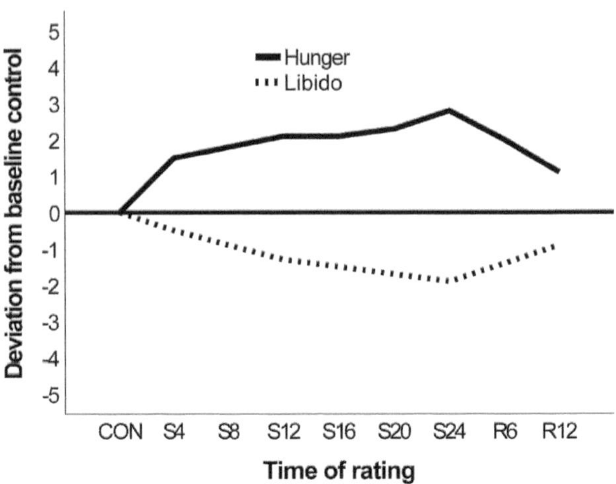

Figure 7.5 Average changes in participants' self-reported hunger and libido in the Minnesota Starvation Study.

perceptual capacity was tracked throughout the study and the changes here were negligible (Brožek et al., 1951). However, each participant progressively abandoned other thoughts, interests, and even relationships, as they became more and more preoccupied with food (e.g., Franklin et al., 1948; Guetzkow & Bowman, 1946). Reports of hunger were as varied as in Benedict et al.'s (1919) study. Participants were asked to make hunger ratings at various points in the study, and the average progressively increased across the semi-starvation period (see Figure 7.5). However, some reported hunger intermittently, while others were hungry all the time. This included both abdominal sensations (varying from mild discomfort to intense pain), craving more after eating, and a strong desire to eat, especially around mealtimes (Franklin et al., 1948).

The desire to eat was so compelling that Keys had to introduce a buddy system, so that any trip outside the laboratory area required taking along another participant as a chaperone. Part of the reason for this was that four participants were either caught or suspected of cheating (Brožek et al., 1951). One participant ate food in town, another stole food in the lab, and both also developed significant depressive episodes, resulting in hospitalisation. One took extra food and coincidentally was also found to have a kidney disorder and another's weight did not reduce, suggesting they were cheating. Both participants were removed from the study but were retained to help with its completion. While these four out of thirty-six succumbed to temptation, the remaining thirty-two did not (or at least for food – one stole coffee cups). Their desire to eat made them think in ways that they found disturbing, especially the intensity of hatred felt to those who got slightly more food, the 'fat' laboratory staff, and people going about their daily business who just happened to be seen eating (Kalm & Semba, 2005). It must be remembered that these men were devoutly Christian, intelligent, well-educated, and highly motivated to take part. This is what makes these changes so striking.

Another manifestation of their preoccupation with food was the alteration in eating habits (Franklin et al., 1948). To obtain their food, participants had to queue, and any delay in serving was a major cause of irritability and angry outbursts. The food had to be very hot, and participants – hunched over the food in a possessive manner – either gulped it down very quickly or excessively extended their mealtimes (up to 2.5 hours). Soups had all their liquid eaten, after which hot water and salt would be added to 're-make' the dish in a process termed 'soupification'. Concoctions of food (e.g., jam with macaroni) were common, and all food preferences vanished. There was heavy use of cigarettes, chewing gum, tea, and coffee drinking, with Keys introducing restrictions on the use of some of these food substitutes.

The study revealed other changes in personality. Libido was reduced (see Figure 7.5) throughout the starvation period. Participants also became depressed and irritable, with the former indicated on the recently developed Minnesota Multiphasic Personality Index. Concern over personal appearance declined, the participants became more egocentric, introverted, their sense of humour became darker and more cynical, and they were less social (Franklin et al., 1948). The preoccupation with food also led to poor concentration, and a difficulty in making even simple decisions (walk this way or that?).

From the end of July 1945 until late October 1945, the third and final phase of the study commenced – refeeding (Keys et al., 1945, 1950). The remaining thirty-two participants were allocated to one of eight conditions, varying in the number of calories offered (four levels), protein content (two levels), and vitamin enrichment (two levels). Gradually, the physical and psychological manifestations of semi-starvation started to remit. Weight was regained, but most of this was as fat rather than muscle mass. Appetites were often insatiable, and most of the participants reported that it took up to two years to return both their body and mind to the state prior to study involvement (Kalm & Semba, 2005).

The legacy of the study is an interesting one. Although the results were disseminated to relief workers in the field (e.g., Guetzkow & Bowman, 1946) and probably helped many understand the psychological effects of starvation, the study was too late to shape policy decisions about refeeding. Refeeding 'in the field' occurred on an ad hoc basis, with more concern for refeeding syndrome (and rightly so) than for the specifics of the refeeding process as studied by Keys. In addition, the unfolding food crisis in Europe and Asia was not as bad as expected. Instead, the main impacts of the study lay elsewhere. As refeeding seemed to eliminate many of the adverse psychological effects of starvation, including depression, early students of anorexia nervosa reasoned that refeeding would similarly alleviate many of the symptoms of that disease too – a rather optimistic conclusion. Keys was suspicious of drawing such parallels, noting that the Minnesota study was conducted on individuals with no pre-existing psychopathology and that starvation in 'less balanced' people would have very different consequences. At a more individual level, the study participants did not seem to suffer any long-term adverse outcomes. Eckert et al. (2018) followed many of them up (nineteen out of the original thirty-six). All had led healthy and productive lives, and all reported that they would do the study again.

7.2.3 Starvation Studies: Conclusion

Long-term semi-starvation experiments are difficult to do, and as the scrutiny attendant on any human study has increased in recent years, the likelihood of there being anything like Benedict's or Keys' studies again seems remote. Perhaps the last of the major starvation studies was Cahill et al. (1966). This included participants of normal weight (alongside heavier and diabetic participants) undertaking a 7.5 day total fast to examine the fuel shift that occurs in starvation. By the final day of Cahill's study participants were generating the energy to stay alive primarily from their fat stores (85 per cent) – generating ketone bodies – but also to a lesser extent from their protein stores (15 per cent). No mention was made of whether the participants were hungry, and based on the studies described so far, it would be hard to predict if they were.

7.3 Hunger as a Weapon

Hunger has been used as a weapon since humans first lived in settlements where one group of people could besiege another. By preventing food entering the besieged area, and perhaps water too, the people under siege would eventually be forced into submission. Of all historic sieges, and indeed of all occasions where hunger has been used deliberately as a weapon, none were more systematic in this regard than the Nazis during the Second World War. Consequently, the examples in this section, on starvation in prison camps, in the Leningrad siege, and the Dutch Hunger Winter, all come from the actions of the Nazi authorities (and noting that the other Axis powers, especially Japan, engaged in similar crimes but on a smaller scale).

The Nazi regime had a general overarching idea to use hunger as a weapon (e.g., Kay, 2006). In just the same way that the Wannsee conference of 1942 laid out the logistics for the Holocaust, a less well-known but potentially more lethal plan was hatched some months earlier in May 1941 – Operation Hunger. Under the general direction of Herbert Backe, Reich Minister of Food and Agriculture, the plan was to starve the population of the former Soviet Union once its territories had been seized by the Nazi armed forces. Food was to be redirected to feed the civilian population in Germany and the military occupying forces, with the local population left to fend for themselves. By Nazi estimates this would have involved somewhere between thirty and forty million deaths, but in the end Operation Hunger was only partially enacted, resulting in *only* three to four million deaths from starvation in Russia, Belorussia, and the Ukraine.

Across occupied Europe, but especially in Germany, the Nazi authorities ran a network of 30,000 forced labour camps, 1,150 ghettos, 980 concentration camps, 1,000 prisoner-of-war camps, and 500 military brothels (van Pelt, 2014). Dietary regimes differed across the camps, varying from adequate to lethal, with inmates at Belsen, for example, receiving just 250 g of 'bread' and 1 litre of watery turnip soup per day (Niremberski, 1946). In the concentration camp system, where life was even more expendable than in other types of camp, the grim process of starvation (see Figure 7.6) was chillingly described by doctor and Neuengamme camp survivor Stanislav Sterkowicz (Sterkowicz, 1971/2022).

He outlined a four-stage process. In the first stage, lasting two to four months, the intelligent inmates used their wits to try to secure more food (e.g., marching on the outside of a column to better collect cigarette butts, as tobacco could be swapped for food), while the crafty stole. Sterkowicz (1971/2022) then described a gradual process of mental and physical deterioration, characterised by increasing egocentricity. In the second stage, lasting one to three months, weight was lost more rapidly, there was a greater interest in camp food, and even in dry grains, slightly mouldy

Figure 7.6 Concentration camp survivors.
Source: US Holocaust Museum

bread, and withered vegetables. Behavioural scruples were shed, bones were sucked for their marrow, and then sucked again and again by other prisoners. Attacks on fellow prisoners for their food were common, and any form of self-abasement– licking an SS soldier's boot for a crust – was tolerated. In the third stage, lasting three to six weeks, the starving prisoner started to adopt a particular set of physical and behavioural characteristics, which were called '*muselmann*' in the camp vernacular. *Anything* was eaten – rotting food, non-food items – and this was accompanied by a growing passivity and indifference to surrounding events. In the final stage, lasting one to three weeks, all will to live was lost and the person slowly faded into death. This was the fate of hundreds of thousands of prisoners.

Of all the sieges in recorded history, none exceed that of Leningrad (St Petersburg) in terms of the number of people killed. Invading Nazi and Finnish forces had surrounded Leningrad by September 1941. While some of the civilian population had been evacuated, many remained. The siege lasted 872 days and, during this period, the Soviet forces were able to secure a tenuous supply line into the city. However, even with rationing, food was still in very short supply and, at its worst, people were subsisting on 125 g of 'bread', made from a mix of milled wheat and sawdust (Gruszka, 2022). The desperation of those besieged in Leningrad is revealed by arrest data from the NKVD (the People's Commissariat for Internal Affairs). Between July 1941 and July 1943, 1,700 people were convicted for engaging in cannibalism, of which 364 were executed and 1,366 imprisoned. Executions were performed when a person had been deliberately killed and eaten, and there was imprisonment for eating the flesh of a dead person. Far more common were instances of people either murdering others for their ration cards (1,216 murders in January–June 1942) or simply stealing them. Across the course of the whole siege, it is estimated that 1.5 million people died, primarily from starvation, aided by intense cold and disease.

Following the Normandy landings, and as Allied forces started to liberate Europe, the exiled Dutch government asked its railway workers to strike to hamper the Nazi war effort. In response to their strike, Reich commissioner Seyss-Inquart stopped all food supplies reaching the civilian population in the Nazi-controlled area of western Holland. While the food embargo itself was short-lived (six weeks), when combined with the severe winter of 1944/1945, transportation difficulties from Allied bombing, and loss of farm land due to deliberate flooding, the consequence was a major shortage of food. In the cities, official intakes were around 4,200 kJ in November 1944, but by February 1945 this had dropped to 2,090 kJ. Even with supplementation from the black market, and using bush foods (e.g., dried tulip bulbs), many people were malnourished and around 25–30,000 died. The consequences of the Dutch Hunger Winter extended well beyond those who died. Many who were children, such as the actress Audrey Hepburn (see Figure 7.7) had long-term health consequences from their period of malnourishment. Moreover, and as discussed in the final part of this chapter, so did the children of women pregnant during this time *and* so did their grandchildren (Imam & Ismail, 2017).

7.4 Delayed and Transgenerational Effects of Hunger

The longer-term effects of wartime starvation have been explored in both Holocaust and prisoner-of-war camp survivors. While many Holocaust survivors experienced post-traumatic stress disorder in the years following the war, the impact on their eating behaviour seems to have been limited. Some studies suggest an aversion to queuing for food, anxiety when food was not immediately available, the need to store excessive amounts of food, and a dislike of throwing food away (e.g., Sindler et al., 2004). There does

Figure 7.7 Audrey Hepburn, a survivor of the Dutch Hunger Winter.
Source: ETH-Bibliothek Zürich, Bildarchiv

not, however, appear to be any increase in eating disorders, especially bingeing (e.g., Sindler et al., 2004), which has been considered by some to be a consequence of significant periods of hunger. The prisoner-of-war literature suggests a rather different conclusion. Here, there is evidence for abnormal eating – especially bingeing – and particularly in those who suffered the greatest degree of weight loss (i.e., starvation) during their captivity (e.g., Favaro et al., 2000). Why these two populations, both exposed to life-threatening situations and significant starvation, should react differently is not understood.

A further impact of mass starvation is the consequence for women who were pregnant when exposed to significant food deprivation. A well-understood consequence of this is low birth weight babies, who then show rapid growth in infancy (Vaiserman, 2011). But there are other less obvious impacts as well. Much of this work has come from studying the offspring of mothers pregnant during the Dutch Hunger Winter, the Leningrad siege, and the Chinese famine (see Chapter 5). For the Dutch Hunger Winter, lower birth weight was most notable for those *in utero* during the third trimester, while those *in utero* early in the gestation period had higher likelihoods of metabolic syndrome and schizophrenia. These effects seem to be caused by epigenetic changes in the foetus, which manifest their effect via insulin-like growth factor (Vaiserman, 2011). For the Leningrad siege, offspring had significantly low birth weight, but follow-up studies have not identified a higher likelihood of metabolic syndrome. For the Chinese famine cohort, the most consistent finding has been for a higher likelihood of schizophrenia in the offspring of women pregnant during this time. It is not clear why these three famines should produce different outcomes. It could be exposure *in utero* to toxic famine foods, environmental contrasts (i.e., the Dutch cohort developed in a food environment very different to the one experienced *in utero*), or some other factor.

More recent studies have examined if the grandchildren of people exposed to famine bear any consequences of this exposure, as might be expected if epigenetic changes are present (González-Rodríguez et al., 2023). Three different cohorts have been studied. The first is a Swedish cohort, where records indicate if a future mother-to-be or father-to-be was exposed to starvation as a child. When a father-to-be is exposed, his *grandsons* live longer and have lower incidence of diabetes and heart disease, but there is no effect on his *granddaughters*. When a mother-to-be is exposed, her *granddaughters* have a higher chance of cardiovascular disease, with no effects for her *grandsons*. For the Dutch Hunger Winter cohort, the sons of mothers starved during pregnancy have children who are less healthy and have higher BMI. For the Chinese famine cohort, the sons and daughters of mothers starved during pregnancy have children who are less physically and mentally healthy and have a higher BMI. There is good evidence that these effects have an epigenetic origin, one, as noted earlier, that involves insulin-like growth factor and another that uses the mTOR signalling pathway, with both involved in regulating cellular metabolism (González-Rodríguez et al., 2023; Vaiserman, 2011).

7.5 Conclusion

It should be apparent after reading this chapter that starvation progressively leads to a narrowing of focus, where the only important thing, indeed the whole point of being, becomes to eat. There seems to be a significant degree of variation in how this manifests in each individual. Understanding the source of this variation, particularly as it applies to hunger, is of some importance, because therapeutic weight loss would presumably be far easier if it were not accompanied by a growing desire to eat.

CHAPTER 8

Absent Hunger

8.0 Introduction

This chapter focusses on diseases and states that are linked to reduced or absent hunger. The largest part of the chapter (Section 8.1) is devoted to anorexia nervosa, and the abnormalities in hunger that occur in this disease. A section on constitutional thinness follows (Section 8.2), where a person is healthy and does not restrict food intake yet remains unusually thin. Certain chronic diseases, as well as old age, are linked to loss of hunger, and wasting (Section 8.4). The final section explores several other sources of restriction (Section 8.5). These include orthorexia (attempts to achieve dietary purity), meat-free diets, and the effects of stress, anxiety, and melancholic depression. The chapter ends with the most theoretically interesting topic, avoidant and restrictive feeding disorder and its related entity, paediatric feeding disorder. These conditions may reflect dysfunctional acquisition of hunger, and so provide further evidence for a learning perspective on human hunger.

8.1 Anorexia Nervosa

8.1.1 Introduction

One case where abnormalities of hunger would be expected is in people with anorexia nervosa (AN). This disease, occurring primarily in young females (see Figure 8.1), is characterised by restriction of energy intake, leading to abnormally low body weight, fear of weight gain, and disturbed body image (Mitchell & Peterson, 2020). In an early study, Silverstone and Russell (1967) reported: (1) that some of their participants experienced persistent loss of hunger; (2) some claimed they had forgotten what it was like to be hungry; and (3) others said their experience of hunger was perfectly normal and that they enjoyed eating. While this suggests that hunger may be

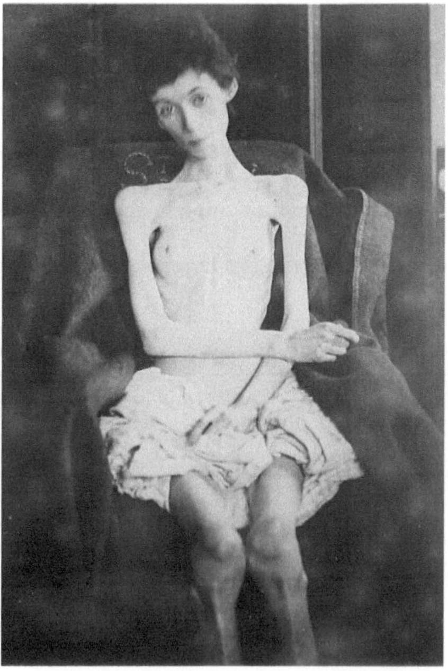

Figure 8.1 Woman suffering from anorexia nervosa.
Source: Barts Health, NHS. https://www.calmview.co.uk/BartsHealth/CalmView/Record.aspx?src=CalmView.Catalog&id=SBHB%2fMU%2f14%2f49%2f16%2f1&pos=2

abnormal in people with AN, it also reflects another feature of research with this population – the variability of findings. This can result from small samples, different subtypes of AN, variation in body weight, disease history, and so on – all reflective of this heterogenous disease.

The diagnostic criteria for AN (from the American Psychiatric Association) are presented in Box 8.1. Currently, two subtypes are identified, one where the person with AN focusses on restriction and/or exercise, and another which involves periods of bingeing, followed by purging (e.g., vomiting) to expel the excess calories. The restricting subtype has an earlier age of onset and a better prognosis relative to the binge eating and purging subtype. Many people do not fit neatly into these diagnostic categories, most notably in respect of their body weight. In this case they may receive a diagnosis of 'other specified feeding and eating disorder – atypical anorexia (OSFED-AN)'. Apart from a higher body weight, and a greater proportion of both men and non-white people, there is little to differentiate OSFED-AN from AN (Walsh et al., 2022).

Box 8.1 Diagnostic Criteria for Anorexia Nervosa (Drawing on the Diagnostic and Statistical Manual of Mental Disorders, Fifth Edition, of the American Psychiatric Association)

Diagnostic criteria and *subtypes*

1. Energy restriction relative to need, resulting in abnormally low body weight*
2. Fear of weight gain or becoming obese
3. Disturbed body image, including an inability to see that current weight is markedly abnormal

   Restricting, via dieting, fasting, and/or exercise

   Binge eating and purging, via vomiting, laxatives, diuretics, enemas, etc.

Note: *Degree of severity is determined by how low body weight is, being ranked from mildly severe (BMI $\geq$17) to extremely severe (BMI <15).

Anorexia is associated with several medical complications, which are often linked to the loss of body mass that occurs with self-starvation (Westmoreland et al., 2016). Some of these may be present before, and be exacerbated by starvation, notably gastroparesis, reflux, functional digestive problems, and constipation – and these warrant mention as they may interfere with perceptions of hunger and satiety. Other medical complications are potentially more serious, notably those involving the heart (arrhythmias), endocrine (including amenorrhea and hypoglycaemia), and renal (including kidney failure and electrolyte disturbances) systems. Risk for these complications increases with weight loss. Severe weight loss is also associated with cognitive impairment across all domains of function (Stedal et al., 2021). This is accompanied by brain atrophy, which is especially marked for the cerebellum, hippocampus, insular cortex, amygdala, and prefrontal and cingulate cortices. Many of these brain areas are central to interoceptive processing (Berntson & Khalsa, 2021), which again might be expected to interfere with the experience of hunger and satiety.

Anorexia is difficult to treat, which partly reflects a lack of understanding about its causes. Weight increase by the end of treatment can usually be accomplished, but these gains are often not maintained. Improvement in psychological functioning, at least from the clinical trial data, does not seem to improve with any form of treatment – pharmacological, psychological, or medical (S. B. Murray et al., 2019). Longitudinal studies over a twenty-year period suggest that between one-third and two-thirds of people with AN experience a full remission. The remainder continue to experience some symptoms, with around 20 per cent exhibiting a chronic form of the disease. The risk of dying from AN is heightened by the medical complications of starvation, and also by an elevated risk from suicide (Mitchell & Peterson, 2020).

8.1.2 Epidemiology

Anorexia is primarily a disease of women (around 92 per cent of cases). It typically manifests during the teenage years around menarche (van Eeden et al., 2021). In women, the number of new cases of AN per year in Western countries is between 40 and 60 per 100,000 and, for men, 4–6 per 100,000. The proportion of the population with AN at one time is around 0.1–3.6 per cent for females, and <0.1–0.3 per cent for males. Standardised mortality rates in people with AN are six times the base rate, and up to sixteen times so with malnourishment.

8.1.3 Cause

As AN is a relatively infrequent disease, with a patient group that may not recognise they have a psychiatric disorder, this has made large-scale studies difficult. Consequently, there has then been a lot of interest in studying animal models of the disease. While animal models have their limitations (e.g., cultural influences are unlikely to be significant here) they are instructive. For rodents, which have been studied the most, the paradigm that has attracted the greatest attention is activity-based anorexia (ABA). This involves restricted availability of food (one to two hours per day) with largely continuous access to a running wheel (Scharner & Stengel, 2021). In young animals, who are most susceptible, this procedure results in excessive wheel running (i.e., modelling the hyperactivity that is observed in people with AN), hypophagia, and weight loss.

Lots of findings in this field are conflicting, including gender and strain-related effects, but it is hard to escape the fact that this procedure is likely to be stressful (Scharner & Stegel, 2021). Indeed, relatively few studies have explored linkages between corticosterone levels and other biological aspects of the hypothalamic-pituitary-adrenal (HPA) stress response, and the behavioural and weight changes in the ABA model. Other animal data suggest the importance of this relationship. Many farm animals are now selectively bred for leanness. In pigs, sows are prone to hyperactivity, hypophagia, and weight loss after farrowing (thin sow syndrome) and after weaning (wasting pig syndrome). Both conditions are quite common, being observed in 6–30 per cent of lean sows (Treasure & Owen, 1997). The basis for this anorexia of sows can be traced to a maladaptive response to their stress-inducing housing conditions (i.e., crowding and bullying by other pigs).

While the animal data point to a probable role for stress (e.g., restraint stress is another model that induces hypophagia, along with reduced fluid intake), it also suggests a further relevant factor – genetics. Older breeds of pigs that are typically fatter and not bred for leanness are not as vulnerable to stress-related anorexias. Rodent genetic models prone to hypophagia have also been developed, including ones that only demonstrate this behaviour when combined with a stressor (e.g., restraint, social isolation, food access restriction; Scharner & Stegel, 2021). This includes gene variants that are associated with increased risk of AN in humans, such as $HDAC4^{A778T}$.

Evidence for genetic susceptibility to AN is robust. People with a family member with AN are eleven times more likely to develop the disease than people with no such history, and twin studies suggest heritability estimates in the range of 50–60 per cent (de Jorge Martinez et al., 2022). Gene-wide association studies indicate around twenty-five genes are involved so far, with these suggesting functional associations to metabolic pathways (Bulik et al., 2021). In addition, several gene variants identified in people with AN overlap with those observed for other psychiatric conditions, including autism spectrum disorder, anxiety, and depression, and those for a heightened risk of suicide. By far the strongest associations are, however, to genes known to be involved in cancer biology, either reflecting a common propensity for cachexia or the greater investigation of gene variants in this field. Finally, the gene variants identified in AN are also found to associate with various phenotypical features, including physical activity and anthropometric and metabolic measures.

Another approach to studying the causes of AN is to examine risk factors. This has been done in two ways, retrospectively and prospectively. The more common retrospective studies converge in identifying a history of trauma (e.g., neglect, abuse, bullying), childhood anxiety, and certain personality traits – perfectionism and rigidity (Mitchell & Peterson, 2020). Prospective studies are rarer, in which a cohort is followed and the factors that predict AN are identified. Four variables have been found in such studies – low body weight alone, low body weight and its interaction with concerns about body image, negative affect (i.e., low mood), and perfectionism (Charrat et al., 2023). People who go on to develop AN may then have inherited traits that, when combined with other factors (e.g., stress, living in a culture that values thinness) at a time when the body is undergoing fat redistribution (i.e., menarche), manifests the disease (Zanella & Lee, 2022). Stress is particularly important here, with an adverse life event often preceding disease onset, and a dysfunctional HPA axis, with a blunted stress response, observed in AN (Keeler et al., 2020; Schmalbach et al., 2020).

8.1.4 Hunger in Anorexia Nervosa

In early descriptions of AN by psychiatrist Hilde Bruch, she described how perceptions and interpretations of eating-related sensations were disturbed. This included difficulty perceiving hunger and fullness, and confusing emotional responses with other interoceptive sensations. Indeed, people with AN score lower relative to healthy controls on the interoceptive dimension subscale of the Eating Disorders Inventory, with this deficit remaining post-treatment, being worse in those with lower BMI and a younger age (Jenkinson et al., 2018).

The literature suggests that the interoceptive deficits in people with AN, and particularly hunger, have four possible causes. The most obvious is that people with AN do not wish to acknowledge that they experience hunger. This might suggest that all that needs to change is a willingness to report what is, in fact, present. One reason to doubt this explanation (more later) is that there are both physiological deficits that may impair hunger perception and abnormalities in hunger even after recovery.

Although early studies reported that gastric hunger signals (e.g., a rumbling empty stomach) were present and detectable in AN (e.g., Silverstone & Russell, 1967), more recent work suggests that significant gastrointestinal problems are present in many people with AN. These gastrointestinal problems may in some cases predate the onset of the disease, with swallowing problems, stomach dysrhythmia, delayed gastric emptying, and longer transit times through the gut being common (Norris et al., 2016). While these physiological changes may not be present in every person with AN, and abnormal patterns of eating and semi-starvation may make them worse, they do suggest that some interoceptive hunger cues related to gut function may be atypical. This may contribute to abnormal sensations of general hunger, and fullness.

Several other biological signals that can form the basis for interoceptive hunger cues are abnormal in people with AN. For example, blood glucose control in people with AN may be impaired, as may glucagon and insulin secretion (e.g., Kumai et al., 1988), and so, to the extent that changes in all or any of these parameters can be used as a signal for hunger, it would not be surprising that hunger judgements based upon them might be abnormal. These are not the only deficits. Abnormalities in incretins, ghrelin, and leptin release have been observed in people with AN (e.g., Hebebrand et al., 2022), and if the bodily sensations these hormones create are either abnormal or absent, then again so to may be any judgements of hunger that depend on them. Many of these hormones have a circadian pattern, especially leptin, and there is also evidence of disruption to circadian patterns in people with AN (Menculini et al., 2019). Not only can eating be tied to the circadian pattern (i.e., daylight feeding), it is also possible to entrain timers for particular meals, such that general hunger occurs at mealtimes. This type of entrained mealtime general hunger pattern is absent in some people with AN (Cugini et al., 2014), which may reflect impairments in underlying circadian biology.

While dysfunctional biological systems are a likely contributor to atypical reports of hunger in people with AN, two further possible causes need to be considered. The first is simply that biological changes are just not perceived (e.g., changes in gastric sensations are not consciously available) and, second, that they are perceived but have an aberrant meaning. Two early studies suggested that what people with AN experienced as hunger was similar to hunger as reported by controls. Using Monello and Mayer's (1967) hunger sensations questionnaire, Garfinkel (1974) found relatively few differences in reports, although the sample sizes were small. In people with AN, negative emotions featured more prominently as indications of hunger, and bloating was a more common sign of fullness. Silverstone and Russell (1967) investigated detection of gastric hunger signals, and found both the nature of the signals and the capacity to detect them was similar between their small group of people with AN and controls.

A further study (Nakai & Koh, 2001) examined variability in blood glucose and hunger following an insulin challenge. While the blood glucose profiles were similar between the (again) small sample of people with AN (restricting) and controls (see Figure 8.2), hunger ratings were very different. While control's hunger spiked with the insulin-induced drop in blood glucose, the reverse occurred in people with AN (restricting) – they reported being *less* hungry. This suggests they may have noticed the bodily change linked to the insulin injection, but this signal had a different meaning to controls. A further finding concerns perception of time. While the ability to know/understand clock time is unlikely to be affected in people with AN, perception of the passage of time may differ. People with AN judge time to pass around 10–15 per cent slower than

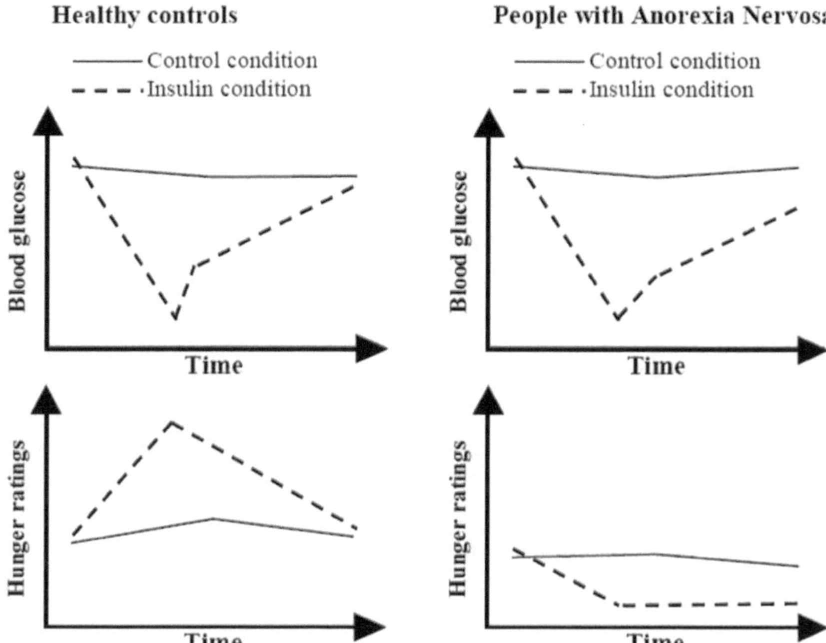

Figure 8.2 Changes in blood glucose and hunger following either control (saline) or insulin injection in healthy controls and people with anorexia nervosa.
Source: Data from Nakai, Y., & Koh, T. (2001). Perception of hunger to insulin-induced hypoglycemia in anorexia nervosa. *International Journal of Eating Disorders*, *29*(3), 354–357. https://doi.org/10.1002/eat.1030

controls (Meneguzzo et al., 2022). Practically, if hunger occurs on the basis of a fixed amount of time elapsing since the last meal, then there would be greater intervals between meals for people with AN. Except for this last study on time, which does suggest a perceptual abnormality, the remaining studies imply that people with AN can perceive bodily changes that are linked to hunger. Rather, what may change is the meaning that this bodily change has. Interestingly, Silverstone and Russell (1967) remarked: 'They [people with AN] *interpret* them [the gastric sensations] abnormally.'

In the material on hunger covered so far, there is a combination of effects in play. People with AN may choose not to report being hungry, so as to explain to others why they are not eating. There is evidence for multiple impairments in the various biological changes (e.g., hormonal) that signal that food will be rewarding to eat now. Moreover, there are several instances where these biological changes are detected but their meaning is aberrant (i.e., they no longer signal hunger). If these effects are all combined, one would expect impairments in hunger in people with AN, and several studies over the last thirty years seem to confirm this.

Some of the most extensive hunger investigations were undertaken by Halmi et al. (1989, 1991), all being conducted with relatively large clinical sample sizes (30+) and contrasting different subtypes. Both studies obtained multiple hunger and fullness ratings across a laboratory-based straw-fed liquid meal, which allowed assessment of eating rate. Across both studies, people with both AN subtypes reported being less hungry before the meal, and fuller after the meal, than controls. Indeed, for many participants with AN there was often little net change in either hunger, which remained low, or fullness, which remained high. These abnormalities persisted even following treatment, and the more significant the hunger-report abnormality, the less the participant ate at the test meal. Eating rate was also found to be slower in people with AN. The basic finding of low hunger/high fullness, with little change across a meal, with limited recovery post-treatment, has now been observed in several subsequent studies, suggesting it is a common aspect of this disease (e.g., Herpertz et al., 2008; Klastrup et al., 2020).

8.1.5 Conclusion

Anorexia nervosa is a disorder characterised primarily by weight loss and inadequate energy intake. Abnormal hunger (and fullness) seems to be a component of this disease, and this may arise from multiple causes – a reluctance to acknowledge hunger, biological dysfunctions in the gut, abnormal food-related hormonal changes, dysregulated circadian patterns, and impaired meaning, such that biological signals that cue hunger in healthy people do not do so in people with AN. Apart from our poor understanding of cause and effect, namely whether, for example, the biological dysfunctions occur prior to any hypophagia, a particularly striking observation is the aberrant meaning that hunger cues have in people with AN. Meaning is critical for general hunger to occur (e.g., if an empty stomach *means* 'illness' rather than 'food will be rewarding now'). It is possible that if meaning can serve to facilitate appetite in the normal way of things, then meaning could also acquire the reverse property, namely robbing foods of their excitatory capacity. Some suggestion of this possibility can be seen in Figure 8.2, and a phenomenon of this sort is discussed in Frank (2021), albeit from the perspective of reward processing (shifting from desire to dread). While normally, palatable foods excite specific hunger via simple Pavlovian associations, these would either never have been formed (i.e., energy-dense food not tried) or would have been extinguished (i.e., tried, but not subsequently eaten for a long time) in people with AN. If general hunger cues then serve to dampen desire to eat, because they had come to acquire an aversive meaning, then there would indeed be little motivation to eat.

8.2 Constitutional Thinness

Constitutional thinness refers to a state of being persistently underweight (i.e., BMI <17.5) with no symptom of physical or mental illness and with no evidence of energy restriction or excessive exercise. Over the last fifty years around forty studies have been published on this topic. Bailly et al. (2021) undertook a systematic review, pooling data from studies of 3,396 people with constitutional thinness. They had a mean BMI of 16.5, with more women than men, and their psychological (i.e., disordered eating, psychiatric history) and biological (i.e., cortisol, IGF, ghrelin, leptin) measures readily differentiated them from people with AN. Some studies suggest higher rates of anxiety in people with constitutional thinness, which is a risk factor for eating disorders and associated with a lower body weight, as discussed later. There do not appear to be any studies looking directly at hunger, but two findings address this indirectly. First, as in people with eating disorders, those with constitutional thinness have higher rates of post-prandial distress syndrome – particularly early satiety and post-prandial fullness (Santonicola et al., 2012). Second, some studies report lower scores on the hunger scale of the Three Factor Eating questionnaire, suggesting a generally lower desire to eat. It remains unknown whether responsiveness to food cues, interoceptive hunger cues, and temporal hunger cues are atypical in people with constitutional thinness.

8.3 Cachexia

Cachexia was first described by Hippocrates as a fatal wasting disease in which 'the shoulders, clavicles, chest and thighs melt away' – *in which all you can eat is yourself* (von Haehling & Anker, 2010). There is no formal definition of cachexia, but across reports three characteristics are present: (1) a chronic disease; (2) a loss of muscle mass; and (3) systemic inflammation (e.g., Morley et al., 2006; Nakamura et al., 2024). Cachexia is distinct from both starvation, with its utilisation of fat for fuel and its

Table 8.1 *The diseases most frequently associated with cachexia, and its prevalence in each case*

Disease	Prevalence, with range estimates if available
Head and neck cancers	57%
Lung cancers	36%
Pancreatic cancers	41–54%
Colorectal cancers	28%
Late stages of cancer generally	60–80%
Chronic heart failure	16–42%
Chronic kidney disease	30–60%
Chronic obstructive pulmonary disease	27–35%
Chronic liver disease	50%
Rheumatoid arthritis	10–67%
HIV-AIDS	10–35%

Source: Data sourced from von Haehling & Anker, 2010, and Morley et al., 2006.

involuntary anorexia, and from age-related muscle loss, which can occur without disease.

Cachexia accompanies some chronic diseases more than others. Prevalence rates, by disease, are presented in Table 8.1. Cachexia is particularly common among cancers that affect food ingestion, digestion, and absorption; however, it becomes more common in other cancers during their final stages. Other chronic illnesses also linked to cachexia are heart failure, kidney disease, chronic obstructive pulmonary disease, HIV-AIDS, and rheumatoid arthritis (Baracos et al., 2018). A common element among these conditions is their capacity to induce systemic inflammation, which appears to be an important mechanism in driving cachexia (Amano et al., 2022).

In cancer, tumours release pro-inflammatory cytokines, and elevated cytokine levels are found in all the conditions linked to cachexia (Morley et al., 2006). These cytokines have two main effects. First, they are catabolic mainly for muscle, triggering their breakdown via several pathways, which liberates amino acids for the generation of immune-related proteins in the liver. Second, these cytokines generate sickness behaviour via their action on the brain, and especially the hypothalamus. The subsequent malaise, fever, pain, drowsiness, depression, fatigue, and nausea impair the person's capacity to experience positive affective memories of food. This is because the mind is not seemingly capable of simultaneously feeling opposing affects, as functionally the malaise serves to predict how unrewarding eating (or anything else) will be now. Hence, with malaise present, and chronically so, hunger is no longer felt, and so food intake reduces. These effects are further amplified by the release of cortisol and prostaglandins, which also exert catabolic effects, and, in the case of chronic cortisol release, augment the sickness behaviours induced by cytokines (Morley et al., 2006). Finally, the direct effects of the chronic disease such as oral pain, difficulty swallowing, chemosensory alterations, and so on all serve to rob eating of giving any pleasure.

Baracros et al. (2018) describes the experience of cachexia thus: 'negative interactions with food and eating are described at every stage of cachexia because of alterations in the perception of taste, smell, and texture of food, usual and even favourite foods become unpleasant or even repulsive' (p. 12). What this further suggests is that, as the disease progresses, food cues start to elicit recollections of how unpleasant food and eating have become. It is hardly surprising then that energy intake is significantly reduced in cachexia, with weight loss culminating at around 20 per cent of initial body mass, and that this condition is so difficult to treat.

8.4 Loss of Hunger in the Elderly

Loss of hunger in the elderly is usually documented on self-report questionnaires, notably the Simplified Nutritional Appetite Questionnaire (SNAQ). This asks four questions, concerning appetite (very poor to very good), how rapidly the person gets full, how food tastes (very bad to very good), and the number of meals eaten per day. Using any type of measure in any type of aged population (65+) produces prevalence estimates of hunger loss ranging from 0.2 per cent (people spontaneously reporting to their general practitioner they are experiencing anorexia) to 63 per cent (in-patient settings using the SNAQ; Fielding et al., 2023). Prevalence estimates, using the SNAQ, for community-dwelling older adults range from 3 to 33 per cent, and for those receiving institutional care from 38 to 63 per cent. These estimates suggest that loss of hunger is more common in institutionalised older adults, but there is some uncertainty over its prevalence in community-dwelling populations. This uncertainty is compounded by the fact that reductions in hunger can seemingly occur with little awareness by the person experiencing it – perhaps because of an insidious onset – which would imply an under-reporting of this problem.

Loss of hunger in the elderly has multiple causes (Landi et al., 2017). These are organised into eight categories in Table 8.2. As a person ages, their capacity to perceive tastes, odours, and textures declines, making food seem bland and so reducing their desire to consume it. There are also

Table 8.2 *Potential causes of hunger loss in the elderly, organised by category*

Category	Examples
Flavour perception	Impaired olfaction, gustation, and somatosensation
Gut	Delayed stomach emptying, slower gut motility
Mouth and throat	Lack of saliva, poor dentition, swallowing problems
Mobility	Difficulty getting about and preparing food
Illness	Acute and chronic illness generates sickness behaviour
Medication side effects	Hypophagia, nausea, fatigue, gastrointestinal symptoms
Psychological factors	Cognitive impairment, depression, knowledge and beliefs
Socio-economic	Poverty, access to food, loneliness, isolation

alterations to the digestive system. These include slower stomach emptying and gut motility, which mean getting full faster and staying full for longer, in addition to a greater likelihood of feeling bloated. Alterations occur in gut-related hormones, with changes to ghrelin release, and increases in satiety-related hormones such as cholecystokinin and PYY. The process of eating may also be problematic, with reduction in saliva, poor dentition, and difficulties swallowing.

At a more macro level, an elderly person's mobility may be limited, making getting and preparing food difficult, with this made worse by vision and hearing impairments. Any chronic illness is likely to reduce appetite, as will more frequent bouts of acute illness (Maki et al., 2019). Drugs taken to manage chronic health conditions can also reduce appetite directly or indirectly through nausea, fatigue, or gastrointestinal symptoms. In addition, psychological factors can play a prominent role. People may believe they do not need to eat as much (Dismore et al., 2024), and cognitive impairment (see Chapter 9 for discussion of dementia) may affect all aspects of eating behaviour from obtaining food, cooking, to feeling hungry (e.g., age-related decline in episodic memory performance will affect specific hunger, impairing retrieval of food-specific memories). Depression in the elderly also manifests via a loss of hunger, weight loss, and digestive symptoms (Landi et al., 2017). Finally, a variety of social and economic factors also serve to accentuate these other causes. Attractive and tasty food may be too expensive, local shops may have little choice, the person may live alone and have never cooked, and they may experience loneliness and social isolation.

Hunger loss has several consequences in older people. First, it can occur in *apparent* isolation, namely without sarcopenia (i.e., muscle loss), malnourishment (i.e., low body weight irrespective of composition), or frailty (i.e., a set of characteristics that place a person at heightened vulnerability to disease and death). However, this may just reflect recent onset of hunger loss, as longitudinal studies suggest that hunger loss is strongly predictive of later weight loss and malnutrition (Fielding et al., 2023). Second, hunger loss is linked to an increased risk of sarcopenia (Ali & Garcia, 2014; A. P. Cerri et al., 2015). Sarcopenia can occur in the absence of nutritional deficit, as muscle strength declines from the age of 30, with this accelerating into old age (Rodrigues et al., 2022). While sarcopenia has many causes, including mechanistic overlaps with cachexia, it is accelerated in ageing by immobility, impaired gut absorption of food, and alterations in the gut microbiota. Sarcopenia enhances the risk for falls, and so there has been some examination of how to reverse it. A protein-rich diet helps (i.e., almost double that recommended for an adult – 1.3 g/kg/day) as does strength training (Rogeri et al., 2022).

A third consequence of hunger loss is malnourishment – as indexed by measures such as the Mini Nutritional Assessment (MNA). The MNA asks about changes to food intake and weight, illness, mobility, neuropsychological problems, and BMI/calf circumference, with a total score used to assess if malnourishment is present. In community-dwelling samples of older adults, in wealthy countries, around 3% are classed as malnourished (Volkert et al., 2019). This increases to 6% among older people presenting at accident and emergency departments, 9% for those receiving home care services, 18% in nursing homes, 22% in hospitals, and 29% in those in long-term care.

The fourth consequence, which overlaps with all the preceding ones, is frailty. This condition is identified when three or more of the following are present – unintentional weight loss, exhaustion, low grip strength, slow walking speed, and low levels of activity (Rudzińska et al., 2023). Not surprisingly, frailty is strongly associated with hunger loss, with this occurring in between 21 and 49 per cent of frail elderly persons.

All these interrelated consequences of hunger loss – sarcopenia, malnourishment, and frailty – increase the risk of morbidity and mortality in older people (e.g., de Souto Barreto et al., 2022; Fielding et al., 2023). While increasing food intake is the most obvious remedy, doing so can be problematic when the person has less desire to eat, pointing to the importance of hunger in maintaining adequate food intake.

8.5 Other Agents of Restriction

8.5.1 Orthorexia, Vegetarianism, and Hunger

Orthorexia is a portmanteau term composed of 'orthos' meaning correct, and 'orexis' meaning appetite (Dell'Osso et al., 2016). This putative disorder was first described in the popular rather than the scientific literature by Dr Steven Bratman and is characterised by attempts to attain 'dietary purity' (Dunn & Bratman, 2016). It involves dysfunctional cognitions and behaviours, such as spending excessive amounts of time thinking about or preparing food, obsessions with food purity, stringent rules of food preparation, significant restrictions over what can be eaten, and self-punishment with fasts/exercise when rules are broken (Bhattacharya et al., 2022). Prevalence estimates for this condition range from 2 per cent up to *80 per cent of the population*, suggesting some issues with the instruments designed to measure it (Ng et al., 2024).

There are two grounds to think that orthorexia is either the same clinical entity as anorexia nervosa or closely related to it. First, historically, attaining spiritual purity was noted as the reason why certain young women engaged in excessive dietary restriction (see Chapter 6). This obsessive focus on attaining spiritual purity through fasting would often lead to weight loss, ill health, and death – as with Saint Catherine of Siena (e.g., Dell'Osso et al., 2016). While anorexia nervosa is currently associated with a focus on attaining an ideal body form, attaining spiritual purity or, as with orthorexia, dietary purity, are all just different reasons for the same behaviour – food restriction. Second, and more significantly, there seems to be little clinical difference between people presenting with orthorexia and those with anorexia nervosa (i.e., comparisons of gender balance, age of presentation, personality traits, insight, role of stress, and so on all suggest similarity; Bhattacharya et al., 2022). What then is different here is the reason, but even this converges in the obsessional attempt to obtain an ideal.

Vegetarianism is by far the commonest form of long-term dietary restriction, namely the avoidance of meat and animal-based foods. Prevalence estimates vary between 1 and 9 per cent of the adult population of Western countries opting for some form of vegetarian diet (Dorard & Mathieu, 2021). The degree of restriction varies from the avoidance of just red meat, to all meat, all meat and dairy (with and without eggs), to the avoidance of any animal-based products altogether (i.e., veganism). There is general agreement – when contrasted with omnivores – that a vegetarian (and probably a vegan diet too) is associated with a lower body weight, a healthier metabolic profile, and a reduction in cancer and heart-disease risk, but not in all-cause mortality (Dinu et al., 2017; Tonstad et al., 2009). An obvious confound of comparing vegetarian/vegans with omnivores is that people who adopt a vegetarian or vegan diet may generally engage more with healthy lifestyles, making it difficult to determine if diet is the cause. However, several studies now indicate that when people are prescribed a vegetarian/vegan diet, with no specific instruction to lose weight, weight loss of 3–5 kg is typically observed (Barnard et al., 2015).

That adopting a vegetarian diet leads incidentally to weight loss might suggest a reduction in hunger. In one of the only studies with relevant data, Medawar et al. (2023) found that omnivores were reportedly more hungry than vegetarians/vegans – although this was a small difference (2 per cent of the scale) with a small effect size ($d = 0.1$) in a large sample. There may be two reasons for this difference. One may relate to the type of person who becomes a vegetarian/vegan. While not all studies have observed this, the data suggest overall consumption of a vegetarian/vegan diet is linked to a higher incidence of anorexia nervosa, and dimensionally to energy-restrictive dietary practices (Dorard & Mathieu, 2021; Sergentanis et al., 2020). As discussed earlier, lower levels of hunger are reported in people with anorexia nervosa.

The second reason is that a mainly plant-based diet may exert an effect on hunger by a longer period of satiety leading to a longer period of memory inhibition after a meal. Exposing healthy participants in randomised order to either a cheeseburger meal or a plant-based tofu burger meal, matched for energy and macronutrients but differing in fibre, revealed greater satiety with the plant-based meal, alongside greater increases in gut hormones involved in the satiety cascade (Klementova et al., 2019). This would mean being full for longer – so less hunger in aggregate.

8.5.2 Stress, Anxiety, Melancholic Depression, and Hunger

Stress is a psychological state generated by some form of challenge – the stressor – that is accompanied by a characteristic set of biological responses (see Figure 8.3). For humans, the most significant stressor is death of kin, with then a full spectrum of stressors through to everyday hassles (e.g., dealing with difficult colleagues). The biological response to stressors is known to affect brain systems involved in hunger, and this was discussed earlier in relation to anorexia nervosa – although the outcomes are different in this disease (i.e., reduced hunger and food intake) perhaps due to genetic influences and a resultant maladaptive or abnormal stress response.

When a stressor is present, especially a potent one (e.g., imminent threat to life) the resulting sympathetic nervous response – fight or flight – is linked acutely to reduced hunger, as too is the initial phase of the slower hormonal stress response (and it may be the *persistence* of these responses that is a contributory abnormality in people with anorexia nervosa).

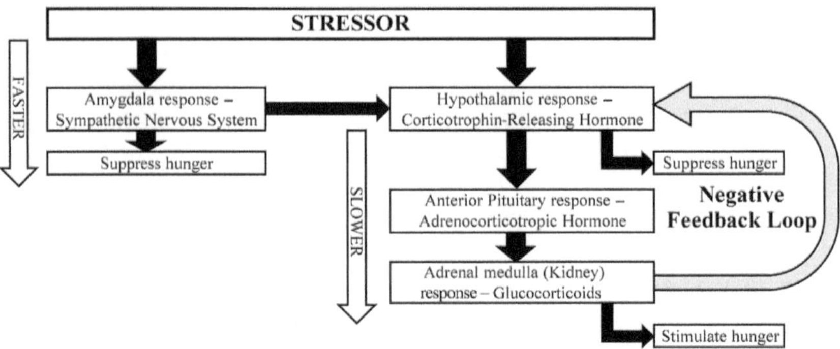

Figure 8.3 Key biological pathways of the human stress response with their associated effects on hunger (typically indexed via food intake).

However, the end point of the stress hormone pathway is the release of glucocorticoids, and these are associated with both increased hunger and food intake (Stammers et al., 2020). If the stressor is chronic, then increased hunger may become the dominant outcome, if elevated glucocorticoid levels persist.

Empirical data for the effect of stress on food intake (which is used here as a proxy for hunger), in humans and animals, reflect these divergent impacts of stressors, and is illustrated in Figure 8.3. In animals, acute severe stressors are associated with reduced food intake, while the availability of palatable food, and more chronic stress, is linked to increased food intake (Groesz et al., 2012; Torres & Nowson, 2007). In humans, a similar pattern emerges. Acute severe stressors are linked to appetite suppression, while chronic stress is linked to weight gain (Torres & Nowson, 2007).

A systematic review and meta-analysis of the extant human data (fifty-four studies) suggests that stress is associated with a small increase in food intake (d = 0.1) – when *all* findings are pooled (Hill et al., 2022). However, pooling here may not be a useful analytic strategy. First, it eliminates individual differences in response to stress that may be considerable (e.g., Stone & Brownell, 1994). Second, it does not account for the intensity of the stressor, nor its chronicity, which the biology suggests will be important (Stammers et al., 2020). Indeed, the meta-analysis revealed significant heterogeneity across studies, with seventeen indicating an appetite-suppressive effect of stress, two no effect, and thirty-five with an appetite-enhancing effect. The presence of palatable food was linked to increased hunger, while the presence of healthy food was linked to a suppressive effect. Gender had no impact, contrary to the widely held view that women are more susceptible to stress-induced eating than men (Hill et al., 2022). In sum, the human data suggest that potent acute stressors will be linked to a reduction in hunger and food intake, while chronicity and availability of palatable food will be associated with enhanced food intake and hunger.

The stress response shares many of the same biological pathways involved in the related emotions of fear (often in response to a stressor) and anxiety (in anticipation of a stressor; Daviu et al., 2019). Anxiety has several distinct clinical manifestations, but its broadest one is generalised anxiety disorder (GAD). The presence of a GAD is associated with heightened rates of fasting in women, persistent thinness in men, and excessive exercise and lower BMI in both men and women (e.g., Thornton et al., 2011). Apart from the association between anxiety disorders and anorexia nervosa, which is well established, generally high levels of anxiety seem to be linked to reduced food intake, and so presumably also to reduced levels of hunger.

Major depressive disorder (MDD), characterised by pervasive low mood, has several variants. The one of interest here is melancholic depression, which occurs in around a quarter of all MDD cases. Melancholic depression is associated with weight loss, lack of interest in food, and reduced hunger (Woelfer et al., 2019). Significant cognitive deficits are also found in melancholic depression, particularly for declarative memory tasks, suggesting hippocampal impairment. Consistent with this are neuroimaging findings that reveal a disconnection between hippocampal and striatal brain areas in melancholic depression, with the greater this disconnection the greater the loss in appetite (Kroemer et al., 2022). What this disconnection seems to imply is that food memories are no longer able to bring to mind representations of their reward value, as reward-processing areas cannot be accessed. Consequently, food no longer looks appealing (i.e., little hunger).

8.5.3 Disgust, Nausea, and Hunger

In 2019, there was considerable media interest in the case of a seventeen-year-old male who had become blind and deaf as a consequence of vitamin deficiency. This had occurred due to his unusual diet, which consisted solely of chips and crisps (R. Harrison et al., 2019). This case is a particularly serious example of avoidant/restrictive food intake disorder

(ARFID). ARFID is prevalent in people with an eating disorder (2–60 per cent), fairly common in non-clinical child/adolescent samples (1–15 per cent), but far less so in adults (0.3 per cent), with more males affected than females (Bourne et al., 2020). Many children and adolescents with ARFID had feeding problems when they were infants. Paediatric feeding disorder (PFD), characterised by serious undernutrition in children <4 years old, is also quite common (4 per cent prevalence), and especially so in those with medical problems and/or developmental delays (Parent et al., 2024). Many children with PFD go on to manifest ARFID, and some 80 per cent of those with ARFID have had a significant medical condition in childhood. This often involves pain, fatigue, or malaise.

ARFID is formally defined as a persistent disruption in feeding, which can cause malnutrition and weight loss and can impair both growth and psychosocial functioning (Bourne et al., 2020). ARFID has three common clinical presentations: (1) a lack of interest in eating; (2) avoidance of food due to its sensory characteristics; and (3) concern about the consequences of eating. Many of the children, adolescents, and adults diagnosed with ARFID have a range of comorbidities, including attention deficit disorder, autism spectrum disorder, and anxiety. A history of abdominal pain, *no* body image concerns, long-standing feeding difficulties, and often a clear origin of the condition because of some external cause (e.g., surgery, drug use) is observed (Bourne et al., 2020). Reading through the case summaries in the Bourne et al. (2020) systematic review, it is apparent that reduced hunger, indifference to food, and food/eating-related nausea and disgust are common problems. Indeed, disgust and nausea towards food have been identified as significant predictors of picky eating, texture intolerance, neophobia, and ARFID (e.g., Harris et al., 2019).

The primary (and often successful) treatment of ARFID (and PFD) involves learning new and more functional behaviours and extinguishing dysfunctional ones. This is not surprising, as the genesis of this condition seems to lie in maladaptive learning outcomes, due to early, unpleasant, and unrewarding feeding experiences (Parent et al., 2024). ARFID has not been explored within the framework of the type of hunger system outlined in Chapter 3. Normally, food-related cues signal that food will be good to eat now. In ARFID they come instead to signal pain, malaise, and discomfort. The broadness of this avoidance – such as in the case of the seventeen-year-old chip-and-crisp-eating adolescent – points to impairments in both specific and general hunger. For specific hunger, because unfamiliar foods are avoided due to heightened neophobia, few rewarding associations (i.e., memories) are then formed between food and its consumption. There are then few cues in the environment to trigger specific hunger.

For general hunger, these cues can be abnormal to start with (e.g., abdominal pain), which may then prevent learning about positive consequences. In addition, the consequences of eating when a typical interoceptive cue (e.g., a stomach rumble) is present can be aversive. In this case, what is learned is that a cue, such as an empty stomach, signals that eating now will be *unrewarding* – that is, it will lead to discomfort and pain. In sum, what is being acquired in ARFID is tantamount to an *anti-hunger*, where cues that normally result in some form of hunger instead result in fear, disgust, and avoidance. While the nature of hunger in ARFID and PFD does not appear to have been well studied, these disorders seem to reflect the consequences of impaired hunger acquisition during development. Indeed, ARFID and PFD may be further grounds to suggest the importance of learning to hunger.

A phenomenon that shares some similarity with the process described earlier for ARFID is the formation of conditioned taste aversions. Normally, specific hungers form when a person learns an association between a particular food and its rewarding immediate and post-ingestive consequences. Later, when the food is seen or smelled (or some other related cue is encountered) this serves to retrieve an episodic memory of the eating experience including its positive affective component – the basis for a specific hunger. For conditioned taste aversions, a target food or drink, and often an unfamiliar one, is followed later by nausea, vomiting, and gastrointestinal discomfort/pain (Chambers, 2018). When the target food is later encountered, it evokes discomfort, nausea, and disgust, ensuring it is not eaten. While there is debate about the exact properties of the negative experience that induces the conditioned taste aversion (cf. Lin et al., 2017; Parker, 2003), the outcome of this form of learning – conditioned taste aversion – can again be regarded as an *anti-hunger*.

Nausea and vomiting are very common during the early part of pregnancy, being experienced by some 70 per cent of women (Fejzo et al., 2019). Severe nausea and vomiting are also quite common (14 per cent), but persistent vomiting, with weight loss, nutritional deficiencies, and the like, as occurs in hyperemesis gravidarum, is unusual, occurring in just one out of a hundred pregnancies. This condition is the leading cause of hospitalisation in women during the first trimester of pregnancy, reflecting its adverse impact on the mother's health. Extended periods of nausea, and frequent vomiting, would be expected to impact on eating behaviour (i.e., conditioned aversions, etc.). Tian et al. (2017) found that nearly half of mothers who had experienced hyperemesis gravidarum underwent significant dietary changes after the pregnancy was complete, suggesting that many foods which had been acceptable no longer were, by virtue of their association with the nausea and vomiting of pregnancy. This can be viewed as a change of multiple specific hungers into disgust-inducing aversions or *anti-hungers.*

8.6 Conclusion

Multiple factors can lead to reduced or absent hunger, but three stand out. The first is stress, which not only occurs as a potentially important factor in the causal pathway of anorexia nervosa, but also, when acute, can reduce desire to eat in most people. While stress in anorexia nervosa may have unusual effects because of genetic predisposition, so that the acute stress state (and hypophagia) may persist, in most people the persistence of stress results in an increase in food intake. The second factor is cytokine-induced malaise. This persistent state of malaise may prevent the retrieval of positive food-related memories into consciousness (i.e., due to the incompatibility of these states) and so inhibit hunger. If sickness persists, and eating is then followed by malaise, new learning will occur due to the unrewarding consequence (i.e., nausea, malaise), further impairing hunger. The third factor concerns the effect of experiencing frequent disgust, nausea, pain, and malaise during early childhood, as in ARFID. Here, the child learns that food and interoceptive cues signal an unrewarding state – the opposite of what is typically learned at this time. The consequence is a highly restrictive diet, and presumably abnormal hunger, again suggesting the importance of learning and memory.

CHAPTER 9

Strong Hunger

9.0 Introduction

This chapter concerns strong hungers. These are examined for in obesity, in neuropsychiatric and endocrine conditions, and for whether drugs or specific diets can generate them. Two caveats apply to this chapter. First, in many instances, weight gain/obesity is used as a *potential* indicator of greater hunger, and an attempt is then made to see if other factors that may drive weight gain are significant (i.e., reduced activity, increased fatigue, reduced basal metabolic rate, and increased satiety/satiation). The aim is to try to isolate any specific role for strong hunger. Second, distinctions are made in this book about types of hunger. While some of these can be discerned in the literature, in many cases the only measure available is self-report hunger. This can make it hard to pin down the precise form a strong hunger may take.

9.1 Obesity

This section considers obesity – its relationship to hunger, the contribution of genes and cognitive impairments to excess hunger, and whether experiences of hunger can be learned or relearned in this population.

An implicit assumption in the title to this section is that obesity is 'one thing'. This is almost certainly not the case (e.g., Rodin, 1981). First, the nature of fat deposition matters, with subcutaneous versus visceral and organ fat each having different impacts (e.g., Piché et al., 2020). Second, there are many potential routes to gaining excess weight, which span the gamut from physiology (e.g., metabolic slowing, gastric emptying rate; Blundell & Cooling, 2000; Ghusn et al., 2024), to psychology (e.g., emotional eating, greater cue reactivity, binge eating; Acosta et al., 2021) and nutrition (e.g., dietary pattern, macronutrient intake; Paradis et al., 2009). Thus, to compare samples of people with and without obesity is potentially fraught. This is because, in all likelihood, the sample of people with obesity will be heterogenous both in the nature of their obesity and in its cause. For these reasons, it is more appropriate to think of 'obesities' (Piché et al., 2020) and to view the literature here, and its ambiguities, as a probable consequence of this heterogeneity.

9.1.1 Hunger in Obesity

For specific hunger, three approaches are relevant. The first concerns self-reports, especially as measured by the Power of Food Scale (PFS; Cappelleri et al., 2009). This asks participants about their desire to consume palatable food when: (1) it is not readily visible but available in the environment (e.g., in a cupboard); (2) when it is present (e.g., visible); and (3) on first tasting. Several studies have examined whether higher scores on the PFS are linked to obesity, as would be expected if greater reactivity (i.e., greater desire/hunger) to food cues (e.g., thinking about or seeing food) is a characteristic of this condition. While some studies do find differences, with the strongest effects for the food available and food present subscales of the PFS (Ribeiro et al., 2018), several find no difference (Espel-Huynh et al., 2018). A further self-report approach is to examine food cravings, which can be considered as intense specific hungers (Potenza & Grilo, 2014). The literature suggests that craving may be more frequent and intense in people with obesity; however, this may only be the case in the subset who have binge-eating disorder (e.g., Reents & Pedersen, 2021; and see later in this chapter for further discussion). In sum, the self-report literature is inconclusive as to whether people with obesity report more intense specific hungers.

A second approach is to examine experimentally the impact of food cue exposure. Most research has looked at the effect of food cues on subsequent food intake, and this was systematically reviewed by Boswell and Kober (2016). In all participants, normal weight and obese, exposure to food cues increased food intake, but this effect is not moderated by body weight. There are other more specialised approaches that do find effects. A few studies have examined the acquisition of cue–food associations. Meyer et al. (2015) found that participants who were obese more rapidly acquired cue–food associations, as indexed by greater salivation to the associated cue. Another study, this time comparing children who were either obese or of normal weight, found greater facial ingestive reactivity in those with obesity, at the prospect of ingesting food (from pictures and smells; Soussignan et al., 2012). While these individual findings are suggestive, the general picture is akin to that for self-report – little if any group difference.

A third approach has been to explore neural reactivity to food cues, by presenting participants of normal weight or obesity with pictures of food, while their brain is imaged. This approach has also produced conflicting reports. One older meta-analysis reported greater activations in brain areas involved in recalling food memories in participants with obesity, after food deprivation (J. Kennedy & Dimitropoulos, 2014). Another more recent meta-analysis, which included several of the same studies, but did not account for deprivation status, observed no differential activations (Morys et al., 2020). All these approaches converge on the same outcome – they are inconclusive – and probably because of the heterogenous nature of obesity.

Turning to general hunger, interoceptive cues have been consistently of interest. Schacter (1968) and Nisbett (1968) suggested reduced usage of internal hunger cues and greater use of external ones by people with obesity, prompting much research (e.g., Rodin, 1981). Early work tended to favour this distinction. Stunkard (1959) reported the relationship between the contractions of an empty stomach and reports of hunger in women who were either obese or of normal weight. He found the women with obesity could not perceive their stomach contractions, suggesting an interoceptive abnormality. However, a later study by Stunkard and Fox (1971), using a larger sample, found that the detection of stomach contractions was as likely in people with obesity as it was in the non-obese controls, suggesting no difference between groups.

Hunger and satiety are also affected by certain physiological parameters connected with the stomach such as its volume and emptying rate (Janssen et al., 2011). However, whether these systematically vary in people with obesity has also been hard to resolve. Some studies found that people with obesity had much larger stomachs, while others have not reached this conclusion (e.g., Geliebter, 2001). Similarly, filling the stomach with fixed amounts of food has been reported to result in little change in reports of hunger or fullness in participants who are obese (e.g., Cornier et al., 2004), but other studies find that it is only certain participants with obesity who report a smaller change (Barkeling et al., 2007).

Other interoceptive differences have also been examined, especially using the heartbeat-counting task that measures the capacity to track one's heartbeat. Using a systematic review and meta-analysis, Robinson et al. (2021) found, for adults with obesity, across all interceptive tasks, a very small but significant interoceptive deficit (Cohens d = 0.1), which was somewhat larger (Cohens d = 0.2) when just considering differences on the heartbeat-counting task. There was no evidence for interoceptive deficits in children with obesity. Overall, the picture that emerges for interoceptive capacity, and in particular interoceptive capacity as it applies to hunger in obesity, is inconclusive.

A smaller set of studies have examined time perception in people with obesity. In the first study, Rodin (1975) found evidence that male participants who were obese experienced time as passing more slowly than normal weight male controls, when there were no other distractions. Gardner et al. (1984) found that people with obesity were more variable in judging short time intervals than normal weight participants, but in their second study on time discrimination this was poorer only in female participants with obesity. In contrast, Nail et al. (1981) using a procedure such as Rodin's (1975) found no evidence for time perception differences in male participants with obesity, but did in females. Most recently, using a large sample of adults with eating disorders, Mennguzzo et al. (2022) found that those with binge-eating disorder – which commonly co-occurs with obesity – also reported that they found time to pass more slowly. So again, as with the interoception data, it is a conflicting picture, with no clear conclusion.

As noted at the start of this section, obesity is a heterogenous condition and so it is unlikely that all its forms would present with the same pattern of impairment. Consistent with this expectation, the research literature presents an inconsistent picture for all the differences explored. Advancing this literature requires finding how to best identify the separate pathways of causation that lead to obesity and making comparisons on this basis.

9.1.1.1 Genes and Hunger

Most of the work in this area, excepting De Castro's, has been a by-product of studying the genetic basis of obesity. Starting with De Castro (e.g., 1999), he had monozygotic and dizygotic twins keep one-week food diaries, which included self-reports of hunger. Reported levels of hunger, both before and after a meal, change in hunger across a meal, and the correlation between pre-meal hunger and subsequent food intake, all had significant heritable components. While such reports of hunger combine many sources of information – including both general and specific hungers – these findings suggest a heritable component to the experience of hunger, although it is not clear what specific form/s this takes.

The study of obesity genetics can be split into that examining typically rare Monogenic causes (and usually with early onset obesity) versus polygenic causes, which reflect the combined impacts of multiple genes (Concepción-Zavaleta et al., 2024). Monogenic causes and their relation to hunger are examined in Section 9.1.1.2. The focus here is on polygenic causes.

An important body of work has emerged from Wardle's behavioural susceptibility model of obesity (e.g., Llewellyn et al., 2023). Wardle's model assumes that appetite (i.e., desire to eat palatable foods) mediates the interaction between the genetic susceptibility to obesity and exposure to an obesogenic environment. Wardle and colleagues conceive of appetite as having two components, responsiveness to food cues (i.e., resembling specific hunger), which was examined in some detail in the first three paragraphs of Section 9.1.1, and sensitivity to internal satiation/satiety signals (i.e., fullness). Across a range of study populations, they explored how successful the cue responsiveness and satiety components were, in their hypothesised mediational role (Llewellyn et al., 2023). Overall, the evidence is more favourable to gene–environment mediation via satiety responsiveness, than by responsiveness to food cues (i.e., specific hunger).

Other relevant findings concern polygenic influences on obesity. Several large-scale studies (with n's in the 100,000s), suggest that around 750+ genetic loci (i.e., a genetic location that may or may not be on a gene) are implicated in obesity, and these involve around 550+ genes (Duis & Butler, 2022; Loos & Yeo, 2022). The individual influence of each loci or gene is generally tiny and, overall, all of those identified so far account for just 6 per cent of the variability in BMI (Loos & Yeo, 2022; Rohde et al., 2019). This is notably discrepant from the known genetic susceptibility to obesity, which is in the order of 40–70 per cent of variability in BMI (Farooqi, 2023). Clearly, much remains to be discovered about its genetic basis.

What is more pertinent here is what this has to say about the causes of obesity, and hunger. Examination of the functions of genes implicated in obesity indicates that they are broad, but with important neural, metabolic, and immune components (e.g., Rohde et al., 2019). Three neural components have been of interest. One is the leptin-melanocortin system, which has an inhibitory effect on hunger when activated by leptin (e.g., Concepción-Zavaleta et al., 2024; Loos & Yeo, 2022). Another is the dopaminergic system, with its role in reward processing (Teixeira et al., 2025). Finally, other brain systems have also emerged as having important links to obesity; notably, the hippocampus and insular (Loos & Yeo, 2022).

Overall, from the perspective of hunger, this would suggest that: (1) genes exert important inhibitory effects on hunger (i.e., via the leptin-melanocortin system); (2) genes impact reward processing, perhaps affecting how desirable food appears, and/or how pleasurable it is to eat; and (3) genes affect brain systems of learning and memory (hippocampus) and interoception (insula).

9.1.1.2 *Monogenic Influences*

There are currently seventy-nine identified syndromes that involve significant abnormalities in body weight that have a genetic basis (Rohde et al., 2019). For many of these syndromes, the specific genetic cause is not known. What has been remarked on in children with these syndromes is the common overlap between learning difficulties and the accumulation of excess body weight (Duis & Butler, 2022). Most of these syndromes are rare, and those about which more is known are summarised in Table 9.1.

Of these conditions, the one studied in most depth is Prader–Willi (PW) syndrome. PW syndrome occurs in around 1 in 15,000 people and is the most common Monogenic cause of obesity (Butler et al., 2019) – see Figure 9.1. While three different genetic causes may contribute to syndrome variability, all result in abnormalities to the same area of chromosome 15 (Kweh et al., 2023). Apart from developing obesity and an insatiable hunger, PW syndrome is associated with significant intellectual impairment, short stature, and hormonal abnormalities, which include most of those involved in food intake regulation, including ghrelin and insulin (e.g., Grootjen et al., 2024; Kweh et al., 2023).

The eating-related problems in PW syndrome go through up to seven developmental stages, although the chronological age when these are reached, and indeed whether they are reached at all, varies between individuals (see Table 9.2). During pregnancy, there is foetal growth restriction, which is followed at birth by difficulty feeding via breast or bottle, a consequence of poor muscle tone and difficulty coordinating sucking and swallowing. These feeding difficulties are severe, with 90 per cent of babies with PW having to be tube fed (McAllister et al., 2011). With maturation, sucking and swallowing improve and the infant gains weight, but metabolic changes that may be linked to a high-fat to low-muscle ratio body result in weight increases that are a precursor for increased interest in food. Whether the intellectual impairments, and resultant developmental delays, impair learning about interoceptive and temporal hunger cues, and more broadly in the acquisition of memories of specific foods (i.e., for specific hunger) has not been examined. It might be expected that this learning would be delayed, if not impaired, as presumably it would be for other learning disorders. This may be one reason for

Table 9.1 *Monogenic causes of obesity*

Syndrome	Features
Angelman syndrome	Abnormality on chromosome 15 with infant feeding problems and increased risk for adult-onset obesity (UBEA3 gene)
Albright hereditary osteodystrophy	Skeletal abnormalities and early onset obesity (GNAS1 gene)
Alstrom syndrome	Ciliopathy with early onset and lifelong obesity, and insulin resistance (ALMS1 gene)
Bardet–Biedl syndrome	Ciliopathy with early onset, lifelong central obesity, and insulin resistance (multiple genes)
Borjeson–Forssman–Lehmann syndrome	Developmental delay and childhood obesity (PHF6 gene)
Carpenter syndrome	Cognitive impairment and mild-to-moderate obesity of face, neck, trunk, forearms, and thighs (RAB23 gene)
Cohen syndrome	Developmental delay, low birthweight, failure to thrive in infancy followed in childhood by central obesity (VPS13B gene)
Cornelia de-Lange syndrome	Behavioural problems and obesity (multiple genes)
CHOPS syndrome	Cognitive impairment and obesity ((AFF4 gene)
Chudley–Lowry syndrome	Mental retardation and mild obesity (ATRX gene)
Fragile X syndrome	Mental retardation, hyperphagia, and often obesity (FMR1 gene)
Kallmann syndrome	Hypogonadism, and obesity (multiple genes)
Kleefstra syndrome	Intellectual disability, childhood obesity (EHMT1 gene, 9q34.3 locus)
Leptin deficiency and mutations to the leptin receptor gene	Resulting in early onset and lifelong obesity
MC4R gene mutations	Commonest monogenetic cause of early-onset childhood obesity and hyperphagia
MORM	Mental retardation and truncal obesity (INPP5E gene)
POMC deficiency	Disrupts leptin-melanocortin system with early onset and lifelong obesity
Rubinstein–Taybi syndrome	Cognitive impairment and obesity (CREBBP, EP300 genes)
Smith–Magenis syndrome	Cognitive impairment and onset of obesity in childhood (17p11.2 locus, Ral1 gene)
SRC1 deficiency	Steroid receptor abnormality linked to excessive appetite and early onset and lifelong obesity
Sh2b1 deficiency	Involved in leptin and insulin signalling with loss linked to early onset and lifelong obesity and insulin resistance
WAGR syndrome	Mental retardation, hyperphagia, and obesity (WT1, PAX6 genes)
White–Sutton syndrome	Intellectual disability and obesity (POGZ gene)
Temple syndrome	Developmental delay, infant feeding difficulties, child onset central obesity (14q32.2 locus)

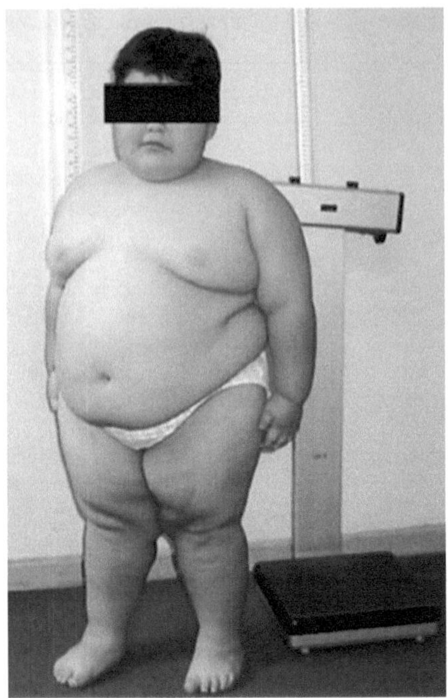

Figure 9.1 An eight-year-old boy with Prader–Willi syndrome.
Source: Cortés, F., Alliende, M. A., Barrios, A., Curotto, B., Santa María, L., Barraza, X., Troncoso, L., Mellado, C., & Pardo, R. (2005). Clinical genetic molecular characterization of 45 Chilean patients with Prader Willi syndrome. Revista Médica de Chile, 133(1), 33–41. https://doi.org/10.4067/S0034-98872005000100005

the linkage between intellectual disability and excess weight gain identified in Table 9.1 (Duis & Butler, 2022).

As the child with PW syndrome continues to grow, their interest in eating and food comes to dominate their thoughts and behaviour. By the time the child is around eight a strict regimen needs to be in place to prevent excess weight gain. This involves two major components. First, strictly time-regulated access to food, with it being available only at mealtimes (i.e., with locked food cupboards, no money to buy food, etc.). Second, careful attention to diet, providing one rich in complex carbohydrates, high in protein, and healthy fats. Without these changes there is progressive and, if unchecked, lethal weight gain (Whitman & Heithaus, 2022).

There has been much interest in the causation of obesity in PW syndrome. It has been suggested that an overarching lens for viewing eating behaviour in PW syndrome is to see it as a 'starvation state', with this initiated by the poor growth of the foetus and infant (Holland et al.,

Table 9.2 *Miller et al.'s (2011) nutrition development phases in people with Prader–Willi syndrome*

Phase	Description
0	Growth restriction during foetal development
1a	In the infant, difficulty breast or bottle feeding, poor appetite, with most being tube fed
1b	In the infant, appetite improves with normal developmental weight gain
2a	Around two years of age, body weight starts to increase more rapidly but without appetite change
2b	Around two years of age, increasing interest in food, but child can still feel full
3	Around eight years of age, insatiable appetite with excess weight gain, with this pattern continuing into adulthood
4	In some adults, insatiable appetite abates

2022). This then sets the stage, alongside presumed neural and hormonal abnormalities, to generate a brain state akin to chronic starvation. There is no doubt that behaviours such as food hoarding, gorging, stealing, and so on, all seen in PW syndrome, are all reminiscent of starving people, but whether there is a deeper link remains unclear.

Two other theoretical perspectives have been advanced (Deweese et al., 2023; McAllister et al., 2011). One suggests that excessive hunger is the driver of obesity, and the other is that weight gain is a consequence of impaired satiety – but noting these are not mutually exclusive (Whitman & Heithaus, 2022). The balance of evidence favours a failure of satiety. First, palatable food cues attract attention in a similar manner in people with PW syndrome as they do in controls. Moreover, there is no neural signature indicative of heightened motivational salience of such cues in PW syndrome (e.g., Deweese et al., 2023). This suggests that when someone with PW syndrome sees a palatable food, their experience of specific hunger may be no different to controls. Second, people with PW syndrome eat longer and want to eat again sooner than controls, suggesting impaired satiation and satiety. They also need to consume around three times as much food to experience the same change in fullness (and reduction in hunger) as controls (McAllister et al., 2011). Third, neuroimaging studies consistently find that when exposed to food images, the most marked abnormalities occur in people with PW when they are sated (e.g., Holsen et al., 2012).

From the perspective of this book, an obvious place to look in terms of impaired satiety is whether there are hippocampal impairments (i.e., relating to memory inhibition). The hippocampus is significantly smaller than in neurotypical controls (e.g., Wu et al., 2022), but so too are other cortical and subcortical structures in PW syndrome. More surprisingly, after a meal, hippocampal activation is significantly *elevated* relative to controls (e.g., Holsen et al., 2012), which is perhaps inconsistent with impaired hippocampal inhibition. In addition, there does not seem to be much long-term memory impairment in PW syndrome (Whitman & Heithaus, 2022), implying intact hippocampal function. This suggests that impaired memory inhibition may not contribute to PW.

Finally, the observation that some individuals with PW syndrome can lose their insatiable hunger implies a certain degree of plasticity, and hence the capacity for experience (i.e., learning and memory) to modify feeding behaviour. Anecdotally, this outcome seems most likely when a rigid and strict dietary regimen is consistently followed from childhood. In sum, impaired satiation and satiety seem to be of key importance in generating excess weight gain in PW syndrome.

9.1.2 Cognitive Impairment, Obesity, and Hunger

Obesity is associated with multiple forms of cognitive impairment, notably in speed of processing, executive function, inhibitory and reward processes, and in learning and memory (e.g., Prickett et al., 2015). The more difficult question is establishing what causes these impairments, namely whether they precede weight gain or are a consequence of it. The evidence suggests that impaired functioning linked to the cerebellum, amygdala, putamen, and nucleus accumbens precedes weight gain, while that to the hippocampus and insula is more a consequence (Weise et al., 2016). The impacts for the hippocampus and insula are relevant for hunger. Impaired hippocampal functioning in humans results in poorer memory inhibition, such that food-related cues are more likely to engender hunger irrespective of the physiological state of the body (e.g., Davidson et al., 2019). Impaired hippocampal functioning has also been associated with blunting of interoceptive changes (i.e., smaller changes in reported hunger/fullness with a meal; e.g., Francis & Stevenson, 2011) and with abnormal time perception (e.g., Richards, 1973). Whether impaired insula function affects interoceptive processing seems probable given this structure's activity (i.e., fMRI) during interoceptive tasks (e.g., Craig, 2002). In sum, neurocognitive impairments associated with obesity probably impact hunger.

9.1.3 Teaching Hunger and Satiety in Obesity

It has been suggested that attending to internal hunger and fullness cues may lead to better weight regulation and reduced energy intake (Palascha et al., 2021a). Four main approaches to achieving these goals have been identified. These are: (1) developing an internally regulated eating style; (2) mindful eating; (3) eating competence (when and how you eat, and what you eat); and (4) appetite awareness training. All four have the same basic theme, namely attending to one's internal state, and utilising this information to consciously regulate eating. Attempts have been made to train people to pay attention to their internal cues, either by using mindfulness manipulations so that they focus on their body (e.g., Ahmadyer et al., 2024; Palascha et al., 2021b; Van der Veer et al., 2016) or by teaching people what a low blood glucose level feels like, and then using this as a hunger cue (e.g., Ciampolini et al., 2013). Although these manipulations have been argued to have beneficial effects on BMI, a recent systematic review found they were ineffective (Grider et al., 2021). A similar picture emerges in the child literature, which again suggests that focussing on internal bodily cues is not associated with better weight outcomes (Beckers et al., 2021). In sum, although there may be certain groups who might benefit from this approach (i.e., regarding the earlier consideration of the heterogeneity of obesity), it does not appear a promising strategy for regulating body weight.

9.2 Neuropsychiatric Conditions That Can Promote Hunger

9.2.1 Bulimia Nervosa

Bulimia (etymology, Greek, for ravenous hunger) nervosa (BN) is characterised by: (1) repeated episodes of binging (i.e., more food eaten in a set time than a typical adult would eat, and there is a sense of having no control over eating); (2) purging following a binge (e.g., vomiting, laxatives, exercise, etc.); and (3) this all occurs in individuals of normal weight. Hunger in response to feeding has been examined in BN and appears abnormal. The abnormality is reflected in both the 'chaotic' nature of hunger reports and their observed feeding patterns.

Judgements of hunger (i.e., as a general rating, and so a composite of specific/general forms) were studied by Halmi and Sunday (1991). Hunger was rated from before, to after, a test meal. In controls it started high before the meal, decreased during eating, and stayed low straight after. In people with BN, hunger dropped in anticipation of feeding, *increased* across the meal, and then *increased* again in the immediate post-meal period (Halmi & Sunday, 1991). For meal patterns, this was studied in a small sample of people with BN who were under observation in an experimental hospital setting, with *ad libitum* access to their preferred foods. Their spontaneous meal patterns were described by the study authors as 'chaotic' (Hetherington et al., 1994). While the average number of meals relative to controls did not differ, there was significantly greater variability in the number of meals that those with BN ate, and the energy intake at each one.

Most research attention has focussed on the triggers for bingeing. There is general agreement that a primary trigger is negative affect – namely emotions such as sadness, anger, anxiety, and loneliness (e.g., Smyth et al., 2007). There are several conceptualisations of how this might generate a binge, with the binge offering an escape from negative affect, a means of reducing negative affect, or of substituting a less negative emotion (e.g., guilt) for a more negative one (e.g., anxiety). In addition to negative affect, two other factors have been identified as important. First, cravings for palatable foods are reportedly more frequent in people with BN (e.g., Meule et al., 2018) and, second, they are also more impulsive. It has been suggested that during a negative affective state, bingeing may be facilitated by the presence of craving and impulsivity (e.g., Leenaerts et al., 2023).

These findings are consistent with a learning-based model of hunger – and indeed learning models have featured prominently in thinking about bingeing (e.g., Jansen, 1998). Negative affect is a common interoceptive hunger cue in healthy people (e.g., Monello & Mayer, 1967), where it becomes associated with eating/food in general. In contrast, in BN, negative affect becomes associated with bingeing. This *may* suggest: (1) increased plasticity in BN for interoceptive hunger cues (i.e., a cue (negative affect) previously associated with food in general being good to eat now, becomes 'replaced' with bingeing on palatable foods will be rewarding now); and (2) abnormal or absent patterns of interoceptive hunger cues prior to BN onset (i.e., during childhood). In addition, chaotic eating patterns suggest the absence of time-based hunger, and more intense/frequent cravings to the development of multiple specific hungers (i.e., from frequent consumption of palatable foods).

9.2.2 Binge-Eating Disorder

As the name binge-eating disorder (BED) implies, there are recurrent binges, but these occur without compensation, and so many people with

BED gain weight, becoming obese (Hilbert, 2019). While there are differences with BN, notably the absence of compensation, there are striking similarities. First, bingeing in people with BED is triggered by negative affect (Kober & Boswell, 2018; Stein et al., 2007). Second, relative to people who are obese without BED, those with BED report more intense food cravings and stronger reactions to food cues, as well as showing poorer cognitive control and greater impulsivity (e.g., Kober & Boswell, 2018; Meule et al., 2018). People with BED are also reported to have very varied meal patterns, and although there have been few studies on their experience of hunger, they do report being hungry, and especially so before a binge (Haedt-Matt & Keel, 2011). The remarks earlier linking BN, hunger, and learning also apply here to bingeing in BED.

9.2.3 Craving and Food Addiction

People can develop a harmful compulsion to engage in particular acts (e.g., gambling), which are termed behavioural addictions. People can also develop harmful compulsions for particular drugs (e.g., opiates), which are termed substance use disorders. It has been suggested that people can also develop food addictions (Schulte & Gearhardt, 2017). However, this is a problematic notion for at least two reasons (Rogers, 2017). First, food is neither a drug with direct action on the brain nor a behaviour, and so it does not fit neatly into current categories of addiction. Second, food is necessary for survival, but addictive drugs and gambling are not. One way round this second problem is to suggest that certain foods, notably those that are designed to be highly palatable (Schulte & Gearhardt, 2017), may be dependence forming, and to conceptualise this in a similar manner to addictive drugs. Presumably then, animals would show dependency if exposed to the type of highly palatable foods that seemingly create problems in people, as they do for addictive drugs. The evidence for this idea is contentious. While mice can develop a dependency-like syndrome for sugar (Wiss et al., 2018), it only occurs under restricted conditions (i.e., limited access to sugar daily for three weeks) and not when available *ad libitum*. There is also no evidence for any dependency-like syndrome for fatty foods (e.g., Hone-Blanchet & Fecteau, 2014). In humans, neuroimaging data are also equivocal, with no compelling evidence that highly palatable foods consistently produce a pattern of anticipatory striatal activity seen with substance use disorders (e.g., Burger & Stice, 2014).

Another place to look for parallels with addiction are cravings, which are important as they have been consistently identified in the maintenance and relapse of problem behaviours such as gambling and in drug use (e.g., Vafaie & Kober, 2022). Craving for high-palatability foods is common in people who consume them (Boswell & Kober, 2016) but note that this is *most people*. Most people do not report cravings for opiates, stimulants, and the like. However, there is some evidence that those who score more highly on the Yale Food Addiction Scale – the main means of determining 'food addiction' – also report more intense cravings than comparable controls (Pursey et al., 2014). While this is suggestive, it is not known if such people also show other addiction-like features, such as excessive preoccupation with high-palatability foods and an incapacity to regulate their consumption. What this does imply though is that some people may experience intense cravings (i.e., specific hungers) for palatable food, but the evidence for food addiction is not so compelling.

9.2.4 Post-Traumatic Stress Disorder

Post-traumatic stress disorder (PTSD) results from exposure to events that are perceived as life-threatening. It has been associated with excess weight gain (Suliman et al., 2016) and it seems that PTSD causes this. The causal pathway from PTSD to excess weight gain involves disordered eating, with bingeing (such as in BN or BED) being the most prevalent type (Murray & Holton, 2021). The strongest evidence for a causal role of PTSD in generating eating-related problems comes from the Millennium Cohort study. This is a longitudinal study of US military personnel, which found that the initial PTSD diagnosis predicted the later occurrence of binge eating (Mitchell et al., 2016). Just as with studies of BN and BED it seems that the driver is negative affect, which may initiate bingeing (Vanzhula et al., 2019). In addition, people with PTSD seem to have diets that feature more high-palatability foods (Kim et al., 2021), which may place them at higher risk for craving (i.e., specific hungers). In sum, PTSD may lead to excess weight gain via binge eating, with this driven by a poorer diet and negative affect.

9.2.5 Depression

Depression affects around 280 million people at any one time. The commonest form is major depressive disorder (MDD), with low mood and anhedonia the core symptoms. The DSM-V identifies six subtypes of MDD, with the melancholic (see Chapter 8) and atypical forms being the commonest – respectively 25–30 per cent and 15–30 per cent. Both increases and decreases in hunger and body weight are encountered in MDD, but this *tends* to be differentiated by subtype. On average, people with the atypical subtype are 2.5 BMI units heavier than those with the melancholic subtype (Silva et al., 2020), and so it is the atypical subtype that is of most interest here (but note that obesity is common in MDD).

Atypical MDD features excessive hunger, dysfunctional eating styles – emotionally and externally cued eating – weight gain, psychomotor slowing, rejection sensitivity, and low mood (Mills et al., 2018). The association between obesity and MDD is particularly strong in the atypical subtype, and longitudinal data indicate that obesity *precedes* its onset (Milaneschi et al., 2019). This would suggest that events prior to the onset of MDD may be responsible for the excessive hunger. Indeed, it has been suggested that atypical depression is a relatively recent condition (Privitera et al., 2013), and one that may result from the obesity epidemic. In this case, the increased hunger in atypical MDD may have a cause linked to obesity (e.g., hippocampal dysfunction and impaired memory inhibition) rather than to depression.

9.2.6 Bipolar Disorder

The core feature of bipolar disorder is the cycling between mania, normal mood, and depression. Psychiatric comorbidity is common, with most people having another psychiatric illness (McIntyre & Calabrese, 2019) – anxiety disorders, drug abuse, personality disorders, and ADHD. So too are medical comorbidities (McIntyre & Calabrese, 2019), including obesity, hypothyroidism, type II diabetes, impaired glycaemic control, and raised levels of leptin and insulin. People with bipolar disorder have almost double the risk of being obese, with 30–40 per cent obese, relative to 20 per cent in controls (e.g., McElroy & Keck, 2012).

The cause of obesity in bipolar has been examined. The medicines used to treat this disorder are linked to weight gain and metabolic syndrome (e.g., atypical antipsychotics, mood stabilisers). Another cause is binge eating, with rates of BED and BN, respectively, 3–5 and 5–7 times higher than in controls (Cuellar-Barboza et al., 2019). Even among those without BED or BN, elevated rates of subclinical binge eating are observed (e.g., Cuellar-Barboza et al., 2019). As with BED and BN populations, impulsivity is also a feature of bipolar disorder (e.g., McElroy & Keck, 2012) alongside a diet rich in high-palatability foods (Koning et al., 2022). Low mood (i.e., negative affect), combined with impulsivity and poor diet, is likely to drive binge eating, just as it does for BN and BED.

In addition to binge eating, two other contributory factors are also present. Although people with bipolar disorder have higher fat mass on average, and so might be expected to have elevated leptin, insulin, and blood glucose, increased levels of all three occur independent of BMI, suggesting pre-existing metabolic abnormalities (Misiak et al., 2022). Relatedly, there is marked circadian dysfunction, with abnormal sleep patterns and irregular meal patterns (Koning et al., 2022). In sum, metabolic abnormalities from both medications and the disorder, dysfunctional time-based hunger, and binge eating, all contribute to the disordered eating and weight gain seen in this condition.

9.2.7 Dementia

There are multiple forms of dementia, with most having some impact on eating. This is especially true in the later stages, when recognition of food, poor coordination, swallowing difficulties (dysphagia), and agitation can all impair feeding (see Table 9.3). The impact on feeding in two dementias has received some study. In both cases, for Alzheimer's disease (AD) and frontotemporal dementia (FTD), eating-related problems are common, can occur early in the disease, and can be difficult for caregivers to manage (Kazui et al., 2016).

In AD, people may develop either hyperphagia or hypophagia (e.g., Keene & Hope, 1998; Shea et al., 2018). Hypophagia seems more common, alongside loss of hunger, with this being reported in over two-thirds of some samples (Keene & Hope, 1998). In contrast, hyperphagia is rarer, occurring in around 18 per cent of people with AD, being more common in men and in Asian samples (Shea et al., 2018). The hyperphagia in AD may have several causes. It could be linked to increased hunger, but both self-report and behavioural measurements of hunger can be difficult (Keene & Hope, 1996). Evidence for a reduction or absence of satiety, with intact hunger, has also been suggested (Keene & Hope, 1996). It may also arise from increased disinhibition, with some forms of AD impacting frontal function more than others (Cipriani et al., 2016). Another suggestion is that hyperphagia is a consequence of greater disease progression, and several studies have noted correlations between hyperphagia and behavioural markers of severity (e.g., more wandering, more unpredictable behaviour, inappropriate body concerns, threats of self-harm, etc.; G. Smith et al., 1998). Finally, it does not appear related to medication use. While hypophagia has been attributed to loss of hunger in AD (Keene & Hope, 1996), hyperphagia may have several causes.

Table 9.3 *Summary of the impacts on ingestive behaviour of different forms of dementia*

Dementia	Impact
Alzheimer's disease	Hypophagia (e.g., forgetting to eat, apathy, not recognising food) more common than hyperphagia; Late-stage dysphagia and eating coordination problems
Frontotemporal dementia (FTD)	
Behavioural variant FTD	Hyperphagia more common than hypophagia; Sweet preference; Late-stage dysphagia and eating coordination problems
Semantic dementia	Loss of interoceptive hunger and satiety cues; Impaired flavour perception
Progressive non-fluent aphasia	Unclear
Vascular dementia	Hypophagia often from dysphagia and eating coordination problems
Huntington's disease	Hypophagia often from dysphagia and eating coordination problems
Lewy body dementia	Hypophagia often from dysphagia and eating coordination problems
Progressive supranuclear palsy	Hypophagia often from dysphagia and eating coordination problems, and hyperphagia (bingeing)

FTD has three forms, but it is only the behavioural variant (bvFTD) that is associated with disordered eating, and especially with hyperphagia and sweet-food preference (Aiello et al., 2016; but note hypophagia has been documented; Cipriani et al., 2016). The cause of hyperphagia in bvFTD is not well understood, but may relate to: (1) increased hunger and decreased satiety; (2) metabolic abnormalities (elevated insulin, leptin, and AgRP; reduced ghrelin and cortisol); (3) abnormal reward processing, with food having a higher than normal expected reward value; and (4) autonomic dysfunction, with changed evaluations of bodily hunger and satiety signals (Aiello et al., 2016). While hyperphagia clearly occurs in bvFTD, its causes remain unclear and may involve increased hunger.

9.2.8 Brain Tumours

Craniopharyngioma (CP) is a type of brain tumour that can invade or press on the hypothalamus, occurring especially in children and older adults (Roth, 2015). When the CP affects the hypothalamus, this can cause changes in body weight. Usually this manifests as obesity (20 per cent at diagnosis), although a smaller percentage can show weight loss (4 per cent at diagnosis – although they tend to later gain weight; Müller, 2016). In the aftermath of surgery or irradiation for treatment, over half of all CP patients become obese. People report being hungrier with a CP (Roemmler-Zehrer et al., 2015) and being hyperphagic (Roth, 2015); however, the evidence suggests that these may not be significant drivers of weight gain and obesity. Food intake as measured by one-week diet diaries completed by carers indicates *lower* food intake (by 20 per cent) relative to that observed in age-matched controls with obesity (Harz et al., 2003). This is *one reason* why traditional weight management techniques – dieting, exercise, pharmaceutical and bariatric interventions – are ineffective in CP (Müller, 2016).

As the tumour invades the hypothalamus, or following surgery/irradiation that damages hypothalamic tissue, patients demonstrate three other significant changes. First, there are disturbances to circadian rhythms, with daytime sleepiness and fatigue, which substantially reduces voluntary energy expenditure. Relative to healthy matched controls with obesity, voluntary movement may be reduced by 30 per cent (Harz et al., 2003). Second, basal metabolic rate (BMR) is also reduced, with lowered heart rate, body temperature, and blood pressure. Damage to the dorsal and dorsomedial hypothalamus is most strongly linked to weight gain, and these structures are particularly involved in regulating BMR (Müller, 2016). Third, there are reductions in post-meal satiety hormones and weaker inhibitory responses in the brain to food cues during satiety (Roth, 2015). In sum, while people with CP may be hungrier, they eat *less*, they are less active, have much reduced BMR, and impaired satiety. This may explain the observed weight gain better than an increase in hunger.

9.2.9 Brain Injury

There are some data suggesting hyperphagia (e.g., Rowell & Faruqui, 2010) and excess food intake (e.g., Henson et al., 1993) following traumatic brain injury (TBI). However, a large cross-sectional US study (n = 7,287) of people who had survived a mild or moderate TBI indicated a far lower rate of overweight/obesity (59 per cent) relative to what would be expected for this demographic (i.e., around 70 per cent). Even when examining for length of post-injury amnesia and acute hospital stay – markers of severity – there was little evidence of any relationship with body weight. Hyperphagia and excess weight gain appear to be rare sequalae of TBI.

9.2.10 Conclusion

This section examined several neuropsychiatric conditions where hyperphagia – and by implication excessive hunger – have been implied or reported. Setting aside brain injury, where the evidence for body weight change is weak, hyperphagia was present to some degree in each study population. Two things are noteworthy. First, learning plays an important role in the genesis of binge eating, which features in BN, BED, PTSD, and bipolar disorder. Whether this is facilitated by abnormal learning of interoceptive hunger cues in childhood or by new learning during illness is not apparent, but it suggests a key role for learning in hunger, even an extreme one such as bingeing. Second, craniopharyngioma, a tumour that can impact hypothalamic function, is strongly linked with obesity, but this seems to be caused not by an increase in hunger, but by reduced satiety, BMR, and activity. This is important, as it suggests that hunger is not a hypothalamic signal per se, but instead one generated by predictive cues whose outcome may be affected by hypothalamic activity.

9.3 Endocrine Disorders

There are four conditions where an endocrine disorder is associated with increasing body weight but noting the uncertainty as to the direction of the causal arrow (Ylli et al., 2022). These are testosterone deficiency in men, polycystic ovarian syndrome in women, Cushing's syndrome (i.e., elevated cortisol), and hypothyroidism. In all cases, it is unclear if changes in body weight result from alterations in hunger or from changes in BMR, satiety, and activity/fatigue. However, what evidence there is suggests that the latter may be more important (e.g., hypothyroidism decreases BMR).

9.4 Drugs and Hunger

Several pharmaceuticals are known to increase body weight in users (see Table 9.4). It is likely that some of these do so by affecting hunger. Three drugs have been used medically, to stimulate hunger (see top of Table 9.4), but their evidence base is sometimes weak (i.e., multiple small studies), and while there have been successes (i.e., HIV/AIDS – Badowski & Perez, 2016), their effectiveness in other domains is either inconclusive (e.g., cancer anorexia – Turcott et al., 2022; AN – Rosager et al., 2021) or unfavourable (e.g., adult hospital patients – Steiner et al., 2023). Typically, these studies focus on body weight as the primary endpoint, with few measuring hunger (e.g., M. E. Harrison et al., 2019; McTavish &

Table 9.4 *Drugs that can increase body weight and may affect hunger*

Type	Drug or class	Effects/comments
Used as hunger stimulants	Cannabinoids	Notably synthetic dronabinol
	Cyproheptadine	Antihistamine, causes weight gain, hunger effects unclear
	Megestrol acetate	Corticosteroid, causes weight gain, shift in preference to fatty foods
Antidepressants	Tricyclics, SSRIs, MAOIs	Most produce 1–5 kg/year weight gain in first year
Antipsychotics	Atypical	Most produce 1–5 kg/year weight gain in first year. Clozapine and olanzapine are 5 kg+/year weight gain in first year and both reduce BMR, affect satiety hormones, increase food intake, along with adverse metabolic consequences
Anticonvulsants	Gabapentin, pregabalin	1–5 kg/year weight gain in first year
	Valproate, carbamazepine	5 kg+/year weight gain in first year, can affect BMR
Mood stabilisers	Lithium	5 kg+/year weight gain in first year, increased thirst, food preference changes, affects hypothalamus
Blood pressure medications	Beta blockers	1–5 kg/year weight gain in first year, reduces BMR and activity levels
	Flunarizine	Calcium channel blocker, up to 4 kg/year weight gain in first year and increases hunger
Diabetic medications	Sulfonylurea	4 kg/year weight gain in first year, hunger stimulant, and reduces BMR
	Thiazolidinediones	1–4 kg/year weight gain in first year, via increased water retention and promotion of fat storage
Others	Other corticosteroids	Prednisolone can cause 10 kg+/year weight gain in around 20 per cent of users, with most increasing in weight
	Antiretrovirals	Obesogenic and alter body fat distribution

Thornton, 2022). None assess the more specific aspects of hunger identified at the start of the book. More generally, while many aspects of the pharmacology of the drugs in Table 9.4 are understood, how they cause changes in body weight or hunger is often not (Ylli et al., 2022). Consequently, it is difficult to know whether any changes in body weight result from an increase in hunger, or from reduced satiation/satiety, greater inactivity (e.g., fatigue), and/or lower basal metabolic rate.

9.5 Diets That May Affect Hunger

Diets that are associated with excess weight gain are those characterised by higher amounts of added sugar, fat, and salt, comprising mainly processed foods (i.e., a Western or ultra-processed food (UPF) diet). These foods tend to be highly palatable, cheap, abundant, and energy dense (Drewnowski, 2004). It is difficult to determine what in a Western diet drives weight gain: is it their high energy density and/or their palatability? There is no doubt that palatability is an important factor (Kringelbach et al., 2012), but how this leads to excess energy intake is another question. One possible route is hunger. Palatable foods are frequently advertised. Exposure to these advertisements could increase the frequency of specific hungers, but only in consumers of this diet (i.e., more adverts hence more bouts of desire to eat the advertised food). In addition, their palatability might make the specific hunger more intense. Hypothetically, more frequent and intense hunger could drive more snacking, and hence generate greater energy intake.

There is also an indirect route by which diet can affect specific hunger. As discussed earlier, hippocampal-dependent processes serve to inhibit rewarding food-related memories when sated. That is, if a person who has just eaten looks at palatable food, they are less likely to find that food desirable because their memory of its rewarding properties is inhibited by hippocampal-dependent processes. This form of memory inhibition has been well studied in animals (e.g., Kanoski & Davidson, 2011). It also seems to operate in humans; however, it is less efficient in people who consume a Western diet, as this diet impairs hippocampal function (Taylor et al., 2021). When a Western diet consumer sees palatable food after a meal, they report feeling greater specific hunger to consume it than a person who eats a more healthful diet (Attuquayefio et al., 2016). Moreover, this effect is strongly related to performance on neuropsychological tests of hippocampal-dependent learning and memory, suggesting it has a hippocampal origin. A more recent study tested the causal role of a Western diet in this effect, finding that exposure to this diet led to greater specific hunger when sated for palatable foods (Stevenson et al., 2020). These findings all suggest that Western diet-induced impairment to hippocampal memory inhibition can cause greater specific hunger for palatable foods.

9.6 Conclusion

Strong hungers may be unusual, and limited to bingeing (observed in BN, BED, PTSD, bipolar disorder), craving for palatable foods (observed in frequent consumers of these foods, 'food addicts', and in BN, BED, PTSD, and bipolar disorder), and genetically determined alterations in the experience of affect (i.e., from recalling an episodic memory of food with its links to brain reward systems). For bingeing, this has long been suspected to involve learning processes (e.g., Jansen, 1998). However, as outlined in Section 9.2, how exactly bingeing develops from the negative affect, which is quite common in interoceptive hunger cue, is unclear. One possible route is dysfunctional acquisition of interoceptive hunger in childhood and/or re-learning the meaning of emotional hunger cues in adulthood. An interesting consideration is whether persistent negative emotional states such as anxiety or depression may make it more difficult to perceive changes in internal bodily states, which may weaken the potential for learning the meaning of these cues in susceptible populations. Equally, the onset of persistent anxiety and depression in adulthood might also serve to mask bodily changes, making it harder to know if one is hungry or sated. In addition, specific hungers (i.e., cravings for high-palatability foods) also seem to be affected in people who binge, irrespective of their diagnostic label. This is often associated with the consumption of a Western/UPF diet, leading to strong cravings for these foods. While the issues listed earlier are all psychological phenomena, it was clear from the polygenic influences on obesity that one biological pathway that may affect hunger is reward processing. As hunger involves activating mental states that have affective components, alterations in affect should impact the meaning of these experiences (i.e., all other things being equal, a food that appears delicious is more likely to be interpreted as meaning 'food will be good to eat now' than a food that just appears edible).

There were also several important examples of weight gain and obesity, which could be attributed to causes other than hunger. Three were notable. First, in Wardle's behavioural susceptibility model, satiety and satiation seem to be more important in mediating the gene–environment link in obesity, than responsiveness to food cues (i.e., akin to specific hunger). More generally, there is little evidence for any general deficit in hunger in samples of people with obesity, but as noted earlier, this may be a consequence of causal heterogeneity in this condition (i.e., multiple types of obesity). A second example concerned Prader–Willi syndrome. Available data suggest that persistent hunger here was a consequence of dysfunctional satiety/satiation processes, rather than hunger being abnormal. A third example is craniopharyngioma, a tumour that affects the hypothalamus and that often results in obesity. In this case, hypothalamic effects driving this weight gain relate to reduced BMR, reduced activity, and increased fatigue, rather than excessive hunger. This last-mentioned case is interesting because it suggests again that the hypothalamus does not cause hunger.

Finally, there was a rather perfunctory section on drugs that may stimulate hunger. This is not to say that drugs cannot do this, it is just to say that the evidence that they do in humans is hard to find. It is relatively straightforward to show that a drug is linked to weight gain. It is less straightforward to explain why, namely whether it impacts basal metabolic rate, activity, satiation/satiety, and so on – and if it does, the extent to which these factors are responsible for weight gain relative to those linked to hunger (and, of course, the type of hunger).

CHAPTER 10

General Discussion

10.0 Introduction

This chapter has two goals. The first is to discuss predictions that arise from the learning and memory model of hunger. The second is to examine some more general problems, identified in the book, that concern hunger and starvation, but fall either on the margins of or outside the model.

10.1 Testing the Learning and Memory Model of Hunger

10.1.1 Development

Relatively few animal or human studies have examined the development of hunger (see Chapter 3). As the learning and memory model suggests that hunger is acquired, this process presumably occurs during childhood. Two key periods may be relevant. The first is during breast or bottle feeding in newborns. This has not been given much attention in the book as it is unclear how important events during breast or bottle feeding are for the development of hunger. It may be that much of the infant feeding process (i.e., breast or bottle feeding) is shaped by a combination of biology in the baby – suckling reflexes, reflexive feedback signals to the brain from the stomach/gut to cease suckling, and generalised distress signals indicating need – alongside psychological processes in the mother. That is her responsiveness and interpretation of infant signals – do they *mean* that the infant needs food, a nappy change, has colic, is teething, is tired, or full?

While views have differed over the importance of these early feeding experiences in the later development of behaviour, and feeding, two things seem clear. One is that significant disruption of infant breast/bottle feeding can be problematic (e.g., a failure to thrive, links to the development of avoidant restrictive food intake disorder). The other is that where the infant feeds and gains weight – in other words, in the typical case –

infant feeding experiences may have little impact on later feeding behaviour. In sum, breast or bottle feeding may not be a major learning occasion for hunger, but rather an interaction between infant biological dispositions and the mother's capacity to learn how to interpret and respond to her baby's needs – in other words, the mother's capacity to learn.

The other period that may be important is weaning. It is during weaning when it seems most likely that learning about specific and general hungers first occur. Weaning is when the infant starts being exposed to a varied range of foods. Thus, infants have the opportunity to learn associations between each food's external cues – its name, appearance, sound, smell, and feel, and its immediate (oro-sensory pleasure vs displeasure) and delayed (pleasant filling vs unpleasant nausea/pain) consequences. These types of association should form the basis for specific hungers. This process description would imply the acquisition of specific hungers for *all* foods that have been sampled individually, and so as these would vary in palatability/post-ingestive consequences, then specific hungers would also vary in their excitatory value (i.e., high-palatability foods and/or those with positive post-ingestive consequences will be the ones with the highest excitatory value). This process of accruing new specific hungers should occur primarily during the childhood years, but would continue throughout the lifespan whenever a new food is encountered.

It is also around the time of weaning that the infant is entrained into a more adult-like feeding pattern, and so the cues that signal mealtimes and snacks start to become available. As the child's ability to communicate improves, parents may also provide information related to time of day and impending feeding events (e.g., lunchtime soon!), as well as feedback on interoceptive cues (i.e., you are irritable, you must be hungry, etc.). With these cues being followed by food of varying sorts, this forms the basis for the acquisition of general hunger.

As this process of learning continues throughout the preschool and early school years, multiple specific hungers should be acquired, alongside a more limited set of general hungers based upon those concentrated on by the caregiver. At least for specific hungers, it is noteworthy that these should closely mirror the child's diet. Put another way, the food the child eats will be the food that makes them specifically hungry, and this presumably applies into adulthood as well. As diets differ in the number of environmental cues they afford (e.g., some foods are heavily advertised), then presumably the frequency of specific hunger must also vary too. Where a diet consists of foods that are heavily marketed – such as those depicted in Figure 10.1 – then specific hunger will be more frequent than

Figure 10.1 Advertisements for palatable foods.

for someone whose food is prepared at home – as cues to these foods are less likely to be encountered in the environment.

Most of the developmental processes described earlier have not been tested. Assuming they are broadly correct, then one would imagine that disrupting them would produce significant abnormalities in the experience of hunger. Three manifestations of this hypothetical disruption are considered here.

The first concerns avoidant and restrictive food intake disorder (see Chapter 8). Seen from the perspective of the learning and memory model of hunger, children with this condition would fail to acquire an adequate number of specific hungers – and possibly general hungers too. Instead, maladaptive hunger learning takes place. One important reason for this is the occurrence of negative reinforcement with feeding events, namely pain, malaise, and nausea, and sometimes relatedly, high levels of fear and anxiety surrounding the eating of new foods. So, if a new food is eaten, it may be accompanied immediately (disgust, displeasure) and/or by delayed (pain, nausea) negative consequences – hence that food does not come to induce a specific hunger but rather a desire to avoid.

Whether and how general hunger may be affected is less clear. If the child had a highly restricted diet, with gastrointestinal disturbance as the cause (e.g., pain or nausea), this would make learning about interoceptive general hunger cues difficult (i.e., pain or nausea are not likely to be very effective *cues* for interoceptive hunger). Similarly, fear and aversion surrounding mealtimes would lead to a negative set of time-based and meal-based cues, where these would come to predict an *unpleasant event* is about to occur – eating. So, one would expect that the normal associative structure of hunger that takes place during development would instead be replaced by one characterised by its opposite – a set of anti-hungers or aversions – excepting the few safe foods that still generate a specific hunger.

The second manifestation of disruption concerns the development of hunger in people with anorexia nervosa (AN). As described in Chapter 8, many people with AN have digestion-related issues during childhood, which may make it harder for them to learn associations between stomach-related cues and hunger. This could rob them of one means of feeling hungry. In addition, as specific hungers are presumed to be the product of first-order Pavlovian conditioning, they should be able to be extinguished. So, if the presence of a specific hunger cue is consistently not followed by rewarding consequences (i.e., anhedonia, fear of weight gain), extinction may occur. In addition, new associations may form between the appearance of food (or its other features), and negative emotions, such as fear or disgust (e.g., disgust at fat content). Consequently, either through a process of extinction and new learning, or of counterconditioning, specific hungers may either be eliminated or turned into specific aversions. If time-based eating is also abandoned (and circadian disruptions in AN have been noted), then all the associative structures that normally generate hunger will have been lost or replaced by responses that motivate avoidance, assisting maladaptive weight-loss goals.

A third form of hypothetical disruption may occur in any individual who is experiencing persistent interoceptive sensation, be it from pain, nausea, malaise, or negative or positive emotions/moods. Persistent hard to ignore background interoceptive sensation (i.e., akin to system noise), *may* make it harder to either learn the meaning of new interoceptive states (i.e., in children) or to detect their presence (i.e., in adults). Thus, where a child is experiencing persistent abdominal discomfort, recognising and learning about hunger, predictive interoceptive states may be difficult. In adults, where these may have already been learned, if there is persistent low mood, pain, and so on, this may make it hard to recognise the occurrence of interoceptive hunger cues.

In sum, little is known about the role of learning and memory processes in the normal development of specific and general hunger, and in conditions where these processes may break down.

10.1.2 Time-Based General Hunger

The animal literature has had an important focus on time-based feeding cues (e.g., work by Stephen Woods, Ralph Mistlberger, etc.). Unfortunately, the same interest has not been focussed on human beings, even though there is plenty of evidence that we make extensive use of time-based feeding cues (i.e., eating occurs in the active part of the circadian phase, eating is often at certain times of day, these times are so common they have names, food intake at each meal increases across the course of a day, hunger/mealtimes are disrupted by jet lag, etc., etc.). In humans it is not known how time-based meal patterns become established (i.e., both in terms of development and mechanism), how resistant they are to change, whether people have reliably different eating patterns (e.g., regular vs irregular), and how these hypothetical patterns might relate to metabolic health, weight gain, and hunger. Mechanistically, Mistlberger has described several potential processes that vary in the extent they involve associative learning, but there seems to have been little exploration of how these might apply to humans.

A final issue concerns the nature of the response to the hunger cue. The almost exclusive focus in this book has been on how environmental or bodily cues can serve as signals, where the response is a mental state of positive anticipation that food will be good to eat now. However, there may be instances where this response is accompanied by an action, or even where the cue results in an action without conscious experience of a mental state of positive anticipation that food will be good to eat now. On the one hand, such instrumental responses are not strictly hunger and so fall outside the realm of this book. On the other hand, such action responses, alone, or accompanying the experience of hunger, may be important determinants of eating. And hypothetically this may be more so for certain types of hunger than for others – some may better support action outcomes rather than psychological states. Time-based cues may be one such example. First, it is a presumption that people get hungrier around scheduled mealtimes, perhaps they do not and instead just seek food. Second, Mistlberger suggests that animals have feeding entrainable clocks, which *may* suggest a system less dependent on acquiring meaning, and more focussed on action.

10.1.3 The Nature of Hunger

In Chapter 3, two claims were made. First, that both specific and general hunger are brief punctate experiences, that can vary in frequency and intensity. Second, that both specific and general hunger cues are excitatory, irrespective of the organism's physiological state. Regarding the first point, as mentioned in Chapter 3 there is some evidence that episodes of hunger are discrete in time, but whether this applies for all hunger cues is not known (e.g., time-based ones). Differences in frequency of hunger seem to be assumed (i.e., more frequent in certain environments, such as a sweet shop), but have not been well explored, while differences in intensity are reflected to some extent in self-report ratings of hunger.

For the second point, exposure to high-palatability foods in those who routinely consume them can generate specific hunger, and eating, even when the person has recently consumed food. For general hunger, insensitivity to physiology is a much more interesting problem. With interoceptive hunger cues, these are usually generated by physiological changes that accompany the late post-digestive phase, and so such cues simply do not occur in the early post-digestive phase. However, it is possible to trick the system, by, for example, using the stomach-rumble illusion described in Chapter 3. This illusion does seem to evoke general hunger and eating irrespective of when the person last ate, suggesting an excitatory hunger cue that is independent of physiological state. For time-based cues, this does not appear to have been explored.

How hunger's excitatory nature is regulated is of major scientific and practical importance (e.g., as a target for weight-loss drugs, etc.), but again much remains to be learned. The nature of memory inhibition processes are not well characterised. For example, it is still unclear if they operate on just food memories akin to the foods just eaten, all food memories, memories of all pleasant things food and non-food, or all memories generally. And there is an interesting parallel with the motivation literature, and the theoretical approaches that generate focussed needs (i.e., thirst, hunger, etc.) versus those that generate general propensities for action (i.e., greater activity). The parallel is the issue of specificity; specificity of memory inhibition (i.e., narrow vs broad), and specificity of motivation (i.e., narrow vs broad). It is unclear as to what dictates this specificity.

A further question concerns how the experience of hunger interacts with other motivational states. As suggested in Chapter 8, the idea of anti-hungers (e.g., nausea, abdominal pain, malaise) implies that these interoceptive states may block the experience of hunger, as too may thirst. Why these experiences *may* be mutually exclusive is not readily apparent, other than they seem to share similar perceived bodily locations. It could though be their mutually exclusive meanings that are important.

10.1.4 Linkage to Biology

The argument in this book is that learning and memory construct a network of associations that link food-related environmental and bodily cues to brain networks that support the experience of hunger, and the processes necessary to satisfy it (i.e., see Figure 2.8). Therefore, looking at the linkages between psychological processes (i.e., learning) and biology is crucial for a complete understanding of hunger. At times the book may have appeared to downplay the importance of brain processes, but of course without a brain there is no learning and memory, and no hunger. Rather the purpose has been to focus on what has not been emphasised enough – namely that hunger depends upon the construction of associations. This section looks at linkages between psychology and biology.

Neuropsychology has been instrumental in highlighting the significance of learning and memory for hunger. The study of Henry Molaison was particularly important, as have been other cases of medial temporal lobe damage. Several questions can be addressed by a neuropsychological approach. First, there are only limited data on how semantic dementia affects the meaning of interoceptive signals. As acquisition of meaning is presumed to occur during development, just as it does for words and for many other things, a loss of meaning should rob interoceptive cues of their capacity to generate hunger. While there is indirect support for this idea, there has been no direct test of this notion in people with semantic dementia, nor more general examination of their interoceptive experiences. Second, time-based hunger cues may also depend on the acquisition of meaning, although they likely involve other processes too. If meaning is important then semantic dementia should also affect the capacity of time-based cues to initiate hunger. Third, any impairment of episodic memory should interfere with specific hungers, but this has not been explored either.

Much of the work linking biological phenomena – brain lesions, genetic linkages, or pharmacological agents – to hunger, has relied almost exclusively on the use of self-report hunger ratings of the form 'how hungry are you now?'. If nothing else, this book should have made clear that hunger is not monolithic, and so testing hunger requires a battery that examines its different parts (see Box 10.1). This would include assessing specific hungers (are they present, how intense, how frequent, do they generate affect and imagery, are they diminished by the intake of food, etc.), and the components of general hunger. For the latter, this would entail determining a person's interoceptive hunger cues (recall these vary – see Chapter 3), as well as time-based hunger cues, responsiveness to such cues, and regularity of eating bouts. Such a battery is likely to yield far greater insights into how pharmacological agents, genetics, and brain injuries affect hunger, because hunger is not one thing.

A key set of findings has been that hormones and metabolites strongly linked to ingestive behaviour (e.g., glucose, ghrelin, insulin) have significant roles in learning and memory (e.g., work of Gold, Kanoski, and Messier). If a cue is followed by positive metabolic consequences, then the association between cue and consequence is an important one to learn, and so the metabolic consequences *themselves* should be the ones most able (i.e., pharmacologically) to facilitate learning. And it seems they often are. Moreover, as learning is argued here to be central to hunger, it is probable that the relationship between hormones/metabolic processes linked to ingestive behaviour, and learning and memory, is even closer and more entwined than currently recognised.

Box 10.1 What a Test Battery for Hunger Might Contain

Box 10.1a Specific Hunger

POSSIBLE MEASURES

1. Questionnaires measuring similar constructs (e.g., power of food scale)
2. Pictures of a range of foods (sweet vs savoury, low to high palatability) with each image evaluated for desire to eat, whether the person can imagine eating it (vividness), frequency of wanting that food, salivation
3. Working for specific food items (e.g., progressive ratio task)
4. Ecological momentary assessment of hunger for particular foods

Box 10.1b General Hunger

POSSIBLE MEASURES

1. Questionnaires measuring interoceptive hunger (e.g., Monello and Mayer scale)
2. Questionnaires measuring time-based hunger (e.g., regularity of meals, food diaries, etc.)
3. Induction of interoceptive states (e.g., playing sound of rumbling stomach and impact on food desire and eating)
4. Ecological momentary assessment of general hunger
5. Examination of behaviour at scheduled mealtimes (e.g., activity)

10.1.5 How Important Is Hunger for Eating?

It might seem odd to tackle this question towards the end of the book, as one might want an answer *before* reading on. However, setting aside that this is a hard question to address, it is better thought about in the light of what is known – in other words – after considering the content of this book. For this reason, the end seemed the best place to address it.

A starting point is to define what 'important' means. It is used here to indicate that hunger is a key, possibly *the* key part, in the momentary computation (i.e., the decision) of whether to eat or not. Two caveats are pertinent to using this definition. One is that to be important does *not* require a strong correlation between an episode of hunger and eating. The second caveat stands in contrast to this. For hunger to be important, episodes of eating must (almost) never occur *without* hunger. For the first caveat, when a person feels hungry, food may be unavailable, they may be on a diet, they may not have time to eat, and so on; indeed there are any number of normal day-to-day events/reasons that can disrupt the correlation between hunger and eating. However, for the second caveat, if eating occurs when there is no specific or general hunger, then this is very problematic, as it would indicate that hunger is not necessary for the decision to eat. This would mean it is not important. As discussed later, there do not seem to be any examples of eating in the absence of hunger (and note that the 'eating in the absence of hunger' task is *not* an example, as the palatable foods presented after eating a meal to satiety just engender specific hungers).

When people report no hunger, they usually do not eat (or eat very little if pushed). One such example is Henry Molaison (HM) who did not appear to experience hunger (see Chapter 3). It is clear from reading Suzanne Corkin's book that were HM not in supported living, he would likely have died from inanition. Although HM had a healthy appetite when food was in front of him (i.e., some spared capacity for specific hunger) and he started eating, in its absence he was just not hungry. HM is not alone in this regard. Many people with restrictive AN also report that they have little or no hunger (see Chapter 8), and they too either eat little or not at all. A further group are the frail elderly, who can also experience little or no hunger, and this too is associated with hypophagia and weight loss (see Chapter 8). Finally, several drugs suppress hunger, and this too is linked to reduced food intake and weight loss (see Chapter 6). When there is little or no hunger, there is also little or no food intake.

There are several examples of the reverse relationship, where hunger is present, and this is associated with eating *if* food is available, and so on. Famines and starvation reflect one extreme example (see Chapter 5). More rigorous examination of the effects of semi-starvation are reported in Keys' and Benedict's studies, indirectly in the CALERIE 2 Study (see Chapter 7), and in people completing weight-loss diets. Hunger is common in all these cases, just as it is in many hunger strikers (see Chapter 6). However, there are reports of people undergoing starvation who do not seem to experience hunger, as well as with certain hunger strikers (respectively, see material on Levanzin in Chapter 7; and the hunger strikers in Chapter 6). Why some people may not experience hunger so intensely relative to others, or indeed not at all under these conditions, is not understood. What is clear though, is that if people are hungry, and if food is available, they will usually eat.

In sum, when people report not being hungry, they do not eat. In contrast, when they report being hungry, they often do. None of this can provide a final answer to the question of importance, as there may be cases of eating in the absence of hunger not currently identified *and* the supporting data are correlational (but see Chapter 3 for a causal induction of hunger). As it currently stands, the evidence suggests that hunger is important in the decision to eat.

10.2 Problems in the Hunger and Starvation Literature

One problem concerns psychological stress, the hypothalamic-pituitary-adrenal (HPA) axis, and its relationship to hunger, and hunger-related behaviours. Stress-related effects were identified in several places throughout the book. In animals and people, starvation is stressful, as is semi-starvation, food insecurity, and the like. It seems that acute stress can reduce food intake (and hunger), something that may be important for understanding AN, where the function of the HPA axis may become abnormal. Chronic stress may have different effects, resulting in enhanced food intake in addition to various metabolic changes relating to blood glucose, insulin, and fat storage. Cumulative stress, where food shortage is just one of many stressors, may contribute to the behavioural changes that accompany food deprivation/starvation, notably an increase in impulsive/immoral behaviour (i.e., where obtaining food becomes the only goal). Whether stress is a major contributory factor to such impulsive behaviour is unclear. Similarly, the role of stress in starvation biology, in AN, and in how chronic stress affects hunger, are also poorly understood. As stress and the HPA axis seem involved in several aspects of hunger and food intake, understanding its biology and impact on behaviour would seem important to study further.

A second issue concerns the preoccupation with food that accompanies hunger, food deprivation, and starvation. Food preoccupation can be seen as an aspect of the learning and memory model. As discussed in Chapter 4, memory inhibition is a consequence of feedback from satiation and satiety processes (see Chapter 3; and the work of Davidson and Parent), which progressively wanes with digestion. If many hours, days, or even weeks pass with no food, then there may be little or no memory inhibition.

Consequently, *any* cue linked to food or eating, however distant, will bring to mind an episodic memory of food. This is probably not the only mechanism at work, and what these other mechanisms are, how they relate to hunger and to changes in the brain and bodily systems, is not understood. As food preoccupation is a characteristic part of deprivation, it would seem important to better understand how it works. Indeed, if a thought of food appeared truly unbidden by an environmental or bodily cue (which would be difficult to establish), this would suggest a brain-based cause for hunger.

A third issue concerns starvation biology. The parallels between changes to human bodily systems during starvation, and the biological changes that accompany hibernation and torpor, are notable. Some scientists have claimed that all mammals have a latent capacity for hibernation/torpor. Understanding how hibernation/torpor relate to starvation biology would seem a key step in testing if this claim is correct. If it is, this would be important, as being able to induce this state in humans might be useful for space flight among other things.

A further observation about starvation, and one present in both small mammals and humans, is that when both the parent and child are food deprived, this has an additional negative impact on child development beyond any injury induced by lack of nutrition. This seems to occur because of the reduction in the quality of the interaction between parent and child, effectively impoverishing the environment. This is likely to be a significant factor in why food supplementation alone may be ineffective at remedying the developmental consequences of a nutritional deficit (see Chapter 5). There has been relatively little study of this, yet with a potential animal model now developed, it may be possible to understand its origins and hence how it might be remediated.

A final issue concerns the bodily signs of starvation and whether these reflect a hard-wired emergency system to drive food seeking. Starvation is accompanied by a broad range of bodily sensations that could occur in any number of life-threatening diseases. These include extreme fatigue, low mood, significant gastrointestinal pain, oedema, chills, and many other unpleasant symptoms (see Chapters 5, 6, and 7). None of these are hard-wired hunger cues because in another context (e.g., in a well-nourished adult), this identical set of symptoms would be interpreted by the sufferer or their medical attendant as some form of serious illness *but not* as starvation. What makes it known as hunger/starvation, apart from the likely preoccupation with food, is the *knowledge* that I am starving, and that it is starvation causing these bodily symptoms. None of these bodily manifestations of starvation reflects inborn hunger signals any more than do physiological manifestations of three hours without food. They only have the meaning they do because people attribute that meaning based on what they know (i.e., I am starving) and have learned (i.e., this means food will be good to eat now).

10.3 General Conclusion

Hunger depends on the establishment of associations between predictive food-related cues in the environment and in the body – and neural feeding systems. Hunger cannot be understood at the level of the brain without taking this psychological perspective into account, as it seems to provide the initial cause. Hunger requires learning because it provides flexibility in how we meet our energy needs. This flexibility is adaptive, as it enables a unique network of hunger associations to be constructed for each unique environment and body.

References

Aaseth, J., Ellefsen, S., Alehagen, U., Sundfør, T. M., & Alexander, J. (2021). Diets and drugs for weight loss and health in obesity – An update. *Biomedicine & Pharmacotherapy*, *140*, 111789.

Abete, I., Parra, M. D., Zulet, M. A., & Martinez, J. A. (2006). Different dietary strategies for weight loss in obesity: Role of energy and macronutrient content. *Nutrition Research Reviews*, *19*, 5–17.

Abizaid, A. (2009). Ghrelin and dopamine: New insights on the peripheral regulation of appetite. *Journal of Neuroendocrinology*, *21*, 787–793.

Accurso, E. C., Ciao, A. C., Fitzsimmons-Craft, E. E., Lock, J. D., & Grange, D. L. (2014). Is weight gain really a catalyst for broader recovery? The impact of weight gain on psychological symptoms in the treatment of adolescent anorexia nervosa. *Behaviour Research & Therapy*, *56*, 1–6.

Acosta, A., Camilleri, M., Abu Dayyeh, B., Calderon, G., Gonzalez, D., McRae, A., Rossini, W., Singh, S., Burton, D., & Clark, M. M. (2021). Selection of antiobesity medications based on phenotypes enhances weight loss: A pragmatic trial in an obesity clinic. *Obesity*, *29*, 662–671.

Adelsberger, L. (1946). Medical observations in Auschwitz concentration camp. *Lancet*, *250*, 317–319.

Ahmadyar, K., Robinson, E., & Tapper, K. (2024). The effect of a mindfulness-based body scan exercise on food intake during TV watching. *Appetite*, *192*, 107131.

Aiello, M., Silani, V., & Rumiati, R. I. (2016). You stole my food! Eating alterations in frontotemporal dementia. *Neurocase*, *22*, 400–409.

Airosus, C., Ardabili, N. G., Hyde, A., & Davidson, T. L. (2025). Short-term effects of liraglutide and semaglutide on weight gain and adiposity by rats fed a Western diet. *Physiology & Behavior*, *298*, 114955.

Alaimo, K., Olson, C. M., & Frongillo, E. A. (2002). Family food insufficiency, but not low family income, is positively associated with dysthymia and suicide symptoms in adolescents. *Journal of Nutrition*, *132*, 719–725.

Ali, S., & Garcia, J. M. (2014). Sarcopenia, cachexia and aging: Diagnosis, mechanisms and therapeutic options – a mini-review. *Gerontology*, *60*, 294–305.

Allen, C., & Nettle, D. (2021). Hunger and socioeconomic background additively predict impulsivity in humans. *Current Psychology*, *40*, 2275–2289.

Amano, K., Hopkinson, J., & Baracos, V. (2022). Psychological symptoms of illness and emotional distress in advanced cancer cachexia. *Current Opinion in Clinical Nutrition & Metabolic Care, 25*, 167–172.

Anderson, J. W., Konz, E. C., Frederich, R. C., & Wood, C. L. (2001). Long-term weight-loss maintenance: A meta-analysis of US studies. *American Journal of Clinical Nutrition, 74*, 579–584.

Andersson, L., & Sundin, E. (2021). Mobile bystanders and rubbernecks, disaster tourists, and helpers: Towards a theoretical framework for critically studying action possibilities at accident sites. *Mobile Media & Communication, 9*, 531–545.

Andrade, J. P., Madeira, M. D., & Paula-Barbosa, M. M. (1995). Effects of long-term malnutrition and rehabilitation on the hippocampal formation of the adult rat: A morphometric study. *Journal of Anatomy, 187*, 379–393.

Annese, J., Schenker-Ahmed, N. M., Bartsch, H., Maechler, P., Sheh, C., Thomas, N., Kayano, J., Ghatan, A., Bresler, N., Frosch, M. P., Klaming, R., & Corkin, S. (2014). Postmortem examination of patient HM's brain based on histological sectioning and digital 3D reconstruction. *Nature Communications, 5*, 3122.

Arnold, D. (1993). Social crisis and epidemic disease in the famines of nineteenth-century India. *Social History of Medicine, 6*, 385–404.

Assanand, S., Pinel, J. P., & Lehman, D. R. (1998). Personal theories of hunger and eating. *Journal of Applied Social Psychology, 28*, 998–1015.

Atkinson, J. W., & McClelland, D. C. (1948). The projective expression of needs; the effect of different intensities of the hunger drive on thematic apperception. *Journal of Experimental Psychology, 38*, 643–658.

Attuquayefio, T., Stevenson, R. J., Boakes, R. A., Oaten, M. J., Yeomans, M. R., Mahmut, M., & Francis, H. M. (2016). A high-fat high-sugar diet predicts poorer hippocampal-related memory and a reduced ability to suppress wanting under satiety. *Journal of Experimental Psychology: Animal Learning and Cognition, 42*, 415–428.

Azevedo, E. P., Ivan, V. J., Friedman, J. M., & Stern, S. A. (2022). Higher-order inputs involved in appetite control. *Biological Psychiatry, 91*, 869–878.

Badowski, M. E., & Perez, S. E. (2016). Clinical utility of dronabinol in the treatment of weight loss associated with HIV and AIDS. *HIV/AIDS, 8*, 37–45.

Bailly, M., Boscaro, A., Pereira, B., Féasson, L., Boirie, Y., Germain, N., Galusca, B., Courteix, D., Thivel, D., & Verney, J. (2021). Is constitutional thinness really different from anorexia nervosa? A systematic review and meta-analysis. *Reviews in Endocrine and Metabolic Disorders, 22*, 913–971.

Baracos, V. E., Martin, L., Korc, M., Guttridge, D. C., & Fearon, K. C. (2018). Cancer-associated cachexia. *Nature Reviews Disease Primers, 4*, 1–18.

Bari, A., & Robbins, T. W. (2013). Inhibition and impulsivity: Behavioral and neural basis of response control. *Progress in Neurobiology, 108*, 44–79.

Barkeling, B., King, N. A., Näslund, E., & Blundell, J. E. (2007). Characterization of obese individuals who claim to detect no relationship between their eating pattern and sensations of hunger or fullness. *International Journal of Obesity*, *31*, 435–439.

Barnard, N. D., Levin, S. M., & Yokoyama, Y. (2015). A systematic review and meta-analysis of changes in body weight in clinical trials of vegetarian diets. *Journal of the Academy of Nutrition and Dietetics*, *115*, 954–969.

Barra, R., Morgan, C., Sáez-Briones, P., Reyes-Parada, M., Burgos, H., Morales, B., & Hernández, A. (2019). Facts and hypotheses about the programming of neuroplastic deficits by prenatal malnutrition. *Nutrition Reviews*, *77*, 65–80.

Batool, R., Butt, M. S., Sultan, M. T., Saeed, F., & Naz, R. (2015). Protein–energy malnutrition: A risk factor for various ailments. *Critical Reviews in Food Science and Nutrition*, *55*, 242–253.

Beckers, D., Karssen, L. T., Vink, J. M., Burk, W. J., & Larsen, J. K. (2021). Food parenting practices and children's weight outcomes: A systematic review of prospective studies. *Appetite*, *158*, 105010.

Benau, E. M., Orloff, N. C., Janke, E. A., Serpell, L., & Timko, C. A. (2014). A systematic review of the effects of experimental fasting on cognition. *Appetite*, *77*, 52–61.

Benedict, F. G. (1915). *A study of prolonged fasting*. Carnegie Institution of Washington.

Benedict, F. G., Miles, W. R., Roth, P., & Smith, H. M. (1919). *Human vitality and efficiency under prolonged restricted diet*. Carnegie Institution of Washington.

Benton, D. (2007). The impact of diet on anti-social, violent and criminal behaviour. *Neuroscience & Biobehavioral Reviews*, *31*, 752–774.

Berntson, G. G., & Khalsa, S. S. (2021). Neural circuits of interoception. *Trends in Neurosciences*, *44*, 17–28.

Berridge, K. C. (1996). Food reward: Brain substrates of wanting and liking. *Neuroscience & Biobehavioral Reviews*, *20*, 1–25.

Berriman, J., Stevenson, R. J., Thayer, Z. C., Thompson, E., Mohamed, A., Watson, J., & Miller, L. (2016). Testing the importance of the medial temporal lobes in human interoception: Does it matter if there is a memory component to the task? *Neuropsychologia*, *91*, 371–379.

Berthoud, H. R. (2004). Mind versus metabolism in the control of food intake and energy balance. *Physiology & Behavior*, *81*, 781–793.

Berthoud, H. R., Münzberg, H., & Morrison, C. D. (2017). Blaming the brain for obesity: Integration of hedonic and homeostatic mechanisms. *Gastroenterology*, *152*, 1728–1738.

Bett, W. R. (1946). Benzedrine sulphate in clinical medicine. *Postgraduate Medical Journal*, *22*, 205.

Bettadapura, S., Dowling, K., Jablon, K., Al-Humadi, A. W., & le Roux, C. W. (2025). Changes in food preferences and ingestive behaviors after glucagon-like peptide-1 analog treatment: Techniques and opportunities. *International Journal of Obesity*, *49*, 418–426.

Bhattacharya, A., Cooper, M., McAdams, C., Peebles, R., & Timko, C. A. (2022). Cultural shifts in the symptoms of anorexia nervosa: The case of orthorexia nervosa. *Appetite, 170*, 105869.

Bindra, D. (1974). A motivational view of learning, performance, and behavior modification. *Psychological Review, 81*(3), 199–213.

Blanco, M. B., Dausmann, K. H., Faherty, S. L., & Yoder, A. D. (2018). Tropical heterothermy is "cool": The expression of daily torpor and hibernation in primates. *Evolutionary Anthropology, 27*, 147–161.

Blundell, J. E., & Cooling, J. (2000). Routes to obesity: Phenotypes, food choices and activity. *British Journal of Nutrition, 83*, S33–S38.

Blundell, J., Finlayson, G., Axelsen, M., Flint, A., Gibbons, C., Kvist, T., & Hjerpsted, J. B. (2017). Effects of once-weekly semaglutide on appetite, energy intake, control of eating, food preference and body weight in subjects with obesity. *Diabetes, Obesity & Metabolism, 19*, 1242–1251.

Blundell, J. E., Finlayson, G., Gibbons, C., Caudwell, P., & Hopkins, M. (2015). The biology of appetite control: Do resting metabolic rate and fat-free mass drive energy intake? *Physiology & Behavior, 152*, 473–478.

Boggiano, M. M., Turan, B., Maldonado, C. R., Oswald, K. D., & Shuman, E. S. (2013). Secretive food concocting in binge eating: Test of a famine hypothesis. *International Journal of Eating Disorders, 46*, 212–225.

Booth, D. A. (2008). Physiological regulation through learnt control of appetites by contingencies among signals from external and internal environments. *Appetite, 51*, 433–441.

Borgna-Pignatti, C., & Zanella, S. (2016). Pica as a manifestation of iron deficiency. *Expert Review of Hematology, 9*, 1075–1080.

Boswell, R. G., & Kober, H. (2016). Food cue reactivity and craving predict eating and weight gain: A meta-analytic review. *Obesity Reviews, 17*, 159–177.

Bourne, L., Bryant-Waugh, R., Cook, J., & Mandy, W. (2020). Avoidant/restrictive food intake disorder: A systematic scoping review of the current literature. *Psychiatry Research, 288*, 112961.

Bousfield, W. A., & Elliott, M. H. (1934). The effect of fasting on the eating-behavior of rats. *Journal of Genetic Psychology, 45*, 227–237.

Brobeck, J. R. (1948). Food intake as a mechanism of temperature regulation. *Yale Journal of Biology and Medicine, 20*, 545–552.

Brožek, J., Guetzkow, H., Baldwin, M. V., & Cranston, R. (1951). A quantitative study of perception and association in experimental semistarvation. *Journal of Personality, 19*, 245–264.

Btaiche, I. F., & Khalidi, N. (2004a). Metabolic complications of parenteral nutrition in adults, part 1. *American Journal of Health Systems Pharmacy, 61*, 1938–1949.

(2004b). Metabolic complications of parenteral nutrition in adults, part 2. *American Journal of Health Systems Pharmacy, 61*, 2050–2057.

Buckner, R. L. (2010). The role of the hippocampus in prediction and imagination. *Annual Review of Psychology, 61*, 27–48.

Bulik, C. M., Carroll, I. M., & Mehler, P. (2021). Reframing anorexia nervosa as a metabo-psychiatric disorder. *Trends in Endocrinology & Metabolism*, *32*, 752–761.

Burger, K. S., & Stice, E. (2014). Neural responsivity during soft drink intake, anticipation, and advertisement exposure in habitually consuming youth. *Obesity*, *22*, 441–450.

Butler, M. G., Miller, J. L., & Forster, J. L. (2019). Prader-Willi Syndrome – Clinical genetics, diagnosis and treatment approaches: An update. *Current Pediatric Reviews*, *15*, 207–244.

Cabanac, M. (1971). Physiological role of pleasure: A stimulus can feel pleasant or unpleasant depending upon its usefulness as determined by internal signals. *Science*, *173*, 1103–1107.

Cahill, G. F. (2006). Fuel metabolism in starvation. *Annual Review of Nutrition*, *26*, 1–22.

Cahill, G. F., Herrera, M. G., Morgan, A. M., Soeldner, J. S., Steinke, J., Levy, P. L., Reichard, G. A., & Kipnis, D. M. (1966). Hormone-fuel interrelationships during fasting. *Journal of Clinical Investigation*, *45*, 1751–1769.

Callahan, H. S., Cummings, D. E., Pepe, M. S., Breen, P. A., Matthys, C. C., & Weigle, D. S. (2004). Postprandial suppression of plasma ghrelin level is proportional to ingested caloric load but does not predict intermeal interval in humans. *Journal of Clinical Endocrinology & Metabolism*, *89*, 1319–1324.

Cannon, W. B., & Washburn, A. L. (1912). An explanation of hunger. *American Journal of Physiology*, *29*, 441–454.

Cappelleri, J. C., Bushmakin, A. G., Gerber, R. A., Leidy, N. K., Sexton, C. C., Karlsson, J., & Lowe, M. R. (2009). Evaluating the Power of Food Scale in obese subjects and a general sample of individuals: Development and measurement properties. *International Journal of Obesity*, *33*, 913–922.

Carr, K. D. (1996). Feeding, drug abuse, and the sensitization of reward by metabolic need. *Neurochemical Research*, *21*, 1455–1467.

Casanova, N., Beaulieu, K., Finlayson, G., & Hopkins, M. (2019). Metabolic adaptations during negative energy balance and their potential impact on appetite and food intake. *Proceedings of the Nutrition Society*, *78*, 279–289.

Cassidy, R. M., & Tong, Q. (2017). Hunger and satiety gauge reward sensitivity. *Frontiers in Endocrinology*, *8*, 104.

Castonguay, T. W., Applegate, E. A., Upton, D. E., & Stern, J. S. (1983). Hunger and appetite: Old concepts/new distinctions. *Nutrition Reviews*, *41*, 101–110.

Caudwell, P., Finlayson, G., Gibbons, C., Hopkins, M., King, N., Näslund, E., & Blundell, J. E. (2013). Resting metabolic rate is associated with hunger, self-determined meal size, and daily energy intake and may represent a marker for appetite. *American Journal of Clinical Nutrition*, *97*, 7–14.

Cerri, A. P., Bellelli, G., Mazzone, A., Pittella, F., Landi, F., Zambon, A., & Annoni, G. (2015). Sarcopenia and malnutrition in acutely ill hospitalized elderly: Prevalence and outcomes. *Clinical Nutrition*, *34*, 745–751.

Cerri, M., Hitrec, T., Luppi, M., & Amici, R. (2021). Be cool to be far: Exploiting hibernation for space exploration. *Neuroscience & Biobehavioral Reviews, 128*, 218–232.

Chambers, K. C. (2018). Conditioned taste aversions. *World Journal of Otorhinolaryngology – Head and Neck Surgery, 4*, 92–100.

Changizi, M. A., McGehee, R., & Hall, W. G. (2002). Evidence that appetitive responses for dehydration and food-deprivation are learned. *Physiology & Behavior, 75*, 295–304.

Charrat, J. P., Massoubre, C., Germain, N., Gay, A., & Galusca, B. (2023). Systematic review of prospective studies assessing risk factors to predict anorexia nervosa onset. *Journal of Eating Disorders, 11*, 163.

Ciampolini, M., Lovell-Smith, H. D., Kenealy, T., & Bianchi, R. (2013). Hunger can be taught: Hunger recognition regulates eating and improves energy balance. *International Journal of General Medicine, 6*, 465–478.

Cipriani, G., Carlesi, C., Lucetti, C., Danti, S., & Nuti, A. (2016). Eating behaviors and dietary changes in patients with dementia. *American Journal of Alzheimer's Disease and Other Dementias, 31*, 706–716.

Clottes, J. (2016). *What is paleolithic art?* Chicago University Press.

Cofer, C. N., & Appley, M. H. (1964). *Motivation: Theory and research*. Wiley.

Colman, R. J., Anderson, R. M., & Johnson, S. C. (2009). Caloric restriction delays disease onset and mortality in rhesus monkeys. *Science, 325*, 201–204.

Concepción-Zavaleta, M. J., Quiroz-Aldave, J. E., Durand-Vásquez, M. D. C., Gamarra-Osorio, E. R., Valencia de la Cruz, J. D. C., Barrueto-Callirgos, C. M., Puelles-León, S. L., Alvarado-León, E. J., Leiva-Cabrera, F., Zavaleta-Gutiérrez, F. E., Concepción-Urteaga, L. A., & Paz-Ibarra, J. (2024). A comprehensive review of genetic causes of obesity. *World Journal of Pediatrics, 20*, 26–39.

Contreras, R. E., Schriever, S. C., & Pfluger, P. T. (2019). Physiological and epigenetic features of yoyo dieting and weight control. *Frontiers in Genetics, 10*, 458872.

Conway, M. A. (2009). Episodic memories. *Neuropsychologia, 47*, 2305–2313.

Corkin, S. (2013). *Permanent present tense*. Penguin.

Cornier, M. A., Grunwald, G. K., Johnson, S. L., & Bessesen, D. H. (2004). Effects of short-term overfeeding on hunger, satiety, and energy intake in thin and reduced-obese individuals. *Appetite, 43*, 253–259.

Corsello, A., Trovato, C. M., Dipasquale, V., Bolasco, G., Labriola, F., Gottrand, F., Verduci, E., Diamanti, A., & Romano, C. (2023). Refeeding syndrome in pediatric age, an unknown disease: A narrative review. *Journal of Pediatric Gastroenterology and Nutrition, 77*, e75–e83.

Craig, A. D. (2002). How do you feel? Interoception: The sense of the physiological condition of the body. *Nature Reviews Neuroscience, 3*, 655–666.

Craig, W. (1912). Observations on doves learning to drink. *Journal of Animal Behavior, 2*, 273–279.

(1917). Appetites and aversions as constituents of instincts. *Proceedings of the National Academy of Sciences of the United States of America, 3*, 685–688.

Crosby, S. S., Apovian, C. M., & Grodin, M. A. (2007). Hunger strikes, force-feeding, and physicians' responsibilities. *JAMA*, *298*, 563–566.

Crutchfield, P., Pazdernik, V., Hansen, G., Malone, J., & Wagenknecht, M. (2018). Being hungry affects oral size perception. *i-Perception*, *9*, 2041669518777513.

Cuellar-Barboza, A. B., Winham, S. J., Biernacka, J. M., Frye, M. A., & McElroy, S. L. (2019). Clinical phenotype and genetic risk factors for bipolar disorder with binge eating: An update. *Expert Review of Neurotherapeutics*, *19*, 867–879.

Cugini, P., Ventura, M., Ceccotti, P., Cilli, M., Marciano, F., Salandri, A., Di Marzo, A., Fontana, S., Pellegrino, A. M., Vacca, K., & Di Siena, G. (2014). Hunger sensation: A chronobiometric approach to its within-day and intraday recursivity in anorexia nervosa restricting type. *Eating and Weight Disorders: Studies on Anorexia, Bulimia and Obesity*, *3*, 115–123.

Cummings, D. E., Purnell, J. Q., Frayo, R. S., Schmidova, K., Wisse, B. E., & Weigle, D. S. (2001). A preprandial rise in plasma ghrelin levels suggests a role in meal initiation in humans. *Diabetes*, *50*, 1714–1719.

Dailey, M. J., Moran, T. H., Holland, P. C., & Johnson, A. W. (2016). The antagonism of ghrelin alters the appetitive response to learned cues associated with food. *Behavioural Brain Research*, *303*, 191–200.

Davidson, T. L., Jones, S., Roy, M., & Stevenson, R. J. (2019). The cognitive control of eating and body weight: It's more than what you 'think'. *Frontiers in Psychology*, *10*, 62.

Davidson, T. L., Kanoski, S. E., Chan, K., Clegg, D. J., & Benoit, S. C. (2010). Hippocampal lesions impair retention of discriminative responding based on energy state cues. *Behavioral Neuroscience*, *124*, 97–105.

Davidson, T. L., Kanoski, S. E., Walls, E. K., & Jarrard, L. E. (2005). Memory inhibition and energy regulation. *Physiology & Behavior*, *86*, 731–746.

Davies, R. R., Halliday, G. M., Xuereb, J. H., Kril, J. J., & Hodges, J. R. (2009). The neural basis of semantic memory: Evidence from semantic dementia. *Neurobiology of Aging*, *30*, 2043–2052.

Daviu, N., Bruchas, M. R., Moghaddam, B., Sandi, C., & Beyeler, A. (2019). Neurobiological links between stress and anxiety. *Neurobiology of Stress*, *11*, 100191.

de Castro, J. M. (1991). Seasonal rhythms of human nutrient intake and meal pattern. *Physiology & Behavior*, *50*, 243–248.

(1999). Heritability of hunger relationships with food intake in free-living humans. *Physiology & Behavior*, *67*, 249–258.

de Castro, J. M., & Plunkett, S. (2002). A general model of intake regulation. *Neuroscience & Biobehavioral Reviews*, *26*, 581–595.

de Jorge Martinez, C., Rukh, G., Williams, M. J., Gaudio, S., Brooks, S., & Schiöth, H. B. (2022). Genetics of anorexia nervosa: An overview of genome-wide association studies and emerging biological links. *Journal of Genetics and Genomics*, *49*, 1–12.

de Souto Barreto, P., Cesari, M., Morley, J. E., Roberts, S., Landi, F., Cederholm, T., Rolland, Y., Vellas, B., & Fielding, R. (2022). Appetite loss and anorexia of aging in clinical care: An ICFSR task force report. *Journal of Frailty & Aging*, *11*, 129–134.

Deem, J. D., Faber, C. L., & Morton, G. J. (2022). AgRP neurons: Regulators of feeding, energy expenditure, and behavior. *The FEBS Journal*, *289*, 2362–2381.

Dell'Osso, L., Abelli, M., Carpita, B., Pini, S., Castellini, G., Carmassi, C., & Ricca, V. (2016). Historical evolution of the concept of anorexia nervosa and relationships with orthorexia nervosa, autism, and obsessive–compulsive spectrum. *Neuropsychiatric Disease and Treatment*, *12*, 1651–1660.

Deloose, E., Janssen, P., Depoortere, I., & Tack, J. (2012). The migrating motor complex: Control mechanisms and its role in health and disease. *Nature Reviews Gastroenterology & Hepatology*, *9*, 271–285.

Deschaine, S. L., & Leggio, L. (2022). From "hunger hormone" to "it's complicated": Ghrelin beyond feeding control. *Physiology*, *37*, 5–15.

Devos, E., Pandelaere, M., & Kerckhove, A. V. (2022). Does a single consumption imagery event increase food desire? *Appetite*, *168*, 105773.

Deweese, M. M., Roof, E., & Key, A. P. (2023). Food cue reward salience does not explain hyperphagia in adolescents with Prader-Willi syndrome. *Developmental Neuropsychology*, *48*, 335–346.

Di Germanio, C., Di Francesco, A., Bernier, M., & de Cabo, R. (2018). Yo-yo dieting is better than none. *Obesity*, *26*, 1673–1673.

Dikötter, F. (2010). *Mao's Great Famine: The history of China's most devastating catastrophe, 1958–62*. Bloomsbury.

Dinu, M., Abbate, R., Gensini, G. F., Casini, A., & Sofi, F. (2017). Vegetarian, vegan diets and multiple health outcomes: A systematic review with meta-analysis of observational studies. *Critical Reviews in Food Science and Nutrition*, *57*, 3640–3649.

Dirks, R., Armelagos, G. J., Bishop, C. A., Brady, I. A., Brun, T., Copans, J., Doherty, V. S., Fraňková, S., Greene, L. S., Jelliffe, D. B., Kayongo-Male, D., Paque, C., Schusky, E. L., Thomas, R. B., & Turton, D. (1980). Social responses during severe food shortages and famine [and comments and reply]. *Current Anthropology*, *21*, 21–44.

Dismore, L., Sayer, A., & Robinson, S. (2024). Exploring the experience of appetite loss in older age: Insights from a qualitative study. *BMC Geriatrics*, *24*, 117.

Dorard, G., & Mathieu, S. (2021). Vegetarian and omnivorous diets: A cross-sectional study of motivation, eating disorders, and body shape perception. *Appetite*, *156*, 104972.

Drenick, E. J., Swendseid, M. E., Blahd, W. H., & Tuttle, S. G. (1964). Prolonged starvation as treatment for severe obesity. *JAMA*, *187*, 100–105.

Drewnowski, A. (2004). Obesity and the food environment: Dietary energy density and diet costs. *American Journal of Preventive Medicine*, *27*, 154–162.

Duerrschmid, C., He, Y., Wang, C., Li, C., Bournat, J. C., Romere, C., Saha, P. K., Lee, M. E., Phillips, K. J., Jain, M., Jia, P., Zhao, Z., Farias, M., Wu, Q., Milewicz, D. M., Sutton, V. R., Moore, D. D., Butte, N. F., Krashes, M. J., . . . Chopra, A. R. (2017). Asprosin is a centrally acting orexigenic hormone. *Nature Medicine*, *23*, 1444–1453.

Duis, J., & Butler, M. G. (2022). Syndromic and nonsyndromic obesity: Underlying genetic causes in humans. *Advanced Biology*, *6*, e2101154.

Dunn, T. M., & Bratman, S. (2016). On orthorexia nervosa: A review of the literature and proposed diagnostic criteria. *Eating Behaviors*, *21*, 11–17.

Eckert, E. D., Gottesman, I. I., Swigart, S. E., & Casper, R. C. (2018). A 57-year follow-up investigation and review of the Minnesota study on human starvation and its relevance to eating disorders. *Archives of Psychology*, *2*(3).

Edholm, O. G., Adam, J. M., Healy, M. J. R., Wolff, H., Goldsmith, R., & Best, T. W. (1970). Food intake and energy expenditure of army recruits. *British Journal of Nutrition*, *24*, 1091–1107.

Elbaek, C. T., Mitkidis, P., Aarøe, L., & Otterbring, T. (2022). Honestly hungry: Acute hunger does not increase unethical economic behaviour. *Journal of Experimental Social Psychology*, *101*, 104312.

Espel-Huynh, H. M., Muratore, A. F., & Lowe, M. R. (2018). A narrative review of the construct of hedonic hunger and its measurement by the Power of Food Scale. *Obesity Science & Practice*, *4*, 238–249.

Farooqi, S. (2023). Obesity and thinness: Insights from genetics. *Philosophical Transactions of the Royal Society of London. Series B, Biological Sciences*, *378*, 20220205.

Fava, M., Rappe, S. M., West, J., & Herzog, D. B. (1995). Anger attacks in eating disorders. *Psychiatry Research*, *56*, 205–212.

Favaro, A., Rodella, F. C., & Santonastaso, P. (2000). Binge eating and eating attitudes among Nazi concentration camp survivors. *Psychological Medicine*, *30*, 463–466.

Fejzo, M. S., Trovik, J., Grooten, I. J., Sridharan, K., Roseboom, T. J., Vikanes, Å., Painter, R. C., & Mullin, P. M. (2019). Nausea and vomiting of pregnancy and hyperemesis gravidarum. *Nature Reviews Disease Primers*, *5*, 62.

Felson, R. B., Osgood, D. W., Horney, J., & Wiernik, C. (2012). Having a bad month: General versus specific effects of stress on crime. *Journal of Quantitative Criminology*, *28*, 347–363.

Ferrario, C. R., Labouèbe, G., Liu, S., Nieh, E. H., Routh, V. H., Xu, S., & O'Connor, E. C. (2016). Homeostasis meets motivation in the battle to control food intake. *Journal of Neuroscience*, *36*, 11469–11481.

Fessler, D. M. (2002). Pseudoparadoxical impulsivity in restrictive anorexia nervosa: A consequence of the logic of scarcity. *International Journal of Eating Disorders*, *31*, 376–388.

Fichter, M. M., & Pirke, K. M. (1986). Effect of experimental and pathological weight loss upon the hypothalamo-pituitary-adrenal axis. *Psychoneuroendocrinology*, *11*, 295–305.

Fielding, R. A., Landi, F., Smoyer, K. E., Tarasenko, L., & Groarke, J. (2023). Association of anorexia/appetite loss with malnutrition and mortality in older populations: A systematic literature review. *Journal of Cachexia, Sarcopenia and Muscle*, *14*, 706–729.

Fisher, C. M. (1994). Hunger and the temporal lobe. *Neurology*, *44*, 1577.

Flint, A., Gregersen, N. T., Gluud, L. L., Møller, B. K., Raben, A., Tetens, I., Verdich, C., & Astrup, A. (2007). Associations between postprandial insulin and blood glucose responses, appetite sensations and energy intake in normal weight and overweight individuals: A meta-analysis of test meal studies. *British Journal of Nutrition*, *98*, 17–25.

Florant, G. L., & Healy, J. E. (2012). The regulation of food intake in mammalian hibernators: A review. *Journal of Comparative Physiology B*, *182*, 451–467.

Fogel, R. W. (2004). *The escape from hunger and premature death, 1700–2100: Europe, America, and the Third World.* Cambridge University Press.

Foodbank Australia (2024). *Foodbank hunger report 2023*. https://reports.foodbank.org.au/foodbank-hunger-report-2023

Francis, H. M., & Stevenson, R. J. (2011). Higher reported saturated fat and refined sugar intake is associated with reduced hippocampal-dependent memory and sensitivity to interoceptive signals. *Behavioral Neuroscience*, *125*, 943–955.

Frank, G. K. (2021). From desire to dread—a neurocircuitry based model for food avoidance in anorexia nervosa. *Journal of Clinical Medicine*, *10*, 2228.

Franklin, J. C., Schiele, B. C., Brožek, J., & Keys, A. (1948). Observations on human behavior in experimental semistarvation and rehabilitation. *Journal of Clinical Psychology*, *4*, 28–45.

Fraser, K. M., & Holland, P. C. (2019). Occasion setting. *Behavioral Neuroscience*, *133*, 145–175.

Fraser, S., & Nettle, D. (2020). Hunger affects social decisions in a multi-round Public Goods Game but not a single-shot Ultimatum Game. *Adaptive Human Behavior and Physiology*, *6*, 334–355.

Galef, B. G., Jr (1991). A contrarian view of the wisdom of the body as it relates to dietary self-selection. *Psychological Review*, *98*, 218–223.

Gan, J. J., Lin, A., Samimi, M. S., & Mendez, M. F. (2016). Somatic symptom disorder in semantic dementia: The role of alexisomia. *Psychosomatics*, *57*, 598–604.

Garbe, R. (1900). On the voluntary trance of Indian fakirs. *The Monist*, *10*, 481–500.

Gardner, R. M., Reyes, B., Brake, S. J., & Salaz, V. E. (1984). Reproduction and discrimination of time in obese subjects. *Personality and Social Psychology Bulletin*, *10*, 554–563.

Garfinkel, P. E. (1974). Perception of hunger and satiety in anorexia nervosa. *Psychological Medicine*, *4*, 309–315.

Geary, N. (2023). Energy homeostasis from Lavoisier to control theory. *Philosophical Transactions of the Royal Society of London. Series B, Biological Sciences*, *378*, 20220201.

Geliebter, A. (2001). Stomach capacity in obese individuals. *Obesity Research*, *9*, 727–728.

Ghent, L. (1951). The relation of experience to the development of hunger. *Canadian Journal of Psychology / Revue Canadienne de Psychologie*, *5*, 77–81.

Ghusn, W., Cifuentes, L., Anazco, D., Fansa, S., Tama, E., Campos, A., Gala, K., Hurtado, D. M., & Acosta, A. (2024). Cumulative effect of obesity phenotypes on body weight and body mass index. *International Journal of Obesity*, *48*, 884–890.

Gilboa, A., Winocur, G., Rosenbaum, R., Poreh, A., Gao, F., Black, S., Westmacott, R., & Moscovitch, M. (2006). Hippocampal contributions to recollection in retrograde and anterograde amnesia. *Hippocampus*, *16*, 966–980.

Global Hunger Index. (2024). *Global Hunger Index*. www.globalhungerindex.org

González-Rodríguez, P., Füllgrabe, J., & Joseph, B. (2023). The hunger strikes back: An epigenetic memory for autophagy. *Cell Death & Differentiation*, *30*, 1404–1415.

Grantham-McGregor, S., Cheung, Y. B., Cueto, S., Glewwe, P., Richter, L., & Strupp, B. (2007). Developmental potential in the first 5 years for children in developing countries. *The Lancet*, *369*, 60–70.

Green, M. W., Rogers, P. J., & Elliman, N. A. (2000). Dietary restraint and addictive behaviors: The generalizability of Tiffany's cue reactivity model. *International Journal of Eating Disorders*, *27*, 419–427.

Grider, H. S., Douglas, S. M., & Raynor, H. A. (2021). The influence of mindful eating and/or intuitive eating approaches on dietary intake: A systematic review. *Journal of the Academy of Nutrition and Dietetics*, *121*, 709–727.

Grill, H. J., & Hayes, M. R. (2012). Hindbrain neurons as an essential hub in the neuroanatomically distributed control of energy balance. *Cell Metabolism*, *16*, 296–309.

Groesz, L. M., McCoy, S., Carl, J., Saslow, L., Stewart, J., Adler, N., Laraia, B., & Epel, E. (2012). What is eating you? Stress and the drive to eat. *Appetite*, *58*, 717–721.

Grootjen, L. N., Diene, G., Molinas, C., Beauloye, V., Huisman, T. M., Visser, J. A., Delhanty, P. J. D., Kerkhof, G. F., Tauber, M., & Hokken-Koelega, A. C. S. (2024). Longitudinal changes in acylated versus unacylated ghrelin levels may be involved in the underlying mechanisms of the switch in nutritional phases in Prader-Willi syndrome. *Hormone Research in Paediatrics*, *97*, 343–352.

Grove, J. C. R., & Knight, Z. A. (2024). The neurobiology of thirst and salt appetite. *Neuron*, *112*, 3999–4016.

Grover, Z., & Ee, L. C. (2009). Protein energy malnutrition. *Pediatric Clinics*, *56*, 1055–1068.

Gruszka, S. (2022). The diaries of besieged Leningraders (1941–1944): Representations of a mass famine during World War II. *Literature and Medicine*, *40*, 98–120.

Grzybowski, A., & Pawlikowska-Łagód, K. (2023). Izrael Milejkowski and hunger disease study in the Warsaw Ghetto. *Clinics in Dermatology*, *41*, 159–165.

Gudzune, K. A., Doshi, R. S., Mehta, A. K., Chaudhry, Z. W., Jacobs, D. K., Vakil, R. M., Lee, C. J., Bleich, S. N., & Clark, J. M. (2015). Efficacy of commercial weight-loss programs: An updated systematic review. *Annals of Internal Medicine*, *162*, 501–512.

Guetzkow, H. S., & Bowman, P. H. (1946). *Men and hunger: A psychological manual for relief workers*. Brethren Publishing House.

Haedt-Matt, A. A., & Keel, P. K. (2011). Revisiting the affect regulation model of binge eating: A meta-analysis of studies using ecological momentary assessment. *Psychological Bulletin*, *137*, 660–681.

Hall, K. D., & Kahan, S. (2018). Maintenance of lost weight and long-term management of obesity. *Medical Clinics*, *102*, 183–197.

Hall, S. A., Rubin, D. C., Miles, A., Davis, S. W., Wing, E. A., Cabeza, R., & Berntsen, D. (2014). The neural basis of involuntary episodic memories. *Journal of Cognitive Neuroscience*, *26*, 2385–2399.

Hallowell, N., Badger, S., & Lawton, J. (2021). Eating to live or living to eat: The meaning of hunger following gastric surgery. *SSM-Qualitative Research in Health*, *1*, 100005.

Halmi, K. A., & Sunday, S. R. (1991). Temporal patterns of hunger and fullness ratings and related cognitions in anorexia and bulimia. *Appetite*, *16*, 219–237.

Halmi, K. A., Sunday, S., Puglisi, A., & Marchi, P. (1989). Hunger and satiety in anorexia and bulimia nervosa. In L. H. Schneider, S. J. Cooper, & K. A. Halmi (Eds.), *The psychobiology of human eating disorders: Preclinical and clinical perspectives* (pp. 431–445). New York Academy of Sciences.

Hao, Z., Mumphrey, M. B., Morrison, C. D., Münzberg, H., Ye, J., & Berthoud, H. R. (2016). Does gastric bypass surgery change body weight set point? *International Journal of Obesity Supplements*, *6*, S37–S43.

Harris, A. A., Romer, A. L., Hanna, E. K., Keeling, L. A., LaBar, K. S., Sinnott-Armstrong, W., Strauman, T. J., Wagner, H. R., Marcus, M. D., & Zucker, N. L. (2019). The central role of disgust in disorders of food avoidance. *International Journal of Eating Disorders*, *52*, 543–553.

Harris, A., & Wardle, J. (1987). The feeling of hunger. *British Journal of Clinical Psychology*, *26*, 153–154.

Harrison, M. E., Norris, M. L., Robinson, A., Spettigue, W., Morrissey, M., & Isserlin, L. (2019). Use of cyproheptadine to stimulate appetite and body weight gain: A systematic review. *Appetite*, *137*, 62–72.

Harrison, R., Warburton, V., Lux, A., & Atan, D. (2019). Blindness caused by a junk food diet. *Annals of Internal Medicine*, *171*, 859–861.

Harshaw, C. (2008). Alimentary epigenetics: A developmental psychobiological systems view of the perception of hunger, thirst and satiety. *Developmental Review*, *28*, 541–569.

Haruki, Y., & Ogawa, K. (2021). Role of anatomical insular subdivisions in interoception: Interoceptive attention and accuracy have dissociable substrates. *European Journal of Neuroscience, 53*, 2669–2680.

Harz, K. J., Müller, H. L., Waldeck, E., Pudel, V., & Roth, C. (2003). Obesity in patients with craniopharyngioma: Assessment of food intake and movement counts indicating physical activity. *Journal of Clinical Endocrinology and Metabolism, 88*, 5227–5231.

Haushofer, J., & Fehr, E. (2014). On the psychology of poverty. *Science, 344*, 862–867.

Häusser, J. A., Stahlecker, C., Mojzisch, A., Leder, J., Van Lange, P. A., & Faber, N. S. (2019). Acute hunger does not always undermine prosociality. *Nature Communications, 10*, 4733.

Hebben, N., Corkin, S., Eichenbaum, H., & Shedlack, K. (1985). Diminished ability to interpret and report internal states after bilateral medial temporal resection: Case H.M. *Behavioral Neuroscience, 99*, 1031–1039.

Hebebrand, J., Hildebrandt, T., Schlögl, H., Seitz, J., Denecke, S., Vieira, D., Gradl-Dietsch, G., Peters, T., Antel, J., Lau, D., & Fulton, S. (2022). The role of hypoleptinemia in the psychological and behavioral adaptation to starvation: Implications for anorexia nervosa. *Neuroscience & Biobehavioral Reviews, 141*, 104807.

Heiderstadt, K. M., McLaughlin, R. M., Wright, D. C., Walker, S. E., & Gomez-Sanchez, C. E. (2000). The effect of chronic food and water restriction on open-field behaviour and serum corticosterone levels in rats. *Laboratory Animals, 34*, 20–28.

Henson, M. B., De Castro, J. M., Stringer, A. Y., & Johnson, C. (1993). Food intake by brain-injured humans who are in the chronic phase of recovery. *Brain Injury, 7*, 169–178.

Herman, C. P., & Polivy, J. (1983). A boundary model for the regulation of eating. *Psychiatric Annals, 13*, 918–927.

Herpertz, S., Moll, A., Gizewski, E., Tagay, S., & Senf, W. (2008). Störung des Hunger- und Sättigungsempfindens bei restriktiver Anorexia nervosa [Distortion of hunger and satiation in patients with restrictive anorexia nervosa]. *Psychotherapie, Psychosomatik, medizinische Psychologie, 58*, 409–415.

Hetherington, M. M., Altemus, M., Nelson, M. L., Bernat, A. S., & Gold, P. W. (1994). Eating behavior in bulimia nervosa: Multiple meal analyses. *American Journal of Clinical Nutrition, 60*, 864–873.

Higginson, A. D., McNamara, J. M., & Houston, A. I. (2016). Fatness and fitness: Exposing the logic of evolutionary explanations for obesity. *Proceedings of the Royal Society B: Biological Sciences, 283*, 20152443.

Hilbert, A. (2019). Binge-eating disorder. *Psychiatric Clinics of North America, 42*, 33–43.

Hill, D., Conner, M., Clancy, F., Moss, R., Wilding, S., Bristow, M., & O'Connor, D. B. (2022). Stress and eating behaviours in healthy adults: A systematic review and meta-analysis. *Health Psychology Review, 16*, 280–304.

Hoch, S. J., & Loewenstein, G. F. (1991). Time-inconsistent preferences and consumer self-control. *Journal of Consumer Research, 17*, 492–507.

Holland, A., Manning, K., & Whittington, J. (2022). The paradox of Prader-Willi syndrome revisited: Making sense of the phenotype. *EBioMedicine, 78*, 103952.

Holsen, L. M., Savage, C. R., Martin, L. E., Bruce, A. S., Lepping, R. J., Ko, E., Brooks, W. M., Butler, M. G., Zarcone, J. R., & Goldstein, J. M. (2012). Importance of reward and prefrontal circuitry in hunger and satiety: Prader-Willi syndrome vs simple obesity. *International Journal of Obesity, 36*, 638–647.

Hone-Blanchet, A., & Fecteau, S. (2014). Overlap of food addiction and substance use disorders definitions: Analysis of animal and human studies. *Neuropharmacology, 85*, 81–90.

Hopkins, M., Beaulieu, K., Myers, A., Gibbons, C., & Blundell, J. E. (2017). Mechanisms responsible for homeostatic appetite control: Theoretical advances and practical implications. *Expert Review of Endocrinology & Metabolism, 12*, 401–415.

Hopkins, M., Finlayson, G., Duarte, C., Gibbons, C., Johnstone, A. M., Whybrow, S., Horgan, G. W., Blundell, J. E., & Stubbs, R. J. (2019). Biological and psychological mediators of the relationships between fat mass, fat-free mass and energy intake. *International Journal of Obesity, 43*, 233–242.

Hsu, T. M., Suarez, A. N., & Kanoski, S. E. (2016). Ghrelin: A link between memory and ingestive behavior. *Physiology & Behavior, 162*, 10–17.

Huppert, E., Shaw, A., & Decety, J. (2020). The effect of hunger on children's sharing behavior and fairness preferences. *Journal of Experimental Child Psychology, 192*, 104786.

Imam, M. U., & Ismail, M. (2017). The impact of traditional food and lifestyle behavior on epigenetic burden of chronic disease. *Global Challenges, 1*, 1700043.

Jacquet, P., Schutz, Y., Montani, J. P., & Dulloo, A. (2020). How dieting might make some fatter: Modeling weight cycling toward obesity from a perspective of body composition autoregulation. *International Journal of Obesity, 44*, 1243–1253.

Jansen, A. (1998). A learning model of binge eating: Cue reactivity and cue exposure. *Behaviour Research and Therapy, 36*, 257–272.

Janssen, P., Vanden Berghe, P., Verschueren, S., Lehmann, A., Depoortere, I., & Tack, J. (2011). Review article: The role of gastric motility in the control of food intake. *Alimentary Pharmacology & Therapeutics, 33*, 880–894.

Jenkinson, P. M., Taylor, L., & Laws, K. R. (2018). Self-reported interoceptive deficits in eating disorders: A meta-analysis of studies using the eating disorder inventory. *Journal of Psychosomatic Research, 110*, 38–45.

Jisheng, Y. (2012). *Tombstone: The great Chinese famine, 1958–1962* (J. Guo & S. Mosher, Trans.). Farrar, Straus and Giroux. (Original work published 2008)

Joshi, A., Schott, M., la Fleur, S. E., & Barrot, M. (2022). Role of the striatal dopamine, GABA and opioid systems in mediating feeding and fat intake. *Neuroscience and Biobehavioral Reviews, 139*, 104726.

Kalm, L. M., & Semba, R. D. (2005). They starved so that others be better fed: Remembering Ancel Keys and the Minnesota experiment. *Journal of Nutrition*, *135*, 1347–1352.

Kanoski, S. E., & Davidson, T. L. (2011). Western diet consumption and cognitive impairment: Links to hippocampal dysfunction and obesity. *Physiology & Behavior*, *103*, 59–68.

Kanoski, S. E., & Grill, H. J. (2017). Hippocampus contributions to food intake control: Mnemonic, neuroanatomical, and endocrine mechanisms. *Biological Psychiatry*, *81*, 748–756.

Kant, A. K. (2018). Eating patterns of US adults: Meals, snacks, and time of eating. *Physiology & Behavior*, *193*, 270–278.

Kavanagh, D. J., Andrade, J., & May, J. (2005). Imaginary relish and exquisite torture: The elaborated intrusion theory of desire. *Psychological Review*, *112*, 446–467.

Kay, A. J. (2006). Germany's Staatssekretäre, mass starvation and the meeting of 2 May 1941. *Journal of Contemporary History*, *41*, 685–700.

Kazui, H., Yoshiyama, K., Kanemoto, H., Suzuki, Y., Sato, S., Hashimoto, M., Ikeda, M., Tanaka, H., Hatada, Y., Matsushita, M., Nishio, Y., Mori, E., Tanimukai, S., Komori, K., Yoshida, T., Shimizu, H., Matsumoto, T., Mori, T., Kashibayashi, T., . . . Tanaka, T. (2016). Differences of behavioral and psychological symptoms of dementia in disease severity in four major dementias. *PLoS One*, *11*, e0161092.

Keeler, J., Patsalos, O., Thuret, S., Ehrlich, S., Tchanturia, K., Himmerich, H., & Treasure, J. (2020). Hippocampal volume, function, and related molecular activity in anorexia nervosa: A scoping review. *Expert Review of Clinical Pharmacology*, *13*, 1367–1387.

Keene, J. M., & Hope, T. (1996). The microstructure of eating in people with dementia who are hyperphagic. *International Journal of Geriatric Psychiatry*, *11*, 1041–1049.

Keene, J., & Hope, T. (1998). Natural history of hyperphagia and other eating changes in dementia. *International Journal of Geriatric Psychiatry*, *13*, 700–706.

Kelley, A. E., Baldo, B. A., & Pratt, W. E. (2005). A proposed hypothalamic–thalamic–striatal axis for the integration of energy balance, arousal, and food reward. *Journal of Comparative Neurology*, *493*, 72–85.

Kemps, E., & Tiggemann, M. (2005). Working memory performance and preoccupying thoughts in female dieters: Evidence for a selective central executive impairment. *British Journal of Clinical Psychology*, *44*, 357–366.

(2007). Modality-specific imagery reduces cravings for food: An application of the elaborated intrusion theory of desire to food craving. *Journal of Experimental Psychology: Applied*, *13*, 95–104.

Kennedy, G. C. (1953). The role of depot fat in the hypothalamic control of food intake in the rat. *Proceedings of the Royal Society of London. Series B-Biological Sciences*, *140*, 578–592.

Kennedy, J., & Dimitropoulos, A. (2014). Influence of feeding state on neurofunctional differences between individuals who are obese and normal weight: A meta-analysis of neuroimaging studies. *Appetite*, *75*, 103–109.

Keys, A., Brožek, J., Henschel, A., Mickelsen, O., & Taylor, H. L. (1945). *Experimental starvation in man.* University of Minnesota.

(1950). *The biology of human starvation* (Vol. 2). University of Minnesota Press.

Kim, J. Y. (2021). Optimal diet strategies for weight loss and weight loss maintenance. *Journal of Obesity & Metabolic Syndrome, 30*, 20–31.

Kim, Y., Roberts, A. L., Rimm, E. B., Chibnik, L. B., Tworoger, S. S., Nishimi, K. M., Sumner, J. A., Koenen, K. C., & Kubzansky, L. D. (2021). Posttraumatic stress disorder and changes in diet quality over 20 years among US women. *Psychological Medicine, 51*, 310–319.

Klastrup, C., Frølich, J., Winkler, L. A. D., & Støving, R. K. (2020). Hunger and satiety perception in patients with severe anorexia nervosa. *Eating and Weight Disorders: Studies on Anorexia, Bulimia and Obesity, 25*, 1347–1355.

Klementova, M., Thieme, L., Haluzik, M., Pavlovicova, R., Hill, M., Pelikanova, T., & Kahleova, H. (2019). A plant-based meal increases gastrointestinal hormones and satiety more than an energy-and macronutrient-matched processed-meat meal in T2D, obese, and healthy men: A three-group randomized crossover study. *Nutrients, 11*, 157.

Kober, H., & Boswell, R. G. (2018). Potential psychological & neural mechanisms in binge eating disorder: Implications for treatment. *Clinical Psychology Review, 60*, 32–44.

Kojima, M., & Kangawa, K. (2005). Ghrelin: Structure and function. *Physiological Reviews, 85*, 495–522.

Koliaki, C., Spinos, T., Spinou, M., Brinia, M. E., Mitsopoulou, D., & Katsilambros, N. (2018). Defining the optimal dietary approach for safe, effective and sustainable weight loss in overweight and obese adults. *Healthcare, 6*, 73.

Koning, E., Vorstman, J., McIntyre, R. S., & Brietzke, E. (2022). Characterizing eating behavioral phenotypes in mood disorders: A narrative review. *Psychological Medicine, 52*, 2885–2898.

Kretsch, M. J., Green, M. W., Fong, A. K. H., Elliman, N. A., & Johnson, H. L. (1997). Cognitive effects of a long-term weight reducing diet. *International Journal of Obesity, 21*, 14–21.

Kringelbach, M. L., Stein, A., & van Hartevelt, T. J. (2012). The functional human neuroanatomy of food pleasure cycles. *Physiology & Behavior, 106*, 307–316.

Kroemer, N. B., Opel, N., Teckentrup, V., Li, M., Grotegerd, D., Meinert, S., Lemke, H., Kircher, T., Nenadić, I., Krug, A., Jansen, A., Sommer, J., Steinsträter, O., Small, D. M., Dannlowski, U., & Walter, M. (2022). Functional connectivity of the nucleus accumbens and changes in appetite in patients with depression. *JAMA Psychiatry, 79*, 993–1003.

Kumai, M., Tamai, H., Fujii, S., Nakagawa, T., & Aoki, T. T. (1988). Glucagon secretion in anorexia nervosa. *American Journal of Clinical Nutrition, 47*, 239–242.

Kweh, F. A., Sulsona, C. R., Miller, J. L., & Driscoll, D. J. (2023). Hyperinsulinemia is a probable trigger for weight gain and hyperphagia in individuals with Prader-Willi syndrome. *Obesity Science & Practice*, *9*, 383–394.

Laermans, J., & Depoortere, I. (2016). Chronobesity: Role of the circadian system in the obesity epidemic. *Obesity Reviews*, *17*, 108–125.

Landi, F., Picca, A., Calvani, R., & Marzetti, E. (2017). Anorexia of aging: Assessment and management. *Clinics in Geriatric Medicine*, *33*, 315–323.

Lang, T., & Heasman, M. (2004). *Food wars: The global battle for mouths, minds and markets*. Earthscan.

Larson, J. S., Redden, J. P., & Elder, R. S. (2014). Satiation from sensory simulation: Evaluating foods decreases enjoyment of similar foods. *Journal of Consumer Psychology*, *24*, 188–194.

Larson, L. M., & Yousafzai, A. K. (2017). A meta-analysis of nutrition interventions on mental development of children under-two in low-and middle-income countries. *Maternal & Child Nutrition*, *13*, e12229.

Laus, M. F., Vales, L. D. M. F., Costa, T. M. B., & Almeida, S. S. (2011). Early postnatal protein-calorie malnutrition and cognition: A review of human and animal studies. *International Journal of Environmental Research and Public Health*, *8*, 590–612.

LeBlanc, E. S., Patnode, C. D., Webber, E. M., Redmond, N., Rushkin, M., & O'Connor, E. A. (2018). Behavioral and pharmacotherapy weight loss interventions to prevent obesity-related morbidity and mortality in adults: Updated evidence report and systematic review for the US Preventive Services Task Force. *JAMA*, *320*, 1172–1191.

Leenaerts, N., Vaessen, T., Sunaert, S., Ceccarini, J., & Vrieze, E. (2023). How negative affect does and does not lead to binge eating: The importance of craving and negative urgency in bulimia nervosa. *Journal of Psychopathology and Clinical Science*, *132*, 621–633.

Leibowitz, S. F., & Shor-Posner, G. (1986). Brain serotonin and eating behavior. *Appetite*, *7*, 1–14.

Le Magnen, J. (1981). The metabolic basis of dual periodicity of feeding in rats. *Behavioral and Brain Sciences*, *4*, 561–575.

Lenharo, M. (2023). What scientists are learning about potent new obesity drugs. *Nature*, *618*, 17–18.

Leung, A. K. C., & Hon, K. L. (2019). Pica: A common condition that is commonly missed – an update review. *Current Pediatric Reviews*, *15*, 164–169.

Levin, B. E., Magnan, C., Dunn-Meynell, A., & Le Foll, C. (2011). Metabolic sensing and the brain: Who, what, where, and how?. *Endocrinology*, *152*, 2552–2557.

Levitsky, D. A., Barre, L., Michael, J. J., Zhong, Y., He, Y., Mizia, A., & Kaila, S. (2022). The rise and fall of physiological theories of the control of human eating behavior. *Frontiers in Nutrition*, *9*, 826334.

Levitsky, D. A., & Strupp, B. J. (1995). Malnutrition and the brain: Changing concepts, changing concerns. *Journal of Nutrition*, *125*, 2212S–2220S.

Leyton, G. (1946). Effects of slow starvation. *Lancet*, *2*, 73–79.

Lieberman, H. R., Caruso, C. M., & Niro, P. J. (2008). A double-blind, placebo-controlled test of 2 d of calorie deprivation: Effects on cognition, activity, sleep, and interstitial glucose concentrations. *American Journal of Clinical Nutrition, 88*, 667–676.

Lin, J. Y., Arthurs, J., & Reilly, S. (2017). Conditioned taste aversions: From poisons to pain to drugs of abuse. *Psychonomic Bulletin & Review, 24*, 335–351.

Lipscomb, F. (1945). Medical aspects of Belsen concentration camp. *The Lancet, 246*, 313–315.

Llewellyn, C. H., Kininmonth, A. R., Herle, M., Nas, Z., Smith, A. D., Carnell, S., & Fildes, A. (2023). Behavioural susceptibility theory: The role of appetite in genetic susceptibility to obesity in early life. *Philosophical Transactions of the Royal Society of London. Series B, Biological Sciences, 378*, 20220223.

Llewellyn, C., & Wardle, J. (2015). Behavioral susceptibility to obesity: Gene–environment interplay in the development of weight. *Physiology & Behavior, 152*, 494–501.

Locke, A. E., Kahali, B., Berndt, S. I., Justice, A. E., Pers, T. H., Day, F. R., Powell, C., Vedantam, S., Buchkovich, M. L., Yang, J., Croteau-Chonka, D. C., Esko, T., Fall, T., Ferreira, T., Gustafsson, S., Kutalik, Z., Luan, J., Mägi, R., Randall, J. C., . . . Speliotes, E. K. (2015). Genetic studies of body mass index yield new insights for obesity biology. *Nature, 518*, 197–206.

Loos, R. J. F., & Yeo, G. S. H. (2022). The genetics of obesity: From discovery to biology. *Nature Reviews Genetics, 23*, 120–133.

Lord, G. M., Matarese, G., Howard, J. K., Baker, R. J., Bloom, S. R., & Lechler, R. I. (1998). Leptin modulates the T-cell immune response and reverses starvation-induced immunosuppression. *Nature, 394*, 897–901.

Lowe, M. R., & Butryn, M. L. (2007). Hedonic hunger: A new dimension of appetite? *Physiology & Behavior, 91*, 432–439.

Lowell, B. B. (2019). New neuroscience of homeostasis and drives for food, water, and salt. *The New English Journal of Medicine, 380*, 459–471.

Lykke, M., Hother, A. L., Hansen, C. F., Friis, H., Mølgaard, C., Michaelsen, K. F., Briend, A., Larsen, T., Sangild, P. T., & Thymann, T. (2013). Malnutrition induces gut atrophy and increases hepatic fat infiltration: Studies in a pig model of childhood malnutrition. *American Journal of Translational Research, 5*, 543–544.

Machado, A. M., Guimarães, N. S., Bocardi, V. B., da Silva, T. P. R., do Carmo, A. S., de Menezes, M. C., & Duarte, C. K. (2022). Understanding weight regain after a nutritional weight loss intervention: Systematic review and meta-analysis. *Clinical Nutrition ESPEN, 49*, 138–153.

Machin, A. (2016). Hunger power: The embodied protest of the political hunger strike. *Interface: A Journal on Social Movements, 8*, 157–180.

Maguire, E., Vargha-Khadem, F., & Hassabis, D. (2010). Imagining fictitious and future experiences: Evidence from developmental amnesia. *Neuropsychologia, 48*, 3187–3192.

Maki, N., Nakatani, E., Ojima, T., Nagashima, T., Harada, T., Koike, F., Tosaka, N., Yoshida, H., & Shimada, T. (2019). The cause of anorexia and proportion of its recovery in older adults without underlying disease: Results of a retrospective study. *PLoS One*, *14*, e0224354.

Makimura, H., Mizuno, T. M., & Isoda, F. (2003). Role of glucocorticoids in mediating effects of fasting and diabetes on hypothalamic gene expression. *BMC Physiology*, *3*, 5.

Mars, M., de Graaf, C., de Groot, C. P. G. M., Van Rossum, C. T. M., & Kok, F. J. (2006). Fasting leptin and appetite responses induced by a 44-day 65%-energy-restricted diet. *International Journal of Obesity*, *30*, 122–128.

Mars, M., de Graaf, C., de Groot, L. C., & Kok, F. J. (2005). Decreases in fasting leptin and insulin concentrations after acute energy restriction and subsequent compensation in food intake. *American Journal of Clinical Nutrition*, *81*, 570–577.

Mattes, R. D. (2010). Hunger and thirst: Issues in measurement and prediction of eating and drinking. *Physiology & Behavior*, *100*, 22–32.

Mattison, J. A., Roth, G. S., & Beasley, T. M. (2012). Impact of caloric restriction on health and survival in rhesus monkeys: The NIA study. *Nature*, *489*, 318–321.

Mattson, M. P. (2005). Energy intake, meal frequency, and health: A neurobiological perspective. *Annual Review of Nutrition*, *25*, 237–260.

May, J., Andrade, J., Kavanagh, D. J. & Hetherington, M. (2012). Elaborated intrusion theory: A cognitive-emotional theory of food craving. *Current Obesity Reports*, *1*, 114–121.

Mayer, J. (1953). Glucostatic mechanism of regulation of food intake. *New England Journal of Medicine*, *249*, 13–16.

McAllister, C. J., Whittington, J. E., & Holland, A. J. (2011). Development of the eating behaviour in Prader-Willi syndrome: Advances in our understanding. *International Journal of Obesity*, *35*, 188–197.

McCormick, C., Ciarameli, E., De Luca, F., & Maguire, E. (2018). Comparing and contrasting the cognitive effects of hippocampal and ventromedial prefrontal cortex damage: A review of human lesion studies. *Neuroscience*, *374*, 295–318.

McCue, M. D. (2010). Starvation physiology: Reviewing the different strategies animals use to survive a common challenge. *Comparative Biochemistry and Physiology Part A: Molecular & Integrative Physiology*, *156*, 1–18.

McCurdy, S. A. (1994). Epidemiology of disaster: The Donner party (1846–1847). *Western Journal of Medicine*, *160*, 338–342.

McElroy, S. L., & Keck, P. E., Jr (2012). Obesity in bipolar disorder: An overview. *Current Psychiatry Reports*, *14*, 650–658.

McEwen, B. S. (2007). Physiology and neurobiology of stress and adaptation: Central role of the brain. *Physiological Reviews*, *87*, 873–904.

McIntyre, R. S., & Calabrese, J. R. (2019). Bipolar depression: The clinical characteristics and unmet needs of a complex disorder. *Current Medical Research and Opinion*, *35*, 1993–2005.

McTavish, D., & Thornton, J. (2022). Appetite stimulants for people with cystic fibrosis. *Cochrane Database of Systematic Reviews, 9*, CD008190.

Medawar, E., Zedler, M., De Biasi, L., Villringer, A., & Witte, A. V. (2023). Effects of single plant-based vs. animal-based meals on satiety and mood in real-world smartphone-embedded studies. *NPJ Science of Food, 7*, 1–19.

Mellinkoff, S. M., Frankland, M., Boyle, D., & Greipel, M. (1956). Relationship between serum amino acid concentration and fluctuations in appetite. *Journal of Applied Physiology, 8*, 535–538.

Menculini, G., Brufani, F., Del Bello, V., Moretti, P., & Tortorella, A. (2019). Circadian rhythms disruptions and eating disorders: Clinical impact and possible psychopathological correlates. *Psychiatria Danubina, 31*, 497–502.

Meneguzzo, P., Mancini, C., Ormitti, A., Bonello, E., & Todisco, P. (2022). Time evaluation and its accuracy in eating disorders: Differences in relation to interoceptive awareness. *Eating and Weight Disorders: Studies on Anorexia, Bulimia and Obesity, 27*, 2551–2560.

Meule, A., Küppers, C., Harms, L., Friederich, H. C., Schmidt, U., Blechert, J., & Brockmeyer, T. (2018). Food cue-induced craving in individuals with bulimia nervosa and binge-eating disorder. *PLoS One, 13*, e0204151.

Meyer, M. D., Risbrough, V. B., Liang, J., & Boutelle, K. N. (2015). Pavlovian conditioning to hedonic food cues in overweight and lean individuals. *Appetite, 87*, 56–61.

Miao, D., Young, S. L., & Golden, C. D. (2015). A meta-analysis of pica and micronutrient status. *American Journal of Human Biology, 27*, 84–93.

Milaneschi, Y., Simmons, W. K., van Rossum, E. F. C., & Penninx, B. W. (2019). Depression and obesity: Evidence of shared biological mechanisms. *Molecular Psychiatry, 24*, 18–33.

Miller, I. (2016). *A history of force feeding: Hunger strikes, prisons and medical ethics, 1909–1974*. Springer Nature.

Mills, J. G., Thomas, S. J., Larkin, T. A., Pai, N. B., & Deng, C. (2018). Problematic eating behaviours, changes in appetite, and weight gain in major depressive disorder: The role of leptin. *Journal of Affective Disorders, 240*, 137–145.

Misiak, B., Kowalski, K., Stańczykiewicz, B., Bartoli, F., Carrà, G., Samochowiec, J., Samochowiec, A., & Frydecka, D. (2022). Appetite-regulating hormones in bipolar disorder: A systematic review and meta-analysis. *Frontiers in Neuroendocrinology, 67*, 101013.

Mistlberger, R. E. (1994). Circadian food-anticipatory activity: Formal models and physiological mechanisms. *Neuroscience & Biobehavioral Reviews, 18*, 171–195.

Mitchell, J. E., & Peterson, C. B. (2020). Anorexia nervosa. *New England Journal of Medicine, 382*, 1343–1351.

Mitchell, K. S., Porter, B., Boyko, E. J., & Field, A. E. (2016). Longitudinal associations among posttraumatic stress disorder, disordered eating, and weight gain in military men and women. *American Journal of Epidemiology, 184*, 33–47.

Mogg, K., Bradley, B. P., Hyare, H., & Lee, S. (1998). Selective attention to food-related stimuli in hunger: Are attentional biases specific to emotional and psychopathological states, or are they also found in normal drive states?. *Behaviour Research and Therapy, 36*, 227–237.

Monello, L. F., & Mayer, J. (1967). Hunger and satiety sensations in men, women, boys, and girls. *American Journal of Clinical Nutrition, 20*, 253–261.

Moody, L., Chen, H., & Pan, Y. X. (2017). Early-life nutritional programming of cognition: The fundamental role of epigenetic mechanisms in mediating the relation between early-life environment and learning and memory process. *Advances in Nutrition, 8*, 337–350.

Morell-Hart, S. (2012). Foodways and resilience under apocalyptic conditions. *Culture, Agriculture, Food and Environment, 34*, 161–171.

Morley, J. E., Thomas, D. R., & Wilson, M. M. G. (2006). Cachexia: Pathophysiology and clinical relevance. *American Journal of Clinical Nutrition, 83*, 735–743.

Morris, J. S., & Dolan, R. J. (2001). Involvement of human amygdala and orbitofrontal cortex in hunger-enhanced memory for food stimuli. *Journal of Neuroscience, 21*, 5304–5310.

Morys, F., García-García, I., & Dagher, A. (2020). Is obesity related to enhanced neural reactivity to visual food cues? A review and meta-analysis. *Social Cognitive and Affective Neuroscience, 18*, nsaa113.

Mrosovsky, N., & Powley, T. L. (1977). Set points for body weight and fat. *Behavioral Biology, 20*, 205–223.

Müller, H. L. (2016). Craniopharyngioma and hypothalamic injury: Latest insights into consequent eating disorders and obesity. *Current Opinion in Endocrinology, Diabetes, and Obesity, 23*, 81–89.

Müller, T. D., Nogueiras, R., Andermann, M. L., Andrews, Z. B., Anker, S. D., Argente, J., Batterham, R. L., Benoit, S. C., Bowers, C. Y., Broglio, F., Casanueva, F. F., D'Alessio, D., Depoortere, I., Geliebter, A., Ghigo, E., Cole, P. A., Cowley, M., Cummings, D. E., Dagher, A., . . . Tschöp, M. H. (2015). Ghrelin. *Molecular Metabolism, 4*, 437–460.

Murray, M., & Vickers, Z. (2009). Consumer views of hunger and fullness: A qualitative approach. *Appetite, 53*, 174–182.

Murray, S. B., Quintana, D. S., Loeb, K. L., Griffiths, S., & Le Grange, D. (2019). Treatment outcomes for anorexia nervosa: A systematic review and meta-analysis of randomized controlled trials. *Psychological Medicine, 49*, 535–544.

Murray, S. L., & Holton, K. F. (2021). Post-traumatic stress disorder may set the neurobiological stage for eating disorders: A focus on glutamatergic dysfunction. *Appetite, 167*, 105599.

Myers, K. P., & Hall, W. G. (2001). Effects of prior experience with dehydration and water on the time course of dehydration-induced drinking in weanling rats. *Developmental Psychobiology, 38*, 145–153.

Nagura, H., Nagura, Y., Fukudo, S., & Sasano, H. (2003). Neuroendocrine-immune interactions and starvation in mucosal immunity and mucosal inflammation. *Acta Histochemica et Cytochemica, 36*, 287–292.

Nail, P., Levy, L., Russin, R., & Crandall, R. (1981). Time estimation and obesity. *Personality and Social Psychology Bulletin, 7*, 139–146.

Nakai, Y., & Koh, T. (2001). Perception of hunger to insulin-induced hypoglycemia in anorexia nervosa. *International Journal of Eating Disorders, 29*, 354–357.

Nakamura, Y., Saldajeno, D. P., Kawaguchi, K., & Kawaoka, S. (2024). Progressive, multi-organ, and multi-layered nature of cancer cachexia. *Cancer Science, 115*, 715–722.

NCD Risk Factor Collaboration. (2024). Worldwide trends in underweight and obesity from 1990 to 2022: A pooled analysis of 3663 population-representative studies with 222 million children, adolescents, and adults. *Lancet, 403*, 1027–1050.

Neel, J. V. (1962). Diabetes mellitus: A 'thrifty' genotype rendered detrimental by 'progress'? *American Journal of Human Genetics, 14*, 353–362.

Nettle, D. (2017). Does hunger contribute to socioeconomic gradients in behavior?. *Frontiers in Psychology, 8*, 229550.

Ng, Q. X., Lee, D. Y. X., Yau, C. E., Han, M. X., Liew, J. J. L., Teoh, S. E., Ong, C., Yaow, C. Y. L., & Chee, K. T. (2024). On orthorexia nervosa: A systematic review of reviews. *Psychopathology, 57*, 1–14.

Niremberski, M. (1946). Psychological investigation of a group of internees at Belsen Camp. *Journal of Mental Science, 92*, 60–74.

Nisbett, R. E. (1968). Determinants of food intake in obesity. *Science, 159*, 1254–1255.

Nonaka, T., Suto, S., Yamakawa, M., Shigenobu, K., & Makimoto, K. (2014). Quantitative evaluation of changes in the clock-watching behavior of a patient with semantic dementia. *American Journal of Alzheimer's Disease & Other Dementias, 29*, 540–547.

Norris, M. L., Harrison, M. E., Isserlin, L., Robinson, A., Feder, S., & Sampson, M. (2016). Gastrointestinal complications associated with anorexia nervosa: A systematic review. *International Journal of Eating Disorders, 49*, 216–237.

Nymo, S., Coutinho, S. R., Eknes, P. H., Vestbostad, I., Rehfeld, J. F., Truby, H., Kulseng, B., & Martins, C. (2018). Investigation of the long-term sustainability of changes in appetite after weight loss. *International Journal of Obesity, 42*, 1489–1499.

Oliveira, L., Calvert, A. L., Green, L., & Myerson, J. (2013). Level of deprivation does not affect degree of discounting in pigeons. *Learning & Behavior, 41*, 148–158.

Orquin, J. L., & Kurzban, R. (2016). A meta-analysis of blood glucose effects on human decision making. *Psychological Bulletin, 142*, 546–567.

Osgood, C. E., Suci, G. J., & Tannenbaum, P. H. (1957). *The measurement of meaning*. University of Illinois Press.

Otterbring, T. (2019). Time orientation mediates the link between hunger and hedonic choices across domains. *Food Research International, 120*, 124–129.

Palascha, A., van Kleef, E., de Vet, E., & van Trijp, H. C. M. (2021a). Internally regulated eating style: A comprehensive theoretical framework. *British Journal of Nutrition, 126*, 138–150.

(2021b). The effect of a brief mindfulness intervention on perception of bodily signals of satiation and hunger. *Appetite*, *164*, 105280.

Papies, E. K., Barsalou, L. W., & Rusz, D. (2020). Understanding desire for food and drink: A grounded-cognition approach. *Current Directions in Psychological Science*, *29*, 193–198.

Papies, E. K., Claassen, M. A., Rusz, D., & Best, M. (2022). Flavors of desire: Cognitive representations of appetitive stimuli and their motivational implications. *Journal of Experimental Psychology: General*, *151*, 1919–1941.

Papies, E. K., van Stekelenburg, A., Smeets, M. A., Zandstra, E. H., & Djksterhuis, G. B. (2022). Situating desire: Situational cues affect desire for food through eating simulations. *Appetite*, *168*, 105679.

Paradis, A. M., Godin, G., Pérusse, L., & Vohl, M. C. (2009). Associations between dietary patterns and obesity phenotypes. *International Journal of Obesity*, *33*, 1419–1426.

Parent, M. B. (2016). Cognitive control of meal onset and meal size: Role of dorsal hippocampal-dependent episodic memory. *Physiology & Behavior*, *162*, 112–119.

Parent, M. B., Whitley, K. E., Zafar, U., Zickgraf, H. F., & Sharp, W. G. (2024). Systematic review of pharmacological treatments that reduce conditioned taste aversions in rodents: A potential animal model of pediatric feeding disorder and avoidant/restrictive food intake disorder (ARFID). *Appetite*, *194*, 107172.

Parker, L. A. (2003). Taste avoidance and taste aversion: Evidence for two different processes. *Animal Learning & Behavior*, *31*, 165–172.

Patel, B. P., Aschenbrenner, K., Shamah, D., & Small, D. M. (2015). Greater perceived ability to form vivid mental images in individuals with high compared to low BMI. *Appetite*, *91*, 185–189.

Peel, M. (1997). Hunger strikes: Understanding the underlying physiology will help doctors provide proper advice. *BMJ*, *315*, 829–830.

Peleg-Raibstein, D., Viskaitis, P., & Burdakov, D. (2023). Eat, seek, rest? An orexin/hypocretin perspective. *Journal of Neuroendocrinology*, *35*, e13259.

Pélissier, L., Bagot, S., Miles-Chan, J. L., Pereira, B., Boirie, Y., Duclos, M., Dulloo, A., Isacco, L., & Thivel, D. (2023). Is dieting a risk for higher weight gain in normal-weight individual? A systematic review and meta-analysis. *British Journal of Nutrition*, *130*, 1190–1212.

Peris-Sampedro, F., Le May, M. V., Stoltenborg, I., Schéle, E., & Dickson, S. L. (2021). A skeleton in the cupboard in ghrelin research: Where are the skinny dwarfs?. *Journal of Neuroendocrinology*, *33*, e13025.

Perkins, J. M., Kim, R., Krishna, A., McGovern, M., Aguayo, V. M., & Subramanian, S. V. (2017). Understanding the association between stunting and child development in low-and middle-income countries: Next steps for research and intervention. *Social Science & Medicine*, *193*, 101–109.

Perreault, L., Kramer, E. S., Smith, P. C., Schmidt, D., & Argyropoulos, C. (2023). A closer look at weight loss interventions in primary care: A systematic review and meta-analysis. *Frontiers in Medicine*, *10*, 1204849.

Piché, M. E., Tchernof, A., & Després, J. P. (2020). Obesity phenotypes, diabetes, and cardiovascular diseases. *Circulation Research, 126*, 1477–1500.

Pickel, L., & Sung, H. K. (2020). Feeding rhythms and the circadian regulation of metabolism. *Frontiers in Nutrition, 7*, 39.

Piech, R. M., Pastorino, M. T., & Zald, D. H. (2010). All I saw was the cake: Hunger effects on attentional capture by visual food cues. *Appetite, 54*, 579–582.

Pollard, C. M., & Booth, S. (2019). Food insecurity and hunger in rich countries – it is time for action against inequality. *International Journal of Environmental Research and Public Health, 16*, 1804.

Pool, E., Brosch, T., Delplanque, S., & Sander, D. (2016). Attentional bias for positive emotional stimuli: A meta-analytic investigation. *Psychological Bulletin, 142*, 79–106.

Potenza, M. N., & Grilo, C. M. (2014). How relevant is food craving to obesity and its treatment? *Frontiers in Psychiatry, 5*, 164.

Prentice, A. M. (2001). Fires of life: The struggles of an ancient metabolism in a modern world. *Nutrition Bulletin, 26*, 13–27.

(2005). Starvation in humans: Evolutionary background and contemporary implications. *Mechanisms of Ageing & Development, 126*, 976–981.

Prickett, C., Brennan, L., & Stolwyk, R. (2015). Examining the relationship between obesity and cognitive function: A systematic literature review. *Obesity Research and Clinical Practice, 9*, 93–113.

Prince, A., Murphy, E. S., & Lupfer, G. (2020). Effects of food restriction and pre-training length on delay discounting in male Wistar rats. *Psychological Record, 70*, 91–98.

Privitera, G. J., Misenheimer, M. L., & Doraiswamy, P. M. (2013). From weight loss to weight gain: Appetite changes in major depressive disorder as a mirror into brain-environment interactions. *Frontiers in Psychology, 4*, 873.

Pursey, K. M., Stanwell, P., Gearhardt, A. N., Collins, C. E., & Burrows, T. L. (2014). The prevalence of food addiction as assessed by the Yale Food Addiction Scale: A systematic review. *Nutrients, 6*, 4552–4590.

Qian, S., Chen, H., Weingarth, D., Trumbauer, M. E., Novi, D. E., Guan, X., Yu, H., Shen, Z., Feng, Y., Frazier, E., Chen, A., Camacho, R. E., Shearman, L. P., Gopal-Truter, S., MacNeil, D. J., Van der Ploeg, L. H. T., & Marsh, D. J. (2002). Neither agouti-related protein nor neuropeptide Y is critically required for the regulation of energy homeostasis in mice. *Molecular and Cellular Biology, 22*, 5027–5035.

Radel, R., & Clément-Guillotin, C. (2012). Evidence of motivational influences in early visual perception: Hunger modulates conscious access. *Psychological Science, 23*, 232–234.

Raghuprasad, M. S., & Manivannan, M. (2019). Volumetric and morphometric analysis of pineal and pituitary glands of an Indian inedial subject. *Annals of Neurosciences, 25*, 279–288.

Ramsay, D. S., & Woods, S. C. (2014). Clarifying the roles of homeostasis and allostasis in physiological regulation. *Psychological Review, 121*, 225–247.

Rao, L. L., Wang, X. T., & Li, S. (2015). Investment choice and perceived mating intentions regulated by external resource cues and internal fluctuation in blood glucose levels. *Frontiers in Psychology*, *5*, 119744.

Reber, A. (1985). *The Penguin dictionary of psychology*. Penguin.

Reents, J., & Pedersen, A. (2021). Differences in food craving in individuals with obesity with and without binge eating disorder. *Frontiers in Psychology*, *12*, 660880.

Reichenberger, J., Richard, A., Smyth, J. M., Fischer, D., Pollatos, O., & Blechert, J. (2018). It's craving time: Time of day effects on momentary hunger and food craving in daily life. *Nutrition*, *55–56*, 15–20.

Ribeiro, G., Camacho, M., Santos, O., Pontes, C., Torres, S., & Oliveira-Maia, A. J. (2018). Association between hedonic hunger and body-mass index versus obesity status. *Scientific Reports*, *8*, 5857.

Rice, D., & Barone Jr, S. (2000). Critical periods of vulnerability for the developing nervous system: Evidence from humans and animal models. *Environmental Health Perspectives*, *108*, 511–533.

Richards, W. (1973). Time reproductions by HM. *Acta Psychologica*, *37*, 279–282.

Robinson, E., Foote, G., Smith, J., Higgs, S., & Jones, A. (2021). Interoception and obesity: A systematic review and meta-analysis of the relationship between interoception and BMI. *International Journal of Obesity*, *45*, 2515–2526.

Rode, E., Rozin, P., & Durlach, P. (2006). Experienced and remembered pleasure for meals: Duration neglect but minimal peak, end (recency) or primary effects. *Appetite*, *49*, 18–29.

Rodin, J. (1975). Causes and consequences of time perception differences in overweight and normal weight people. *Journal of Personality and Social Psychology*, *31*, 898–904.

(1981). Current status of the internal-external hypothesis for obesity: What went wrong?. *American Psychologist*, *36*, 361–372.

Rodrigues, F., Domingos, C., Monteiro, D., & Morouço, P. (2022). A review on aging, sarcopenia, falls, and resistance training in community-dwelling older adults. *International Journal of Environmental Research and Public Health*, *19*, 874.

Roemmler-Zehrer, J., Geigenberger, V., Störmann, S., Ising, M., Pfister, H., Sievers, C., Stalla, G. K., & Schopohl, J. (2015). Specific behaviour, mood and personality traits may contribute to obesity in patients with craniopharyngioma. *Clinical Endocrinology*, *82*, 106–114.

Rogeri, P. S., Zanella Jr, R., Martins, G. L., Garcia, M. D., Leite, G., Lugaresi, R., Gasparini, S. O., Sperandio, G. A., Ferreira, L. H. B., Souza-Junior, T. P., & Lancha Jr, A. H. (2022). Strategies to prevent sarcopenia in the aging process: Role of protein intake and exercise. *Nutrients*, *14*, 52.

Rogers, P. J. (2017). Food and drug addictions: Similarities and differences. *Pharmacology, Biochemistry & Behavior*, *153*, 182–190.

Rogers, P. J., & Brunstrom, J. M. (2016). Appetite and energy balancing. *Physiology & Behavior*, *164*, 465–471.

Rohde, K., Keller, M., la Cour Poulsen, L., Blüher, M., Kovacs, P., & Böttcher, Y. (2019). Genetics and epigenetics in obesity. *Metabolism: Clinical and Experimental*, *92*, 37–50.

Rolls, B. J., Rolls, E. T., Rowe, E. A., & Sweeney, K. (1981). Sensory specific satiety in man. *Physiology & Behavior*, *27*, 137–142.

Rolls, E. T. (2016). Motivation explained: Ultimate and proximate accounts of hunger and appetite. In A. J. Elliot (Ed.), *Advances in motivation science* (Vol. 3, pp. 187–249). Elsevier.

Rosager, E. V., Møller, C., & Sjögren, M. (2021). Treatment studies with cannabinoids in anorexia nervosa: A systematic review. *Eating and Weight Disorders*, *26*, 407–415.

Roth, C. L. (2015). Hypothalamic obesity in craniopharyngioma patients: Disturbed energy homeostasis related to extent of hypothalamic damage and its implication for obesity intervention. *Journal of Clinical Medicine*, *4*, 1774–1797.

Rowell, A. M., & Faruqui, R. A. (2010). Persistent hyperphagia in acquired brain injury: An observational case study of patients receiving inpatient rehabilitation. *Brain Injury*, *24*, 1044–1049.

Rowland, C. V. (1968). Psychotherapy of six hyperobese adults during total starvation. *Archives of General Psychiatry*, *18*, 541–548.

Rozin, P., Dow, S., Moscovitch, M., & Rajaram, S. (1998). What causes humans to begin and end a meal? A role for memory for what has been eaten, as evidenced by a study of multiple meal eating in amnesic patients. *Psychological Science*, *9*, 392–396.

Rudzińska, A., Piotrowicz, K., Perera, I., Gryglewska, B., & Gąsowski, J. (2023). Poor appetite in frail older persons – a systematic review. *Nutrients*, *15*, 2966.

Ruf, T., & Geiser, F. (2015). Daily torpor and hibernation in birds and mammals. *Biological Reviews*, *90*, 891–926.

Sakurai, T. (2014). The role of orexin in motivated behaviours. *Nature Reviews Neuroscience*, *15*, 719–731.

Salameh, E., Morel, F. B., Zeilani, M., Déchelotte, P., & Marion-Letellier, R. (2019). Animal models of undernutrition and enteropathy as tools for assessment of nutritional intervention. *Nutrients*, *11*, 2233.

Santonicola, A., Siniscalchi, M., Capone, P., Gallotta, S., Ciacci, C., & Iovino, P. (2012). Prevalence of functional dyspepsia and its subgroups in patients with eating disorders. *World Journal of Gastroenterology*, *18*, 4379–4385.

Sarkar, T., Patro, N., & Patro, I. K. (2019). Cumulative multiple early life hits: A potent threat leading to neurological disorders. *Brain Research Bulletin*, *147*, 58–68.

Sarró, S. (2018). Those courageous boys: 73 years after the Minnesota starvation experiment. A psychiatrist's view. *Neurosciences and History*, *6*, 28–37.

Scammell, T. E., & Winrow, C. J. (2011). Orexin receptors: Pharmacology and therapeutic opportunities. *Annual Review of Pharmacology and Toxicology*, *51*, 243–266.

Schachter, S. (1968). Obesity and eating: Internal and external cues differentially affect the eating behavior of obese and normal subjects. *Science, 161*, 751–756.

Scharner, S., & Stengel, A. (2021). Animal models for anorexia nervosa: A systematic review. *Frontiers in Human Neuroscience, 14*, 596381.

Schemmel, R. A., Vaghefi, S. B., & Bowman, B. A. (2001). Olaf Mickelsen (July 29, l912 to August 8, 1999). *Journal of Nutrition, 131*, 205–210.

Sclafani, A. (2004). Oral and postoral determinants of food reward. *Physiology & Behavior, 81*, 773–779.

Schmalbach, I., Herhaus, B., Pässler, S., Runst, S., Berth, H., Wolff-Stephan, S., & Petrowski, K. (2020). Cortisol reactivity in patients with anorexia nervosa after stress induction. *Translational Psychiatry, 10*, 275.

Schmid, D. A., Held, K., Ising, M., Uhr, M., Weikel, J. C., & Steiger, A. (2005). Ghrelin stimulates appetite, imagination of food, GH, ACTH, and cortisol, but does not affect leptin in normal controls. *Neuropsychopharmacology, 30*, 1187–1192.

Schulte, E. M., & Gearhardt, A. N. (2017). Development of the Modified Yale Food Addiction Scale Version 2.0. *European Eating Disorders Review, 25*, 302–308.

Scrimshaw, N. S. (1987). The phenomenon of famine. *Annual Review of Nutrition, 7*, 1–22.

Sellayah, D., Cagampang, F. R., & Cox, R. D. (2014). On the evolutionary origins of obesity: A new hypothesis. *Endocrinology, 155*, 1573–1588.

Sergentanis, T. N., Chelmi, M. E., Liampas, A., Yfanti, C. M., Panagouli, E., Vlachopapadopoulou, E., Michalacos, S., Bacopoulou, F., Psaltopoulou, T., & Tsitsika, A. (2020). Vegetarian diets and eating disorders in adolescents and young adults: A systematic review. *Children, 8*, 12.

Shah, N. (2022). *Refusal to eat: A century of prison hunger strikes*. University of California Press.

Shanley, D. P., & Kirkwood, T. B. L. (2006). Calorie restriction does not enhance longevity in all species and is unlikely to do so in humans. *Biogerontology, 7*, 165–168.

Shea, Y. F., Lee, S. C., & Chu, L. W. (2018). Prevalence of hyperphagia in Alzheimer's disease: A meta-analysis. *Psychogeriatrics, 18*, 243–251.

Shin, Y., Kim, S., & Sohn, J. W. (2023). Serotonergic regulation of appetite and sodium appetite. *Journal of Neuroendocrinology, 35*, e13328.

Shukitt-Hale, B., Askew, E. W., & Lieberman, H. R. (1997). Effects of 30 days of undernutrition on reaction time, moods, and symptoms. *Physiology & Behavior, 62*, 783–789.

Siemian, J. N., Arenivar, M. A., Sarsfield, S., & Aponte, Y. (2021). Hypothalamic control of interoceptive hunger. *Current Biology, 31*, 3797–3809.

Silva, D. A., Coutinho, E. D. S. F., Ferriani, L. O., & Viana, M. C. (2020). Depression subtypes and obesity in adults: A systematic review and meta-analysis. *Obesity Reviews, 21*, e12966.

Silverstone, J. T., & Russell, G. F. M. (1967). Gastric 'hunger' contractions in anorexia nervosa. *British Journal of Psychiatry, 113*, 257–263.

Silverstone, J. T., Stark, J. E., & Buckle, R. M. (1966). Hunger during total starvation. *The Lancet, 7451*, 1343–1344.

Simansky, K. J. (1996). Serotonergic control of the organization of feeding and satiety. *Behavioural Brain Research, 73*, 37–42.

Sindler, A. J., Wellman, N. S., & Stier, O. B. (2004). Holocaust survivors report long-term effects on attitudes toward food. *Journal of Nutrition Education & Behavior, 36*, 189–196.

Skrynka, J., & Vincent, B. T. (2019). Hunger increases delay discounting of food and non-food rewards. *Psychonomic Bulletin & Review, 26*, 1729–1737.

Skvortsova, A., Veldhuijzen, D. S., Kloosterman, I., Pacheco-López, G., & Evers, A. (2021). Food anticipatory hormonal responses: A systematic review of animal and human studies. *Neuroscience and Biobehavioral Reviews, 126*, 447–464.

Smith, C., & Richards, R. (2008). Dietary intake, overweight status, and perceptions of food insecurity among homeless Minnesotan youth. *American Journal of Human Biology, 20*, 550–563.

Smith, G., Vigen, V., Evans, J., Fleming, K., & Bohac, D. (1998). Patterns and associates of hyperphagia in patients with dementia. *Neuropsychiatry, Neuropsychology, and Behavioral Neurology, 11*, 97–102.

Smyth, J. M., Wonderlich, S. A., Heron, K. E., Sliwinski, M. J., Crosby, R. D., Mitchell, J. E., & Engel, S. G. (2007). Daily and momentary mood and stress are associated with binge eating and vomiting in bulimia nervosa patients in the natural environment. *Journal of Consulting and Clinical Psychology, 75*, 629–638.

Sorokin, P. A. (1975). *Hunger as a factor in human affairs*. The University Presses of Florida.

Soussignan, R., Schaal, B., Boulanger, V., Gaillet, M., & Jiang, T. (2012). Orofacial reactivity to the sight and smell of food stimuli: Evidence for anticipatory liking related to food reward cues in overweight children. *Appetite, 58*, 508–516.

Speakman, J. R., & Hall, K. D. (2023). Models of body weight and fatness regulation. *Philosophical Transactions of the Royal Society of London. Series B, Biological Sciences, 378*, 20220231.

Speakman, J. R., Levitsky, D. A., Allison, D. B., Bray, M. S., De Castro, J. M., Clegg, D. J., Clapham, J. C., Dulloo, A. G., Gruer, L., Haw, S., Hebebrand, J., Hetherington, M. M., Higgs, S., Jebb, S. A., Loos, R. J. F., Luckman, S., Luke, A., Mohammed-Ali, V., O'Rahilly, S., . . . Westerterp-Plantenga, M. S. (2011). Set points, settling points and some alternative models: Theoretical options to understand how genes and environments combine to regulate body adiposity. *Disease Models & Mechanisms, 4*, 733–745.

Squire, L. R., Stark, C. E., & Clark, R. E. (2004). The medial temporal lobe. *Annual Review of Neuroscience, 27*, 279–306.

Squire, L. R., & Zola-Morgan, S. (1991). The medial temporal lobe memory system. *Science, 253*, 1380–1386.

Stammers, L., Wong, L., Brown, R., Price, S., Ekinci, E., & Sumithran, P. (2020). Identifying stress-related eating in behavioural research: A review. *Hormones and Behavior, 124*, 104752.

Staples, J. F. (2016). Metabolic flexibility: Hibernation, torpor, and estivation. *Comprehensive Physiology*, *6*, 737–771.

Stedal, K., Broomfield, C., Hay, P., Touyz, S., & Scherer, R. (2021). Neuropsychological functioning in adult anorexia nervosa: A meta-analysis. *Neuroscience & Biobehavioral Reviews*, *130*, 214–226.

Stein, R. I., Kenardy, J., Wiseman, C. V., Dounchis, J. Z., Arnow, B. A., & Wilfley, D. E. (2007). What's driving the binge in binge eating disorder? A prospective examination of precursors and consequences. *International Journal of Eating Disorders*, *40*, 195–203.

Steiner, J. E., Glaser, D., Hawilo, M. E., & Berridge, K. C. (2001). Comparative expression of hedonic impact: Affective reactions to taste by human infants and other primates. *Neuroscience and Biobehavioral Reviews*, *25*, 53–74.

Steiner, L., Brunetti, L., Roberts, S., & Ziegler, J. (2023). A review of the efficacy of appetite stimulating medications in hospitalized adults. *Nutrition in Clinical Practice*, *38*, 80–87.

Stellar, E. (1954). The physiology of motivation. *Psychological Review*, *61*, 5.

Sterkowicz, S. (2022). Observations on hunger disease in Nazi German concentration camps (M. Kantor, Trans.). *Medical Review – Auschwitz*, 17–22 (Original work published 1971)

Sternson, S. M. (2013). Hypothalamic survival circuits: Blueprints for purposive behaviors. *Neuron*, *77*, 810–824.

Sternson, S. M., & Eiselt, A. K. (2017). Three pillars for the neural control of appetite. *Annual Review of Physiology*, *79*, 401–423.

Stevenson, R. J. (2024). The psychological basis of hunger and its dysfunctions. *Nutrition Reviews*, *82*, 1444–1454.

Stevenson, R. J., Bartlett, J., Wright, M., Hughes, A., Hill, B. J., Saluja, S., & Francis, H. M. (2023). The development of interoceptive hunger signals. *Developmental Psychobiology*, *65*, e22374.

Stevenson, R. J., & Francis, H. M. (2023). *Diet impacts on brain and mind*. Cambridge University Press.

Stevenson, R. J., Francis, H. M., Attuquayefio, T., Gupta, D., Yeomans, M. R., Oaten, M. J., & Davidson, T. (2020). Hippocampal-dependent appetitive control is impaired by experimental exposure to a Western-style diet. *Royal Society Open Science*, *7*, 191338.

Stevenson, R. J., Francis, H. M., Hughes, A., Wylie, F., & Yeomans, M. R. (2023). Predictors of state-based changes in wanting and liking. *Appetite*, *188*, 106640.

Stevenson, R. J., Hill, B. J., Hughes, A., Wright, M., Bartlett, J., Saluja, S., & Francis, H. M. (2023). Interoceptive hunger, eating attitudes and beliefs. *Frontiers in Psychology*, *14*, 1148413.

Stevenson, R. J., Saluja, S., Forsyth, J., Rodgers, S., Brasher, S., Ho, V., & Francis, H. M. (2025). Psychological induction of interoceptive hunger cues and their effect on food desire. *Appetite*, *206*, 107855.

Stevenson, R. J., Serebro, J., Mruk, A., Martin-Rivera, D., Wyver, S., & Francis, H. M. (2024). Caregivers' attention toward, and response to, their child's interoceptive hunger and thirst cues. *Developmental Psychobiology, 66*, e22531.

Stevenson, R. J., Yeomans, M. R., & Francis, H. M. (2024). Human hunger as a memory process. *Psychological Review, 131*, 174–193.

Stewart, T. M., Martin, C. K., & Williamson, D. A. (2022). The complicated relationship between dieting, dietary restraint, caloric restriction, and eating disorders: Is a shift in public health messaging warranted? *International Journal of Environmental Research and Public Health, 19*, 491.

Stone, A. A., & Brownell, K. D. (1994). The stress-eating paradox: Multiple daily measurements in adult males and females. *Psychology and Health, 9*, 425–436.

Stratton, R. J., & Elia, M. (1999). The effects of enteral tube feeding and parenteral nutrition on appetite sensations and food intake in health and disease. *Clinical Nutrition, 18*, 63–70.

Strubbe, J. H., & Woods, S. C. (2004). The timing of meals. *Psychological Review, 111*, 128–141.

Stubbs, R. J., & Turicchi, J. (2021). From famine to therapeutic weight loss: Hunger, psychological responses, and energy balance-related behaviors. *Obesity Reviews, 22*, e13191.

Stunkard, A. J. (1959). Eating patterns and obesity. *Psychiatric Quarterly, 33*, 284–295.

Stunkard, A. J., & Fox, S. (1971). The relationship of gastric motility and hunger: A summary of the evidence. *Psychosomatic Medicine, 33*, 123–134.

Subramaniapillai, M., & McIntyre, R. S. (2017). A review of the neurobiology of obesity and the available pharmacotherapies. *CNS Spectrums, 22*, 29–38.

Sugino, T., Yamaura, J., Yamagishi, M., Ogura, A., Hayashi, R., Kurose, Y., Kojima, M., Kangawa, K., Hasegawa, Y., & Terashima, Y. (2002). A transient surge of ghrelin secretion before feeding is modified by different feeding regimens in sheep. *Biochemical and Biophysical Research Communications, 298*, 785–788.

Suliman, S., Anthonissen, L., Carr, J., du Plessis, S., Emsley, R., Hemmings, S. M., Lochner, C., McGregor, N., van den Heuvel, L., & Seedat, S. (2016). Posttraumatic stress disorder, overweight, and obesity: A systematic review and meta-analysis. *Harvard Review of Psychiatry, 24*, 271–293.

Sun, Y., Ahmed, S., & Smith, R. G. (2003). Deletion of ghrelin impairs neither growth nor appetite. *Molecular and Cellular Biology, 23*, 7973–7981.

Swanson, D. W., & Dinello, F. A. (1970). Severe obesity as a habituation syndrome: Evidence during a starvation study. *Archives of General Psychiatry, 22*, 120–127.

Tahreem, A., Rakha, A., Rabail, R., Nazir, A., Socol, C. T., Maerescu, C. M., & Aadil, R. M. (2022). Fad diets: Facts and fiction. *Frontiers in Nutrition, 9*, 1517.

Taylor, Z. B., Stevenson, R. J., Ehrenfeld, L., & Francis, H. M. (2021). The impact of saturated fat, added sugar and their combination on human hippocampal integrity and function: A systematic review and meta-analysis. *Neuroscience and Biobehavioral Reviews, 130*, 91–106.

Teff, K. L. (2011). How neural mediation of anticipatory and compensatory insulin release helps us tolerate food. *Physiology & Behavior, 103*, 44–50.

Teixeira, M. R., Silva, T., Felício, R. F. M., Bozza, P. T., Zembrzuski, V. M., de Mello Neto, C. B., da Fonseca, A. C. P., Kohlrausch, F. B., & Salum, K. C. R. (2025). Exploring the genetic contribution in obesity: An overview of dopaminergic system genes. *Behavioural Brain Research, 480*, 115401.

Thompson, K. M., Wonderlich, S. A., Crosby, R. D., & Mitchell, J. E. (1999). The neglected link between eating disturbances and aggressive behavior in girls. *Journal of the American Academy of Child & Adolescent Psychiatry, 38*, 1277–1284.

Thomson, T. J., Runcie, J., & Miller, V. (1966). Treatment of obesity by total fasting for up to 249 days. *The Lancet, 7471*, 992–996.

Thornton, L. M., Dellava, J. E., Root, T. L., Lichtenstein, P., & Bulik, C. M. (2011). Anorexia nervosa and generalized anxiety disorder: Further explorations of the relation between anxiety and body mass index. *Journal of Anxiety Disorders, 25*, 727–730.

Tian, R., MacGibbon, K., Martin, B., Mullin, P., & Fejzo, M. (2017). Analysis of pre-and post-pregnancy issues in women with hyperemesis gravidarum. *Autonomic Neuroscience, 202*, 73–78.

Toates, F. (1986). *Motivational systems.* Cambridge University Press.

Tonstad, S., Butler, T., Yan, R., & Fraser, G. E. (2009). Type of vegetarian diet, body weight, and prevalence of type 2 diabetes. *Diabetes Care, 32*, 791–796.

Torres, S. J., & Nowson, C. A. (2007). Relationship between stress, eating behavior, and obesity. *Nutrition, 23*, 887–894.

Treasure, J. L., & Owen, J. B. (1997). Intriguing links between animal behavior and anorexia nervosa. *International Journal of Eating Disorders, 21*, 307–311.

Tulving, E. (1983). *Elements of episodic memory.* Oxford University Press.

Turcott, J. G., Zatarain-Barrón, Z. L., Cárdenas Fernández, D., Castañares Bolaños, D. T., & Arrieta, O. (2022). Appetite stimulants for patients with cancer: Current evidence for clinical practice. *Nutrition Reviews, 80*, 857–873.

United States Department of Agriculture. (2022). *Key statistics and graphics.* https://shorturl.at/wbrD3

Vafaie, N., & Kober, H. (2022). Association of drug cues and craving with drug use and relapse: A systematic review and meta-analysis. *JAMA Psychiatry, 79*, 641–650.

Vågerö, D., Koupil, I., Parfenova, N., & Sparen, P. (2013). Long term health consequences following the Siege of Leningrad. In L. H. Lumey & A. Vaiserman (Eds.), *Early life nutrition and adult health and development* (pp. 209–225). Nova Science Publishers.

Vaiserman, A. (2011). Early-life origin of adult disease: Evidence from natural experiments. *Experimental Gerontology, 46*, 189–192.

Van de Veer, E., Van Herpen, E., & Van Trijp, H. C. M. (2016). Body and mind: Mindfulness helps consumers to compensate for prior food intake by enhancing the responsiveness to physiological cues. *Journal of Consumer Research, 42*, 783–803.

Van den Akker, K., Havermans, R. C., & Jansen, A. (2017). Appetitive conditioning to specific times of day. *Appetite, 116*, 232–238.

Van Eeden, A. E., Van Hoeken, D., & Hoek, H. W. (2021). Incidence, prevalence and mortality of anorexia nervosa and bulimia nervosa. *Current Opinion in Psychiatry, 34*, 515–524.

Van Galen, K. A., Ter Horst, K. W., & Serlie, M. J. (2021). Serotonin, food intake, and obesity. *Obesity Reviews, 22*, e13210.

Van Pelt, R. J. (2014). Nazi ghettos and concentration camps: The benefits and pitfalls of an encyclopedic approach. *German Studies Review, 37*, 149–159.

Vandereycken, W., & van Deth, R. (1994). *From fasting saints to anorexic girls.* The Athlone Press.

Vanzhula, I. A., Calebs, B., Fewell, L., & Levinson, C. A. (2019). Illness pathways between eating disorder and post-traumatic stress disorder symptoms: Understanding comorbidity with network analysis. *European Eating Disorders Review, 27*, 147–160.

Veronese, N., Facchini, S., & Stubbs, B. (2017). Weight loss is associated with improvements in cognitive function among overweight and obese people: A systematic review and meta-analysis. *Neuroscience and Biobehavioral Reviews, 72*, 87–94.

Visscher, P. M., Brown, M. A., McCarthy, M. I., & Yang, J. (2012). Five years of GWAS discovery. *American Journal of Human Genetics, 90*, 7–24.

Volkert, D., Beck, A. M., Cederholm, T., Cereda, E., Cruz-Jentoft, A., Goisser, S., de Groot, L., Großhauser, F., Kiesswetter, E., Norman, K., Pourhassan, M., Reinders, I., Roberts, H. C., Rolland, Y., Schneider, S. M., Sieber, C. C., Thiem, U., Visser, M., Wijnhoven, H. A. H., & Wirth, R. (2019). Management of malnutrition in older patients – current approaches, evidence and open questions. *Journal of Clinical Medicine, 8*, 974.

Volkow, N. D., Wang, G. J., & Baler, R. D. (2011). Reward, dopamine and the control of food intake: Implications for obesity. *Trends in Cognitive Sciences, 15*, 37–46.

von Haehling, S., & Anker, S. D. (2010). Cachexia as a major underestimated and unmet medical need: Facts and numbers. *Journal of Cachexia, Sarcopenia and Muscle, 1*, 1–5.

Wagner, M., Probst, P., Haselbeck-Köbler, M., Brandenburg, J. M., Kalkum, E., Störzinger, D., Kessler, J., Simon, J. J., Friederich, H. C., Angelescu, M., Billeter, A. T., Hackert, T., Müller-Stich, B. P., & Büchler, M. W. (2022). The problem of appetite loss after major abdominal surgery: A systematic review. *Annals of Surgery, 276*, 256–269.

Waismel-Manor, I. (2005). Striking differences: Hunger strikes in Israel and the USA. *Social Movement Studies, 4*, 281–300.

Walsh, B. T., Hagan, K. E., & Lockwood, C. (2022). A systematic review comparing atypical anorexia nervosa and anorexia nervosa. *International Journal of Eating Disorders, 56*, 798–820.

Wang, G., & Speakman, J. R. (2016). Analysis of positive selection at single nucleotide polymorphisms associated with body mass index does not support the 'thrifty gene' hypothesis. *Cell Metabolism, 24*, 531–541.

Wang, L., Sinnott-Armstrong, N., Wagschal, A., Wark, A. R., Camporez, J. P., Perry, R. J., Ji, F., Sohn, Y., Oh, J., Wu, S., Chery, J., Nemati Moud, B., Saadat, A., Dankel, S. N., Mellgren, G., Tallapragada, D. S. P., Strobel, S. M., Lee, M.-J., Tewhey, R., . . . Näär, A. M. (2020). A microRNA linking human positive selection and metabolic disorders. *Cell, 183*, 684–701.

Wang, T., Hung, C. C., & Randall, D. J. (2006). The comparative physiology of food deprivation: From feast to famine. *Annual Review of Physiology, 68*, 223–251.

Wangensteen, O. H., & Carlson, H. A. (1931). Hunger sensations in a patient after total gastrectomy. *Proceedings of the Society for Experimental Biology and Medicine, 28*, 545–547.

Ward, J., Hall, W., & Mattick, R. P. (1999). Role of maintenance treatment in opioid dependence. *The Lancet, 353*, 221–226.

Wardle, J., & Carnell, S. (2009). Appetite is a heritable phenotype associated with adiposity. *Annals of Behavioral Medicine, 38*, S25–S30.

Watts, A. G., Kanoski, S. E., Sanchez-Watts, G., & Langhans, W. (2022). The physiological control of eating: Signals, neurons, and networks. *Physiological Reviews, 102*, 689–813.

Weingarten, H. P. (1985). Stimulus control of eating: Implications for a two-factor theory of hunger. *Appetite, 6*, 387–401.

Weise, C. M., Hohenadel, M. G., Krakoff, J., & Votruba, S. B. (2014). Body composition and energy expenditure predict ad-libitum food and macronutrient intake in humans. *International Journal of Obesity, 38*, 243–251.

Weise, C. M., Piaggi, P., Reinhardt, M., Chen, K., Savage, C. R., Krakoff, J., & Pleger, B. (2016). The obese brain as a heritable phenotype: A combined morphometry and twin study. *International Journal of Obesity, 41*, 458–466.

Weisz, G. M., Grzybowski, A., & Albury, W. R. (2012). The fate of the Warsaw Ghetto Medical Faculty. *Israel Medical Association Journal, 14*, 209–213.

Westmoreland, P., Krantz, M. J., & Mehler, P. S. (2016). Medical complications of anorexia nervosa and bulimia. *American Journal of Medicine, 129*, 30–37.

Weyer, C., Walford, R. L., Harper, I. T., Milner, M., MacCallum, T., Tataranni, P. A., & Ravussin, E. (2000). Energy metabolism after 2 y of energy restriction: The biosphere 2 experiment. *American Journal of Clinical Nutrition, 72*, 946–953.

Whitman, B. Y., & Heithaus, J. L. (2022). Neurodevelopmental and neuropsychological aspects of Prader-Willi syndrome. In M. G. Butler, P. D. K. Lee, & B. Y. Whitman (Eds.), *Management of Prader-Willi syndrome* (pp. 219–246). Springer.

Wilding, J. P., Batterham, R. L., Davies, M., Van Gaal, L. F., Kandler, K., Konakli, K., Lingvay, I., McGowan, B. M., Oral, T. K., Rosenstock, J., Wadden, T. A., Wharton, S., Yokote, K., Kushner, R. F., & STEP 1 Study Group. (2022). Weight regain and cardiometabolic effects after withdrawal of semaglutide: The STEP 1 trial extension. *Diabetes, Obesity and Metabolism, 24*, 1553–1564.

Williams, D. M., Nawaz, A., & Evans, M. (2020). Drug therapy in obesity: A review of current and emerging treatments. *Diabetes Therapy, 11*, 1199–1216.

Williams, E. F., Pizarro, D., Ariely, D., & Weinberg, J. D. (2016). The Valjean effect: Visceral states and cheating. *Emotion, 16*, 897–902.

Wing, R. R., & Phelan, S. (2005). Long-term weight loss maintenance. *American Journal of Clinical Nutrition, 82*, 222S–225S.

Wiss, D. A., Avena, N., & Rada, P. (2018). Sugar addiction: From evolution to revolution. *Frontiers in Psychiatry, 9*, 545.

Woelfer, M., Kasties, V., Kahlfuss, S., & Walter, M. (2019). The role of depressive subtypes within the neuroinflammation hypothesis of major depressive disorder. *Neuroscience, 403*, 93–110.

Woodham-Smith, C. (1962). *The Great Hunger: Ireland 1845–9*. Hamish Hamilton.

Woods, S. C. (1991). The eating paradox: How we tolerate food. *Psychological Review, 98*, 488–505.

Woods, S. C., May-Zhang, A. A., & Begg, D. P. (2018). How and why do gastrointestinal peptides influence food intake? *Physiology & Behavior, 193*, 218–222.

World Food Program. (2023). *Global report on food crises: Number of people facing acute food insecurity rose to 258 million in 58 countries in 2022*. https://shorturl.at/uTaEI

World Health Organization. (2024). *Malnutrition*. www.who.int/news-room/fact-sheets/detail/malnutrition

Wren, A. M., Small, C. J., Abbott, C. R., Dhillo, W. S., Seal, L. J., Cohen, M. A., Batterham, R. L., Taheri, S., Stanley, S. A., Ghatei, M. A., & Bloom, S. R. (2001). Ghrelin causes hyperphagia and obesity in rats. *Diabetes, 50*, 2540–2547.

Wright, C. M., Macpherson, J., Bland, R., Ashorn, P., Zaman, S., & Ho, F. K. (2021). Wasting and stunting in infants and young children as risk factors for subsequent stunting or mortality: Longitudinal analysis of data from Malawi, South Africa, and Pakistan. *Journal of Nutrition, 151*, 2022–2028.

Wu, N., Yu, H., & Xu, M. (2022). Alteration of brain nuclei in obese children with and without Prader-Willi syndrome. *Frontiers in Neuroinformatics, 16*, 1032636.

Wynne, K., Stanley, S., McGowan, B., & Bloom, S. (2005). Appetite control. *Journal of Endocrinology, 184*, 291–318.

Yam, K. C., Reynolds, S. J., & Hirsh, J. B. (2014). The hungry thief: Physiological deprivation and its effects on unethical behavior. *Organizational Behavior and Human Decision Processes, 125*, 123–133.

Yeomans, M. R., & Brace, A. (2015). Cued to act on impulse: More impulsive choice and risky decision making by women susceptible to overeating after exposure to food stimuli. *PLoS One, 10*, e0137626.

Ylli, D., Sidhu, S., Parikh, T., & Burman, K. D. (2022). Endocrine changes in obesity. In K. R. Feingold, B. Anawalt, & M. R. Blackman (Eds.), *Endotext*. MDText.com, Inc. www.ncbi.nlm.nih.gov/books/NBK279053

Zanella, E., & Lee, E. (2022). Integrative review on psychological and social risk and prevention factors of eating disorders including anorexia nervosa and bulimia nervosa: Seven major theories. *Heliyon, 8*, e11422.

Zhang, L., Hernandez-Sanchez, D., & Herzog, H. (2019). Regulation of feeding-related behaviors by arcuate neuropeptide Y neurons. *Endocrinology, 160*, 1411–1420.

Index

For EU product safety concerns, contact us at Calle de José Abascal, 56–1°, 28003 Madrid, Spain or eugpsr@cambridge.org.

www.ingramcontent.com/pod-product-compliance
Ingram Content Group UK Ltd.
Pitfield, Milton Keynes, MK11 3LW, UK
UKHW040046200726
473483UK00007B/97

* 9 7 8 1 0 0 9 4 4 5 1 6 0 *